If Only We'd Known

By Stewart Shale

Copyright © 2021

1

Acknowledgements

First and foremost, I'd like to thank my wife Diane for putting up with me throughout this long exasperating process. Writing this sequel to 'The Hippo in a hairnet' has taken its toll, both on my sanity and Diane's patience. And without her formatting skills and editorial assistance, both books may have lain unpublished in my desk drawer.

Next, I must give thanks to family who are mentioned by name in the books. They all helped us in various ways to live our French dream. Without them to rely on in so many ways, there were times when we could easily have gone under.

Now a thankyou to my writing group, who helped me hone whatever skills I have, and build self-belief. And a special thanks to Oliver and Iona for their help throughout.

Last, and certainly not least, my thanks go to Lady Jane Grosvenor, who despite being an extremely busy lady, came through on her promise to read, then recommend 'Hippo in a hairnet.'

About the author

Born in county Durham, England, Stewart is a 75 year old father of two children, three step-children, and at the time of writing, fifteen grandchildren. After spending most of his working life in the sales and service sector, he took early retirement; and with his then partner Diane, moved to France in 2004. Renovating a small farm they'd bought in 2002, they built up a holiday let business. Though, it was often challenging, they lived there happily until 2010, when the financial crisis forced a move back to the UK. Married in 2015, they now live in the Scottish Borders, where Stewart works seasonally as a vistor attraction guide at a local castle. In addition to writing, his interests include reading, painting, collecting and travel.

As a member of the Kelso writers group, he's had stories published in anthologies, and written a play for a Borders theatre group. He is also a member of the The Federation of Writers Scotland. When not writing, he endeavours to keep up with family and friends.

About this book

'If only we'd known,' is the sequel to the well received 'Hippo in a Hairnet a French adventure,' and follows the couple as they continue the struggle to renovate their farm, while battling French authority, rip-off merchants, and some anti- English in a rural community. Fortunately they have good French neighbours and ex-pat friends to rely on. But even then – are *they* all that they seem?

Throughout their trials and tribulations, they maintain a sense of humour, while the eponymous Hippo in a hairnet continues to give loyal service as a super-trailer. But how will it all all end?

Read on, to find out the *true* cost of a life in the sun.

Part One

New life – New horizons

If Only We'd Known

Chapter 1

Home is where the 'hearth' is

'What do you think it'll look like?' I asked a sleepy Diane as we approached the hamlet. I reckon we'll have a job on our hands, don't you?'

It was a surreal experience, driving through that lush wooded valley and pulling up the drive to the farm. We could have ust been returning from a shopping trip. On the other hand, it felt as if we'd been away for months. And though everything was comfortingly familiar, much had changed in the relatively short time we'd been gone.

In November 2004, we'd taken a break from renovating our French farm to visit Diane's daughter Helen and husband Stewie. Spending time with them and their new baby Aaron had been great, and catching up with other family had been long overdue. But it was time to get back to reality.

Before we left France, Diane had promised to return to the apple orchards for the late apple picking. But once she'd fulfilled her contract, we had decisions to make. We were past the tipping point with our project. If we worked hard through the winter and finished the house, we could be renting it out next summer. It all depended on how far our money stretched. Though, whatever we decided, the next season might prove to be a deal breaker. But right then it was late at night, we'd arrived on the last ferry, and we weren't relishing the long drive ahead of us.

Once we hit the *autoroute,* though, the miles rolled by metronomically; and as dawn smudged the sky, we pulled up outside the farm. After opening up and dumping our luggage, it was time to uncork the Merlot. I agree, it's not your normal breakfast, but after a long hairy drive, we felt we deserved it. Out came the glasses and on went the music. We were back!

Considering the homecoming party the night before, we arose surprisingly early that first morning. It'd gotten kinda wild at one point, as our old friends dropped by to welcome us back. Status Quo, Bon Jovi, Meatloaf and Tina Turner had all made it. Yep – you've got the idea!

Given the circumstances, waking up should've been an absolute nightmare, but miraculously, we both felt fine. Bursting with energy after one of Diane's legendary fry-ups, we began making plans. Skirting the orchards the previous evening, Diane had spotted *balloxes* on the terraces, so leaving me to unpack, she drove off to pick up her outstanding wages and check out the work situation.

Handing Diane her cheque, the *secretaire* said, unfortunately picking was on hold due to bad weather. She'd ring when things changed. A frustrated Diane returned home and loaded the washing machine. We then set off to the *cave de champignons* to collect *my* cheque. Handing it over, the supervisor suggested I return the next morning for my bonus – two kilos of freshly picked mushrooms. Driving off to Noyant, we banked the cheques before heading back to Le Lude for supplies.

Noticing we were back, our neighbours popped over; handing back our bunch of keys like a hot potato. Véronique had been reluctant to take them originally, as it's apparently not the done thing except with family. Business taken care of, the ladies drooled over Aaron's baby photos, while Bertrand magically produced an opened bottle of *rosé* to wet the baby's head. I *still* don't know how he does that.

When they left, we finished unpacking before airing Michael Flately's *Lord of the dance* video. It wasn't a patch on *Riverdance* in our humble opinion, but hey, what do *we* know? Feeling the effects of our journey, Mr Flately was switched off in mid-leap as we crashed out for a nap.

During the week the temperature took a nosedive, which was a cause for concern. Sure, we had logs for the lounge fire; but with no central heating as yet, our situation was dire to say the least. In a bid to remedy the situation, we visited Saumur mid-week looking for some additional form of heating. Settling on two oil-filled radiators, we prayed they'd boost the lounge temperature, then at least we'd be comfortable in the heart of the house. The rest would have to wait for funds.

On the way back, I called in at the *cave* office, where Armand the boss sat at his desk. Welcoming me back, he asked about our UK visit; then we discussed business, which he said was still in the doldrums. With no work on offer, we shook hands and I left, with Armand promising to call if the situation changed.

Home again with the heaters connected, we began feeling the effects immediately. Combined with the log fire, the lounge was moderately comfortable at a heady 17 deg C. Diane even suggested cutting back on wood burning, which, she said might cure the cough I'd developed of late. Whoa! Let's not jump the gun here!

With it being a smidgin warmer, I decided to remodel the fire surround; but while scrubbing the field-stones I'd collected outside, the heavens opened. Returning to the kitchen drenched, I found Diane wrestling with two huge pumpkins.

Our *cave* was piled high with these monsters – the progeny of two plants Véronique had given us. Triffid-like, they'd taken over a huge swathe of the garden, giving birth to twenty enormous orange offspring. We'd given some away but were stuck with the rest. It seems everyone around here grew them for the festival of *Toussaint*. Not wanting to waste them, Diane consulted her recipe books. Dicing them then blending them with spices, she simmered them in pans. On the kitchen worktop, rows of gleaming Kilner jars stood at attention awaiting the metamorphosis to follow.

After tea, we chilled out beside a glowing fire, a hint of wood-smoke blending with the aromas seeping through from the kitchen. Projects taken care of, we chatted contentedly. Clutching glasses of full-bodied red wine, no entertainment was needed.

Though we'd settled back in quickly, we found sleep hard to come by. We were 'wired' and our body-clocks totally out of sync. Up well before five the next morning, I was anything but bright-eyed and bushy-tailed, I can tell you. The problem was, it felt strange not going to work. With coffee in hand, I read until Diane emerged. Like me, she felt restless: drained of all energy as if jet-lagged. So with nothing specific to get up early for, I filled the lone hot water bottle and sent her back to bed. I'd hoped she'd drift off again, but it was no good. After an hour spent tossing and turning fruitlessly, she was up again.

Stood at the dining room window later, we watched workers passing on the way to the *cave*. Feeling a sense of loss, I pointed out drivers in the passing cars. Yes, the work could often be brutal, but I missed being part of the team. Diane admitted she felt the same as she waited for a call from the orchards.

We breakfasted as daylight suffused the horizon; and as Diane had finished in the kitchen by then, I carried in chiselled stones for my project. Unfortunately, with them laid out in situ they just didn't have that '*va va voom*' I was looking for – so back out they went. Seeking inspiration, I picked up a chisel and began carving slabs of discarded mortar. Shaking her head in disbelief, Diane left me to it and began bottling preserves.

Lunchtime arrived, and Diane's '*pièce de jour*' was pumpkin and lardon soup, followed by buttered baguette slathered with pumpkin jam. Simple peasant dishes maybe, but nutritious, hearty and big on flavour. Sadly, my cladding experiment failed miserably, as the cement refused to set. So leaving it in the hope it would dry overnight, I moved on.

Rummaging in the barn mid-afternoon, I found something I'd prayed was there. Moving some boxes, I unearthed an old superser heater we'd transported on our first journey. Set aside in the barn it'd lain forgotten. Checking it out, I discovered a half-full gas cylinder – an absolute godsend now that the weather was changing.

With the cladding still damp the log fire had to remain unlit, so I fired up the two oil-filled radiators and superser to compensate. But with the room feeling depressingly chilly, we discussed having an early night. Opening a bottle of wine while we thought it over helped improve our mood a little. And gradually, through the magic of video we were transported to a rock concert. Though, strangely, the gig we'd attended proved hard to recall the next morning. But whatever and wherever the venue was, it beat the hell out of sitting there freezing our butts off. In fact we went off to bed in a much chirpier mood.

Feeling rather delicate in the cold light of dawn, I stared at the fireplace. Scratching my head, I decided the cement just *had* to be dry by then. *Why don't I just kinda lean against it?* I thought. Oh great! So who needed a stupid fire surround anyway?

While I cleared away the resulting rubble, Diane dug out her cooking utensils. After a consolation breakfast, we prepared to set off for *Bricomarché* with plan B – the one where we roped in the ever cheerful Aurore, a bubbly little girl who was always keen to help us.

Before we could make it to the car, though, Bertrand and François arrived to check on progress. After describing the cladding debacle, then telling them of our plan to visit *Brico*, François told me to forget it. Today was a public holiday, he said, and the shops were all closed.

'Dammit! Which holiday is that then?' I asked, showing little interest ... until he replied. And what he said absolutely *astounded* me.

'It is called Armistice Day,' he said. 'Have you heard of this in England?'

By the time I'd explained what Armistice Day means to Britain, and recounted the lives lost while liberating France in both World Wars, he looked suitably abashed. But in the tactless manner of youth, he just ploughed on undaunted.

'So you say the British fought in the Second World War. Did they fight in the *First* War?' he then asked.

It seemed I *still* hadn't gotten my message across. And as I was seething by then, I told him to visit the war graves stretching across Northern France as Diane and I had. Maybe *then* we could discuss Armistice Day. In retrospect, I suppose I was a bit heavy handed, but realizing that I was furious, he finally dropped the subject.

That was the first time I'd fallen out with my neighbours. Apparently, some French schools teach a *very* different version of the events in both World Wars: hyping up *their* involvement, while downgrading or omitting the sacrifice made by other nations. I suppose it wasn't really François' fault, but what had his *parents* taught him about those conflicts? Surely Bertrand knew the truth. But maybe he

11

didn't want to admit it. Whatever the reason, he stood there passively while I lectured his son.

Forgive me for going off on a rant like this. But like so many others, I've had family who fought in the two World wars. My dad fought in WW2, and I get really angry at how history is glossed over; or worse still re-written – usually for the benefit of the film industry.

With the atmosphere being a tad awkward by then, I changed the subject, asking gruffly why the lounge fireplace was peppered with tiny holes. Was it a feature of the local limestone? Looking surprised, François said he thought I knew. It was where Monsieur Renard had hammered in nails for stringing up freshly killed game to dry out. What an absolute cretin that man was.

With the shops being closed, I decided to trot out the mower; but surprise, surprise, it wouldn't start. While I was yanking away on the pull-cord like a man possessed, Bertrand showed up. Hearing me flogging away, (and possibly hoping to smooth over the Armistice Day fiasco,) he'd come to help.

'*Tous avez un problem avec le tondeuse Steward?*'

Had I a problem with the lawnmower? Oh, not really – just about every time I used the damned thing! Borrowing my tools he stripped the top section, but unable to find the problem, we adjourned to his workshop to conduct a more detailed investigation. In a gesture of consiliation, I nipped back and grabbed a jar of pumpkin and ginger preserve while Bertrand tinkered. Surprisingly Véronique hadn't tasted it before. I'd also picked up the Riverdance video. They'd really liked the snippet they'd seen, and had asked if they could borrow it – confirming the show's universal appeal.

As Véronique was busy in the kitchen, Bertrand and I stripped down the mower; cleaning the fuel system and filters with his air compressor. Noticing something odd, I pointed out a spring dangling off the choke. Smacking his forehead, Bertrand muttered, '*Stupide.*'

Re-connecting it, he tried again; and after a few hefty pulls on the cord it fired, albeit reluctantly. So leaving it clattering away erratically, we washed our hands. Then clutching the preserves and video, I rapped on the kitchen door. As usual the dogs went berserk, clawing at the door to get at me. To my surprise, when it was opened, Veronique's Aunt Anna appeared. Stepping into the kitchen shooing the dogs aside, I handed out kisses to both her and Véronique, who was making aperitifs.

'*Ou est Deanna?*' asked Anna, glancing towards the door.

When I said she was busy cooking, she despatched François to ring her, asking her to join us. On her arrival, snacks and drinks were served and two hours just flew by.

During a wide ranging discussion, the conversation switched to the *armoire* and dining suite we'd arranged to buy from them; planning how and when to move it to La Ferronnerie. Bertrand said the operation had to take place mid-December before their new furniture was delivered. It would be a five man job, he decided, involving 'The Hippo' hitched to their tractor, plus Uncle Maurice, cousin Philippe, François, and myself. The numbers seemed excessive to me, but it promised to be fun.

Discussion over, handshakes and kisses were exchanged and we set off; me pushing the renegade mower ahead of us. By then it was four pm, virtually twilight and extremely cold; so locking everything away, I went inside and lit the fire. Oh boy! Peering through the shutters, it was black and gloomy. It looked like the gateway to hell out there; while inside it was teeth-chatteringly cold, until the fire caught and spluttered into life.

After a late meal, then a reluctant plunge in the cold bathroom, we dived into bed frozen to the marrow. We read for a while until we warmed up a little, but then it was lights out. After all, who knew what the morning would bring?

Chapter 2

Murder most 'fowl'

When we visited Le Lavendu on the Saturday, shocking news awaited us. Sitting down carefully next to Diane, Bertrand said gently, '*Je suis desolate, Diane, mais, Cécile est morte.*'

'What was that*?*' Diane asked, turning to me, 'Did he say Cécile's *dead*?'

Cécile had become Diane's closest friend on the terraces; one of the few she ever made. It was a hell of a shock, as she was only in her early thirties and the mother to young children. Turning to Véronique, Diane queried the bombshell news in case we'd misunderstood; but sadly, she confirmed Bertrand's statement. She didn't know the cause of death, only that it'd occured the previous Sunday. The news completely floored Diane, as Cécile's *pannier*, coat and boots were stored in our barn. Diane had planned to meet-up with her to hand them over. Anyway, we'd been back a week.Why hadn't they told us sooner? But that's how this community were – close-knit and private.

Back home again, Diane pottered about listlessly, distracted and upset. Giving her some space, I went out to try bonding with the mower. You never know, talking to it nicely *might* work. It was ridiculous. Here we were in mid-November, and I was still cutting grass.

Lugging the infernal machine out, I glanced around to make sure no-one was watching. Then, like Basil Fawlty, I gave it a damn good talking to and pulled the cord. *That* did the trick. It spluttered into life; and tying down the throttle bar to prevent it stalling, I set off around the lawn with fingers crossed. (Try it sometime, it's tricky.)

François arrived as I finished the rear lawns, saying, 'If the good weather continues tomorrow, we will begin harvesting the rape seed.'

Breaking off after negotiating the tree roots and fallen fruit in the orchard, I mixed more fuel. But as Diane had finished in the kitchen by then, we changed clothes and drove to the *immobiliere* to see Jane. Using her office phone, she checked on our *Carte Vital* application, then invited us to her house to see the standard required for letting. We arranged the visit for later, as *Brico's* sale beckoned and there were bargains to be had.

Following a quick snack, we hitched up our small trailer. Bought on a recent UK visit, it was ideal for small loads. Leaving the house, I caught a flash of light in my peripheral vision. Turning, I spotted a guy on our top field watching us through binoculars. Nipping back inside, I returned with *my* binoculars, which I trained on *him*. That did it. He scuttled off, with Lupé and Hermé barking furiously as he crossed *their* land. Though their barking often annoyed me, I had to admit they made a great alarm system. Unfortunately, shop-bought alarms could be switched off – they couldn't.

Before driving to *Brico*, we planned showing Annette the baby photos. But *this* time we'd hatched a cunning plan. Allowing for a few minutes of kiddy talk over coffee, I'd then say, 'Oh, is that the time?' Then apologing profusely we'd leave. What could possibly go wrong?

I should've known better. Pulling up at La Minoterie we climbed out of the car … and walked into a scene from a horror movie. In the outhouse, Annette and daughter Jeanne stood ankle deep in feathers and gore. Dead chickens were strewn everywhere; twenty four in total, Annette declared triumphantly. Scrawny creatures compared to Véronique's plump specimens, they'd nevertheless been butchered for sale to friends and family. The pair stood grinning, knives in hands, blood up their forearms and smeared across their faces. 'Processed' carcasses were piled on the worktop dripping blood, while heads, feet and offal lay reeking in the sink. The stench in that enclosed space was overpowering, the air tainted with the coppery tang of blood. Mind you the flies weren't complaining. As to health and hygiene laws – now don't be silly!

Meanwhile, outside in the compound, Henri marched up and down carrying two rifles, aiming them alternately into the sky and shouting, 'Clack.'

Annette rolled her eyes and pouted, saying he'd been out shooting at pheasants. Maybe he'd been on our land, I thought. Best not to ask, though!

Edging away from the deranged looking chasseur wannabee, I bumped into blood-spattered Annette. Waving a knife vaguely as I turned towards her, she asked if I wanted a bird. Well I hoped that's what she'd said. Feeling I needed to display some macho credentials in this charnel house, I hefted a couple of wretched corpses as if weighing them. Kicking my ankle, Diane gave me 'the look.'

Mistaking my intentions, Annette stepped forwards – and offered me her knife.

Now I'm no stranger to the 'necking' and preparation of chickens, I'd helped my dad run a poultry smallholding as a boy. But this seemed like a mass murder. I imagined police cars and ambulances screeching into the yard at any minute; blue lights strobing and sirens wailing. Maybe there'd even be a C.S.I team in Tyvek suits thrown in for good measure.

Slinging another decapitated head casually into the sink, Annette wiped her hands on her apron, and asked if we'd like to adjourn to the sun-lounge for coffee. *'Beh oui,'* we said hurriedly, following her swiftly inside.

With us safely seated, Diane whipped out the baby photos, which a cleaned-up Annette cooed over. Meanwhile, shy Jeanne soldiered on alone in the abattoir.

Extracting myself from the baby- photo orgy and feeling drowsy in the suffocating heat, I imagined a scenario where the chickens – taking advantage of Annette's absence found a way to magically re-incarnate. Rising phoenix-like they'd overpowered Jeanne then flown away. (Difficult without heads, I agree – but work with me here.)

If such a miracle *were* to happen, Annette could be unseated as a major player in the local poultry industry. And what would the local Christmas club do then, eh?

Back to reality, I thought, pulling myself together. After photos and coffee, the conversation moved on to village gossip. Naturally, Annette knew of Cécile's death. It was a small community after all. While Henri 'clacked' away outside, she confided that Cécile had been *diabetique.* Though, she'd been known to enjoy the odd glass of red wine, she whispered, shrugging her shoulders elequently.

While in this serious vein, she said Henri had been to *hopital* for a check-up, as his heartbeat had been erratic lately. After he'd been wired-up on a bed, monitors had begun flashing wildly. He told Annette it was due to the busty young nurse leaning over him.

Just then the old goat made his appearance, and the conversation switched to more prosaic matters – like tools. *Jaman* the dealer was expensive, he said, but Bertrand bought there to get a longer guarantee. However *his* son, Jean had bought a cheap mower from *Brico* with a year's warranty, and so far he'd had no problems. Okay, but I'd seen Jean's tiny garden. Dismissing all of our fields, the grassed areas around our house took more than four hours to mow, so we needed something more substantial.

Leaving our eccentric octogenarians to their pursuits, we shot off to pester Aurore at *Brico*. We needed to find a match for our brick samples. Abandoning her Christmas display, the diminutive assistant and her collegue scoured the outside yard for some. However, search abandoned, it was decided they didn't stock them – so neither would other branches.

Undeterred, we set off for La Flèche, confident that we'd find some there. And just as well we did, as *they* had quite a stock. We paid for sixty at the yard office; and after loading them, we pulled away, trailer creaking. We hoped to get back before twilight fell. Yep – more problems with the trailer's electrics.

Nearing home, I switched off the engine and coasted quietly up to an avenue in the orchards. I'd spotted a stag standing framed in a shaft of late sunlight. Despite our presence it stood motionless watching us. Then after a few priceless seconds, it snorted, tossed its antlers and trotted off into the undergrowth. Though we felt privileged to have seen it, we hoped its next encounter with Homo-Sapiens didn't prove terminal.

After labouring slowly up the drive to the barn, we unloaded the bricks onto a pallet. As I lit the fire, Diane, who'd just made coffee, picked up the ringing phone. It was Nadine, saying, Ben had been driving her crazy. Because of his mood-swings, she'd taken him to the doctor who prescribed a diet excluding E-numbers. It seemed to be working so far, she said. Calm restored, we trawled through our comedy videos, selecting a classic featuring the Trotter family. Once again the programme's theme song asked the question, 'Why do only fools and horses work?'

While boiling the kettle one particular morning, I glared at the thermometer. It didn't alter the reading, though. The temperature in the kitchen was below zero. After making coffee and filling our solitary hot water bottle, I climbed back into bed. Thawed out a little later, I left a shivering

Diane, and braved the icy chill to switch on the superser. However, I couldn't light the fire, as my crafted stonework needed to dry slowly or it could crack.

Hoping for more warmth outside the bedroom, a deranged looking Diane rose swiftly, dressed like a Whirling Dervish and scurried into the kitchen. Switching on the oven, she left its door open to heat the room. After standing in front of it for a few minutes to stimulate her circulation, she began cooking breakfast.

With our *petit dejeuner* out of the way, I examined the fire surround. For some reason the cement still hadn't set. Maybe it was just too cold. Who knows? With extreme reluctance, I asked Diane if she'd drive to *Brico* to buy some fire-resistant mortar, while I demolished the structure I'd poured my heart and soul into.

Standing amid a pile of rubble soon after, I heard a shout. It was François. Would I like to visit *Jaman*? It was tempting, but I'd heard a vehicle coming up the drive. The mortar had arrived!

What Diane dumped on the kitchen table however was a mere four kilo bag. It wasn't nearly enough for the job, and at fourteen euros it was damned expensive. Also, the microscopic print on the bag said, 'Leave for fifteen days before lighting a fire.' And worse still; underneath that was written, 'This product will turn black when dry.'

Saying I'd catch up with François later, I set the bag aside while we had lunch and a re-think.

Following our sanity break, François returned with his *'fazzaire'* to inspect the strimmer. They'd brought a container of fuel they were using in *their* machine. After checking our's over and changing the fuel, Bertrand pulled the cord; and of course it fired up immediately for *him*. Off he went, like some virtuoso conducting a master-class. With swathes of vegetation falling before him, he strode forward like a strimming colossus.

Thinking, '*Okay, you've made your point, pal,*' I tried telling François, that the problem only occured when the machine had warmed up. But after a muffled discussion, François replied, 'My fazzaire, he says there is no problem.'

It was pointless arguing with them, so off we went to *Bricomarché*. And with the mortar returned for credit and chainsaws priced, we drove back to *Jaman*. With François translating, we discussed saws with the owner. He advised checking specifications. (Duh) Also, cheaper saws with plastic uni-bodies are difficult to repairs, so It's often cheaper to buy a new one. And, *Bricomarché* didn't do repairs. They sent them to him! It seemed there was a lot to think about. 'It is a matter of much seriousness,' he stated.

So adjourning to Le Ferroneries's kitchen, we clinked beer bottles in a toast before discussing my options. Spotting Diane in the lounge, François headed over oozing Gallic charm. He'd wanted to try out Diane's computer for ages, and he thought he'd chance his arm again.

'Sorry, there's too much dust in the air,' said the wily Diane, protecting her electronic baby jealously. He looked at me with raised eyebrows. I shrugged wryly. He knew then that he was beaten. Soon afterwards the duo set off home, leaving me to ponder the minefield of chainsaw ownership.

However, my unsuspecting neighbours had no idea what they were in for next. François had returned the Riverdance video saying it wouldn't play on their VCR. No problem! After tea, I asked them over to watch it on *ours*. Hah! They weren't getting off *that* easily.

On their arrival the trio sat down cautiously. Placing a bottle of *rosé* and glasses on the coffee table, I closed the shutters. Then with drinks poured and lighting dimmed, the show began. As my audience settled, Irish pipes began wailing mournfully. Rising steadily in volume they were joined by the crashing of Bodhran drums. Then from the wings, Michael Flately leapt onstage – dozens of 'tap' shoes clattering in unison behind him. The thundering drums, the wailing pipes and staccato shoes soon built to a crescendo of noise, the likes of which the family had probably never experienced before. It was an unqualified success. Even the teenage François couldn't contain his excitement.

As the credits rolled, I thought I'd push my luck. While Diane's back was turned, I inserted my Status Quo video. That did it! As wailing guitars screeched out across the room, I could almost see their hair stand on end and the blood drain from their faces.

'Right, I think that's enough, don't you?' said Diane, emerging swiftly from the kitchen and ejecting the cassette from the VCR.

Well you can't win them all I suppose.

Because of the worsening weather, I fired up the superser before breakfast the next day. And with the dishes cleared away, we began our tasks *de jour*. As Diane tidied up, I mixed cement and began laying new fire-bricks.

Enveloped by a heavy mist, the atmosphere in the valley felt oppressive. Suddenly, like a scene from *The Hound of the Baskervilles,* a blood-curdling howl shattered the silence. Emanating from the next hamlet, the mournful noise grew louder by the second. Within minutes, a baying pack of hounds erupted from the woods. Hot on the trail of the frenzied animals were a rabble of equally crazed hunters, following dog handlers blowing bugles and trumpets. Ah well; just another Sunday morning in the hunting season.

Hearing shots soon after, we hoped they hadn't killed a lovely young doe we'd spotted earlier. Mind you, if someone had knocked on the door and said, 'Here's a haunch of fresh venison,' I'd have taken their hand off – so to speak.

When Bertrand popped over later with François, I described how *le chasse* had crossed the fields. And green with envy, his trigger finger curled as he imagined the action. Our young student had come to say goodbye. He was returning to college for five weeks, and asked if we'd like to accompany his parents when they next visited him. Though we'd have loved to, we had to decline, as Kay, Nadine, and her boys were flying in then. An obviously disappointed, François said he'd be back in mid-December, and shot off home to begin packing.

Once he'd gone, I finished the brickwork. But unhappy with the result, I tore it down and used the cement to repair cracks on the outside walls. Then, after sweeping the floor, I stowed the tools away. Feeling a bit low afterwards, we decided to phone all the kids.

When I got through to Chris, he said he'd been accepted by Nissan UK as an apprentice and was starting college the next day. We congratulated him, knowing he'd had a run of bad luck lately. But sticking at it, he'd been successful. He was absolutely chuffed and as high as a kite. With the kids sorted out, our final call was to Diane's Mum. But unable to keep our eyes open after that, we admitted defeat and went off to bed.

Chapter 3

Getting it all together

At one-thirty am on Monday, we sat there wide awake, our sleep patterns in tatters. Sipping endless cups of tea, we talked until a golden dawn suffused the horizon. Exhausted or not, we were up for the day.

While Diane began breakfast, I tackled my nemesis the fireplace. Making steady progress, I even dared imagine the finished masterpiece. Sadly, I was being a tad presumptious; as laying a brick, I realized a gap needed to be left above the stove. Without one, the next course would bond to the stove itself. That would probably be okay in Monsieur Renard's world, but it was a no-no for me.

Then ping! A light seemed to go on in my brain. Yes, I'd had an idea. I'd construct a support lintel over the fire. Ridiculously pleased with this tiny nugget of ingenuity, I searched the barn for a vaguely remembered length of steel. A 'eureka' moment followed when I unearthed it, and within minutes, the disc grinder was throwing off a shower of sparks.

'Breakfast's ready,' Diane called out.

Laying down the cooling metal, I went to wash my hands.

'How's it going?' she asked, placing a heaped plate in front of me.

'Getting there,' I said. 'It shouldn't be long now.'

Pushing back my empty plate, I sipped my tea.

'What are *your* plans for the day then?' I asked.

'Oh, I've got plenty to keep *me* busy,' she said, picking up my plate while eyeing my cup pointedly.

'Right, I suppose I'd better crack on then,' I said draining my cup. I headed back to the job with renewed vigour. Oh the power of a full English breakfast!

Back in the lounge, I inspected the brickwork, but somehow it lacked that *je ne sais quoi* I'd been striving for. Jumping into the car, I drove to *Brico,* looking for something special. While rummaging through their garden-centre, I discovered some rectangular terracotta *plaquettes* with a scorched patina. They seemed ideal. Mounted vertically across the top of the fire they'd make a bold statement. Seeking out Aurore in the main store, I said I'd need ten of them. But they were in boxes of sixty, could the box be split? '*Helas non Monsieur,*' she replied. I'd need to buy a full box, and they weren't cheap.

Borrowing a sample, I rushed home to show Diane, who liked the look, but a box of sixty, forget it. Then she thought of a use for the others on the patio and it was game on. I arrived back at *Brico* just before closing time; and grabbing the *plaquettes,* I was advised to attach them with a nail-less adhesive called '*Plac-Blanc.*'

In line at the checkout, I chatted to an English couple, who mistook my 'Geordie' accent for Scottish. After correcting this outrageous error, we laughingly compared project disasters. Then saying goodbye, I returned home with my purchases.

Stepping back from the fireplace with the tiling finished, I had a stupid grin on my face. I know that look. I see it in the mirror every day. Now this project might seem like small beer to some, but if you retire to a simpler existence like we did, a job well done can mean a lot.

Inspired by my success, I thought I'd take the bull by the horns. (Be careful what you wish for in the country.) Driving to *Jaman*, I ordered my chainsaw for Friday's delivery. Spurred on, I returned to Le Ferronerie and my next job – grouting the brickwork.

Cleaning my trowel later, I admired the finished job. Illuminated by a shaft of sunlight, the fireplace looked massive. With the black stove now enclosed by russet brickwork, the combination set into the limestone blockwork was almost a sensual experience. (Steady on now – it's only a fireplace.)

With Nadine, Kay, and the boys flying in at the weekend, it was imperative that we finished our other jobs. But of course, Sod's Law reared its ugly head again. The superser chose then to run out of gas. Removing the bottle, I set it aside until the morning. By then the brickwork should be dry and the fire could be lit.

Since settling in France, we'd begun using our ingenuity and inventiveness a lot more. No longer were we part of the Nanny State, where so many people are feather-bedded. We enjoyed the challenges each day threw at us. And with good neighbours and friends to rely on, we couldn't wait to see what came next. But there *were* exeptions.

There was one job I'd been avoiding for a while. The leaking roof had been set aside for a better time, but if we had heavy rain carried on a westerly wind it could bite me on the ass. With the family arriving soon, fixing it became a priority. I wasn't *expecting* bad weather you understand – but you never know do you?

Heart in my mouth, I ascended Monsieur Renard's rickety old ladder. Exhaling deeply at the top, I scanned the roof. But where was the problem tile? It appeared to have been fixed. Bertrand must have done it when we were out sometime, and he'd never even mentioned it. What a guy! Climbing back down, I told Diane, who knowing his sweet tooth said she'd bake him a cake as a thank-you.

Nadine rang later, saying she was excited as their departure grew nearer. Then she casually mentioned that Ben had scribbled on the walls, TV, and carpet in black marker pen. Oh the little Angel! When I thought of his impending visit, I *also* felt excited. In fact my heart-rate seemed to have doubled for some strange reason.

Though it was drizzling the next morning, it didn't stop Bertrand from sawing logs. Walking over, I thanked him for fixing the roof, but he just looked at me blankly. I tried again, asking *when* he'd fixed it. Looking perplexed, he said he *hadn't* fixed it. Ditching his saw, he carried his ladder over and we took turns climbing up and inspecting the roof. It was a mystery. From a distance the hole was unnoticeable. But then we saw it. A slate must have slipped, because on closer inspection it still needed sealing. Shrugging, he said he'd leave the ladder in our barn and return later to fix it.

With it stored away, I asked him in for a chat; and over coffee laced with *eau de vie*, he said he fancied restoring a vintage car. Oh yes! Pulling out some classic car mags, I passed them over. Though they were English, he could read specifications and convert prices to euros. Riffling through the 'for sale' section, he was almost drooling. Suddenly excited, he pointed out a vintage Citroën, the model he wanted. However, he whistled and blew on his fingers when reading the price, saying he'd yet to convince Véronique.

Changing tack, he asked what *I'd* been up to lately. So leading him into the lounge, I showed him the fire surround. He was impressed with the quality of my brickwork, and suggested an acid-based cleaner which would eat off excess cement. *Yeah, and my fingers too*, I thought.

Misunderstanding my reluctance, he said it wouldn't damage the bricks at all. I told him I'd consider it, then with a longing glance at the magazines, he shook my hand and left, saying, 'Non merci,' when I suggested he take them.

He'd just left when Diane returned from shopping. She said she'd met an English guy who lived near Chiné. It was useful developing contacts; someone with a skill you could exchange money or services for. It may sound mercenary, but it's the bartering system used by the expat community. We were happy to embrace it – but on our terms. We didn't move to France to live in a British enclave.

'Fair to middlin,' was how a Yorkshireman would describe Friday.☐☐ In other words, gray and drizzling. Not a day for working outside. With loads to do *inside,* it was a no-brainer then.

Despite the grubby pink bathroom being subjected to a radical makeover, it needed tweaking before our guests arrived. Situated in the house extension, it was jaded and tired. Jerry-built initially, and with little insulation, plaster was crumbling off the inner wall. I'd repaired the shower, renovated the bath and sink unit, then sanded the floor-tiles ready for painting.

After breakfast, I began applying primer; unaware that the door had closed behind me. Feeling whoozy after a few minutes, I realized what'd happened and got the hell out of there. With my head clearing, I sanded the primer, before rolling on a coat of ultramarine tile paint. Removing my socks to avoid contamination, I worked my way back on my knees towards the door. Standing on the threshold later, I admired the finished room. In shades of blue with contrasting white woodwork and chrome fittings, the overall effect was 'mediterranean cool.'

Carrying out the brushes and roller, I passed Diane in the lounge. She'd painted the walls magnolia, and was applying burgundy wallpaper either side of the chimney breast. As a contrast to the creamy limestone fireplace it looked stunning.

Leaving Diane papering, I drove to *Jaman* to collect my promised chainsaw. Being aware of the French two hour lunch-break I arrived at two thirty – unfortunately the saw hadn't. Maybe it would arrive by tomorrow afternoon, the owner said; adding the caviat that if it didn't, nothing much moves on a Monday so it probably be Tuesday.

Driving back following a *deviation* sign, I passed the orchards; and drooling at the bunches of fruit, I felt compelled to pull over and watch. Workers were picking apples from mature trees, some balancing on a pallet held high by a fork lift truck. Yet another blow struck for ingenuity and expediency against political correctness.

Arriving home I did a recce around the garden, assessing possible danger spots for kids. Tidying anything remotely dangerous away, I threw anything burnable on the bonfire amassed during the 'restricted burning'period. I planned lighting it on our visitor's last night at a farewell party. Deciding, better be safe rather than sorry where curious youngsters are concerned, I then blocked off the stairs leading to the granary.

When I finally dragged my weary ass into the house, I was gobsmacked to find that Diane had re-arranged most of the furniture in my absence. I thought *I'd* been motoring, but *she'd* re-arranged the lounge and dining room furniture single-handed. The oxblood Chesterfield settee now took centre-stage, complimenting the burgundy paper abreast the fireplace. With Diane's monochrome sketches gracing the walls, and silk drapes framing the French windows, the room just oozed quality.

Early next morning, Diane tackled the lounge and kitchen. By linking complimentary accessories, she added even more warmth to the rooms. The bedrooms themselves just needed fresh laundry, flowers, and a few personal touches. Leaving her to what she excels at, I drove to *Jaman* to check on the chainsaw. Would you believe it? It was delivered just after I left yesterday, but without my phone number, the guy couldn't let me know. Within minutes he'd checked it over, fuelled and demonstrated it, then given me a handbook containing an English translation – which was becoming something of a rarity lately. Stowing the saw in the car, I set off home.

There was no holding me back after that; so after brunch, Diane drove to La Flèche and left me to it. Donning protective gear, I tooled up and marched off to find wood to cut – any wood really! After decimating a bush on a trial run, I sawed up some rotted old fence-posts. Then hauling out my collection of lengthy poles from the barn, I cut up the wonky ones and re-stacked the rest. With the woodshed doors thrown open, sunlight picked out sawdust motes floating in the air. As they landed on me, I gradually morphed into the Spillers Flour Man – powdery white from head to toe.

With perfect timing, Diane returned just as the saw spluttered out of fuel. Pleased with the amount of logs I'd accumulated, I dusted off the machine and myself before going inside.

Showered and changed, I was served dinner in our re-furbed dining room. Coincidentally, the first video we watched afterwards was a DIY programme unearthed by Diane. A subtle hint maybe? Her face was impassive! However, the video rock section wasn't far away. And it *was* Saturday night after all.

Chapter 4

Massing the troops

While lying in bed the next morning mulling over plans, we thought it wise to have a trial run to Tours airport. Nadine and family were arriving on Monday's flight, and Bertrand said it was tricky to find. After saying he regularly passed it in his truck, he gave us detailed directions including seven roundabouts and an industrial estate!

Before setting off, Diane cooked breakfast while I gave the bathroom tiles another lick of paint. Then after a tidy-up and change of clothes, I closed the door behind me and we were off.

Passing through a bustling Château-la-Valliere later, we turned right for Tours, enjoying a surreal moment when we spotted a herd of reindeer in a field. Huddled together in a paddock behind an *auberge,* they watched us pass by. Who knows? Maybe they'd flown in from Lapland for a vacation in the sun. Yeah right! Odds were that they featured on the menu.

We drove another thirty kilometres before crossing the river bridge and entering Tours, wondering why we hadn't seen a sign for the airport before then. Where the hell was it? Ending up in a city centre bus lane, I did a screeching (and illegal) 180 degree turn, before heading back over the bridge. Fortunately, approaching a mini-roundabout at speed, we spotted a tiny white finger sign marked *Aeroporte*. Barely noticeable among many others, it pointed off to the left.

By the time we arrived, it'd taken over an hour to drive sixty kilometres – only to find the airport closed. It transpired that Ryanair, a glider school, *and* the French Air Force all shared the facilities. But only Ryanair used the main terminal; and that was only twice a week in low season and maybe four times in the summer. They opened just an hour before the incoming flight landed; and with the new arrivals disembarked, the plane was immediately re-fuelled. Once loaded with passengers and luggage, it took off again. After departure, everyone left the concourse and the airport building was closed.

This was explained very carefully to me by an extremely helpful lady at the car rental company next door. It sounded extraordinary, but apparently it worked perfectly well – as we were to find out the next day.

On the way back, we followed a sign for Le Mans and Chartre – crossing six, *possibly* seven roundabouts. With mini roundabouts and so much traffic it was hard to tell. At times it was virtually a race track. However, we steadfastly wove our way home through it, mission accomplished.

There was no time for self-congratulation, though, as Diane had final jobs to do, and I needed to continue strimming. But with the job half-finished, I ran out of spool filament. Returning the strimmer to the shed, I muttered a prayer and rolled out the mower. I wasn't hopeful, but hey, miracles *can* happen. It coughed into life, and after a mad dash around the lawns, I was finished by five pm.

Arriving home another surprise awaited me, as I noticed sumptuous throws and cushions arranged tastefully on both settees.

The evening ended rather sedately after our meal, watching a video while drinking one glass of wine each. Then it was an early night, as the next day would be full on.

Early to bed early to rise they say. We were wide awake by five am reading in bed. But it was no good just lying there, there was too much to do. So getting up, Diane cooked breakfast while I rolled out the small trailer. Before hitching it up, I nipped down to the *boulangerie* for baguettes; returning to find Diane hanging out washing. It was a really gorgeous day by then; ideal for our visitors to see the beautiful countryside at its best.

Setting off at eleven am with the trailer bouncing behind us, we dawdled along on deserted roads. As it was, we *still* arrived early... to be met with absolute pandemonium!

Both short and long term car parks – which had been totally empty the day before, were now jam-packed. And we had a fight on our hands to find a parking space; especially towing the trailer.

We crawled around three times in a line of desperate drivers, like Indian braves circling a wagon-train. It was musical chairs with cars – minus any of the fun element. Finally, I nipped into a space behind a departing driver. It was next to the perimeter fencing, which was perfect towing the trailer. However, my radical manoeuvre really annoyed a circling Frenchman. 'Tough tittie my Gallic friend,' sprang to my fevered mind.

Inside the building the concourse was packed. There was standing room only; with English travellers ready to depart, and ex-pats waiting to pick up visitors. It was very impressive for such a small airport; set up and running so efficiently at such short notice. Indeed it was quite the International Airport, with its compact departure lounge, bijou customs area, and bustling café-cum restaurant.

Could it be true then – size really doesn't matter?

The muffled tannoy announced that the incoming flight was on time, causing outgoing passengers to file through customs into the departure lounge. Soon afterwards, the plane could be glimpsed descending through thin cloud, its wing-mounted lights glowing. Gliding past the loung window with flaps lowered, engines whistling and throttling back, it landed with a thunderous roar. Turning at the end of the runway, it taxied back to the arrival's tunnel. Before it'd come to a standstill, manually operated steps were being wheeled to both front and rear doors. Then as flight crew opened them, lily-white passengers emerged blinking in the fierce midday sunlight.

After the initial rush to disembark, the crowd slowed down to a trickle – then nothing. Where were *our* group? We were starting to worry. Had they even left the UK? Then from the gloomy fuselage, Nadine and Kay emerged, struggling with the boys and their bags. At the base of the steps they collected a buggy from a steward. Panic over!

Hauling their luggage off the carousel they emerged in the concourse, where it was hugs all round. Wrestling the baggage to the car and trailer, we shoe-horned it all in. Then, with our harassed passengers squeezed into the car, the kids in child-seats, I set off.

While I jousted with the traffic on the manic drive back, Diane pointed out the reindeer to Ben as we passed the *auberge*. But he missed them while enthusing over a large red tractor. *Never mind; as long as he's happy,* I thought. Half an hour later, we pulled up at the door.

Chapter 5

The banana incident

Having dumped everything in their rooms, the girls began exploring, checking progress made since their last visits. While they ooed and aghed, Lewis sat peacefully in his buggy. Not Ben though. He couldn't wait to get outside. Only natural after being cooped up in a plane, I suppose, but from the off, he was into everything. I spent a lively afternoon keeping him entertained, while the girls played catch-up with Diane.

First, I took him next door to see the ducks, which he began chasing all over the plot. Their outraged quacking soon attracted Lupé and Hermé, who barked insanely while trying to chew their way out of their wire enclosure. Delighted by their frenzied leaping about, Ben went over to stroke Lupé's nose. I could almost read the mutt's mind as his beady eyes fixed on those waggling little fingers; teeth bared, tongue salivating behind the wire-mesh.

As I reached for Ben's hand, the upstairs shutters opened; and distracted by the noise, he pulled back. Looking up, he saw Bertrand and shouted, 'Hello man.'

'*Bonjour*,' Bertrand replied jauntily – which meant absolutely nothing to Ben.

Within a couple of minutes, Bertrand arrived on the scene. Stooping, he shook Ben's hand, before he shot off chasing the long suffering ducks. (Ben that is, not Bertrand!)

Stood there watching his enthusiasm, we agreed that children were *beaucoup de travais,* or hard work. Then wishing Bertrand, *'Au revoire,'* I grabbed the wriggling Ben and made to leave. Turning his head, Ben waved and said, 'Bye bye man.'

'Bye bye,'replied Bertrand, mouth twitching in a smile.

I eventually wrestled Ben away from the ducks; but only by promising to play football with him. *Oh God, I'm not used to this*, I thought, as I kicked, threw, and dived all over the lawn.

As the first half drew to a close, Diane and Kay came out to watch Grandad the goalie. Without bringing me so much as a slice of orange, they said, as Ben and I seemed to be getting on famously, they'd just drive into Le Lude for a while. Did I mind?

'Of *course* I don't mind,' I *think* I remember saying. And since Nadine had gone for a lie down with Lewis, I had all the fun to myself.

The girls finally returned, (much, much later) in time for the grand screening of Bambi. Though, whether it was for the kid's benefit or Kay's was hard to tell. After the film, Kay and Diane got the boys ready for bed, by which time I could happily have gone myself. Following a tearful wrestling session, Ben finally took the hint and stayed in his room.

Opening a bottle of wine (with a tremor,) I poured four glasses and toasted their holiday. Turning to set down the bottle, I spotted a magnificent stag and two does in the lower field. After pointing them out, we gazed at them spellbound for a brief moment before I closed the shutters. We then relaxed watching Billy Connolly put the world to rights on video. However, we'd all had a long day, (especially Grandad the goalie) so it wasn't long before we gave in to Mister Sandman.

A crying Ben woke me early the next morning. Unsettled in his strange surroundings, he woke Lewis who began coughing hoarsely. Soon we were all in the kitchen, where we then had a lively time getting Ben to eat his breakfast. As most of it seemed destined for the floor or walls, Diane, as an encouragement suggested a shopping trip.

'That'll be nice for you all,' I said pointedly, heading for the door. 'I'll just cut up that fallen tree in the bottom field. I *must* keep the logpile topped up.'

As I waved them off from the woodshed doorway, my brain re-booted itself, warping across into a parallel universe devoid of noise. At first, I thought I'd gone deaf – but in kind of a *nice* way. Sighing contentedly with the saw and tools loaded into my barrow, I set off down the field whistling.

Trundling up to the tree a few minutes later, I set down my load. Stretching my back and with the sun on my face, I heard birds twittering nearby and felt a deep sense of peace. The mushroom *cave* down the road stood silent for the weekend, and apart from the odd passing vehicle, I was alone in my own little world.

After a few moments of quiet contemplation, I got down to business. As I fired up the saw, birds shot out from the hedges up into the clear blue sky. Working methodically, I cut up the tree then barrowed the first logs to the woodshed.

It was mid-afternoon, and I saw the red Peugeot appear on the bottom road. As I stored away my tools, it roared up the drive and braked sharply outside the kitchen. Diane jumped out first, a thunderous look on her face. Slamming the car door, she stormed into the house. Oh oh!

It transpired there'd been an 'incident' in the supermarket. Ben had thrown a tantrum because he couldn't have a banana. The bunch had been placed on the check-out belt with the other shopping, and he'd been told he could have one when the 'nice lady' weighed them. But like many a two year old, he wasn't prepared to wait. He wanted one *right then*. As he began kicking off, Diane took him outside to calm him down. But he continued kicking and screaming until Nadine came out with his banana; by which time, Diane was simmering.

Back home, Nadine carried him inside, laying him down for a nap as he'd exhausted himself crying. With coffee poured peace was restored; and with the boys tucked up in bed after our meal, we watched music videos over drinks. Kay was the first to crash out, going to bed after Meatloaf finished his gig. Next, Status Quo lined up onstage for their spot. Finally, as Tina Turner strutted out into the spotlights on her Louboutin high-heels, I left the ladies to a little mother and daughter time and headed off to bed.

We were all strung out the next morning. Diane had hit the sheets at two fifty am, leaving Nadine watching *Lord of the rings* alone. However, Ben didn't intend lying in; and being up *way* before Nadine, he cried until she appeared doing her Oscar winning zombie impression. He then claimed her complete attention. It was so frustrating. When he was calm he was a blonde-haired little angel; but when he was wound up, he was like a Tasmanian Devil. So, until his tantrums abated, we daren't visit anyone. I felt for Diane, as Ben was her first grandchild, and she'd looked forward to taking both boys to visit our friends. Then again, it was early days.

Following an afternoon of highjinks, Nadine finally got Ben to stay in bed. And as peace descended, we all sat like stunned mullets staring at a video. But we couldn't concentrate, as we expected him to erupt from the bedroom at any moment. So with nerves jangling we went off to bed early, hoping things would improve soon.

Tip-toeing along the corridor at five the next morning, I quietly raked out then lit the fire. Enjoying a little 'me' time, I sat reading until Diane emerged. I'd just made her a cuppa when we heard Ben crying. The noise then grew progressively louder, until the kitchen door burst open, and Nadine carried Ben in kicking and screaming. As she bundled him into his high chair, I went out for firewood to escape the bedlam.

When I returned with the log basket, Kay was just making *her* appearance, yawning mightily and carrying Lewis. It was five thirty and we were all up.

With the breakfast battle finished, we seized a brief window of opportunity, and with the sleeping Ben strapped in his car seat, we set off for Saumur. He woke on the way, but we distracted him by car-spotting, which kept him entertained until we arrived. Parked safely by the riverside, I thought – *so far so good.*

With Ben strapped into his pushchair, Nadine moved off, followed by Kay pushing the docile Lewis. We managed to visit *Intermarché* and *Vetimarché* before Ben became restless. Deciding we'd seen enough anyway, we set off home.

On the way through Noyant, we stopped for pastries at the *boulangerie,* and because of passing traffic, Diane and Kay nipped in for the goodies. But because he wasn't allowed to get out of the car, Ben kicked off big style.

'Right, let's go,' Diane said, when she climbed back in with the treats.

Drive it like you stole it, I thought, pushing the accelerator to the floor; while behind me, Nadine tried to calm Ben, who was screaming and kicking the back of my seat. With the noise drilling into my brain, I risked a speeding ticket getting us home. We arrived none too soon and gave Ben something to eat. But after an afternoon of non-stop screaming we'd had enough. He was in bed at five pm.

Calming down, we finally managed to feed Lewis and ourselves. Then settling down with wine, we watched a Hugh Grant film – coincidentally entitled, *About a boy.*

Chapter 6

The winter market ruckus

The next morning was a revelation. Hearing Ben crying, I tip-toed out of our bedroom and found him sat in the corridor. Picking him up, I carried him to the kitchen and gave him juice; then lighting the superser, I sat reading to him. What a change. He was a totally different child. We sat there for half an hour in companionable absorption as I explained the story to him. Then Nadine got up!

As *soon* as she walked into the room, he began crying for her attention. Before long, Diane and Kay made their appearance and it was game on. Unfortunately, we were trapped inside due to torrential rain; and unable to go anywhere, we sent a worn-out Nadine back to bed. But surprise, surprise, Ben wanted to go with her, and howled when he couldn't. We took turns reading to him and played games, but as soon as Nadine got up he swarmed all over her, demanding her undivided attention. As for Lewis, he couldn't get a look in. This had to stop.

Trying a strategy recommended by so called 'experts,' we began ignoring Ben completely when he kicked off. This new development totally baffled him. But on the flip side, he soon realised that if he behaved, Auntie Kay took him to see the ducks as a reward.

That afternoon, Diane took them all shopping, while I chickened out to increase the logpile. Apparently the trip was a success, and they even managed to call into Le Lavendu where the girls met Bertrand and Anna. As Véronique was at work, Anna cooed over the boys, and as Ben remembered 'the man' from earlier all went well. However, he soon became restless. So using tiredness as an excuse, he was plonked in his buggy outside the kitchen. Meanwhile, Lewis captivated Anna and Bertrand with his ready smile, and using this judicious white lie the visit went well. Unaware of any problem, Anna fussed over everyone.

They left, with Ben 'the sleeping angel' transferred to his child seat. Somehow, Kay had managed to buy some clothes, and they'd also done food shopping. Plus, Diane finally got to show our neighbours her grandkids. Not bad in the circumstances, I suppose. This was the way to play it then – softly softly catchee monkey. It's an old saying, but still relevant today.

We hit lucky again on the Friday, when Henri and Annette called in from Noyant market. Lewis was his usual smiling self, and with Ben behaving admirably for a change, the visit went well. As things were improving daily by then, Nadine could finally relax. With the kids in bed, Diane and I retired early, leaving Nadine and Kay watching Tina Turner in concert. Singing along raucously with their heroine made sleeping impossible for me, but Diane, in training for the snoring Olympics was oblivious to the noise. Steering the girls to bed around two am, I read for a while before crashing out on the settee.

Then things took a spooky turn! Around six am, some gut instinct woke me – to find Ben standing roughly a metre away staring wide-eyed at me in the gloom. *Jesus Christ*! Did he want me to have a *heart attack*?

Switching on the light, I laid him on the settee and lit the fire, talking to him quietly throughout. He seemed content to lie there – until sounds of stirring came from upstairs. Soon everyone was up. But to our surprise, *this* time breakfast got underway harmoniously.

It was the day of Le Lude's *Marché Noel,* or winter market. Unfortunately no-one had informed the weather gods. It was cold and foggy, but come hell or high water, we were going.

With breakfast over by seven-thirty, Diane and I nipped to Le Lude for shopping. After paying off a major chunk of the French national debt for groceries, we drove to the *Place de Marie* to scope out the market. Arriving in the square, though, we found little activity; just a few stalls being set out by depressed looking traders.

'Never mind,' I said, turning back. 'It's still early.'

Approaching our driveway we found the house still standing, which was a relief. And though we were all keen to get out, we thought it advisable to have an early lunch first. Afterwards the kids could have a nap; then suitably refreshed, we'd head out in the afternoon. By then, everything should be in full swing. With lots of lights, decorations and events to see, it would give the kids a festive treat. Hah – If only!

We arrived to find most of the stalls were set up inside the community hall. Worse still, most of them were selling foodstuffs. Where were the decorations and lights? It wasn't looking good. Then, to further enrich my day, I almost caused an international incident!

Behind a stall run by the local school, was a large backdrop painted by the kids. On it, all the countries of the world were depicted – except for the UK and Ireland. When I asked the sour-faced teacher, '*Ou est Angleterre Madame?*' she shrugged derisively and turned away. Well, so much for the European Union then!

Stepping outside into a drizzle, we found a small merry-go-round turned by two ponies; while standing nearby looking incredibly bored, two more Shetlands waited to give kids rides. Quaint and amusing though it was, it wasn't a threat to Disneyworld. Half an hour was stretching it, so we set off home.

On our way back, we passed Henri and Annette walking along the back road. We waved, thinking it was as well they'd called yesterday as they'd seen the boys at their best. They'd also gotten hugs and kisses into the bargain. After the *Marché Noel* fiasco however, all bets were off.

Arriving home damp and dispirited, Diane and Nadine prepared lunch while Kay and I ran Ben ragged playing football, hoping to tire him out. Meanwhile, Lewis just sat smiling in his chair at peace with himself. Soon, Ben's eyelids began to droop. 'I love it when a plan comes together,' I said, paraphrasing Hannibal Smith of 'The A-Team' TV series.

'Right, I'll get him off to bed,' said Nadine picking Ben up. Hah! It was like trying to wrestle an eel. Eventually, though, he gave in, and with him tucked up in bed we relaxed, watching the quirky Aussie cross-dressing movie, '*Priscilla Queen of the Desert.*' Following that, we gorged ourselves on two episodes of Billy Connolly's, '*Travels around Australia,* 'made possible only after Kay sorted out a problem with the VCR. 'You two are such technophobes,' was her withering comment.

A bleary day best spent indoors was our considered opinion of Sunday. After sleeping late, I woke at seven am. As Nadine and Ben were already up, I lit the fire. With it being dismal and depressing, the day was mainly spent watching kid's videos – anything to keep the peace really.

Taking advantage of the calm, Nadine asked Diane if she'd cut Ben's unruly hair. Consenting warily, Diane stipulated there must be no tantrums, or she'd have to stop. Scissors and ears just don't mix. With Ben gowned up she began cutting, but after a few snips he kicked off. Enough!

After that, the day dragged on till the bedtime ritual. With Ben in bed, our tele-fest for the evening was *Moulin Rouge;* followed by Status Quo in concert. It was an eclectic mix no doubt but Lewis loved it, bobbing along with Quo then attempting the can-can in his high chair copying the Follies Bergère. Go Lewis! When he tired, we laid him down in our room to give him a full night's sleep for a change.

In the early hours, I woke up to unnerving scratching and whispering noises and found myself on the settee. Don't ask me how I got there, I couldn't tell you. I hadn't touched a drop of alcohol, so maybe I'd turned to somnambulism as a hobby. Seriously though, what had woken me up?

On her previous visit, Nadine swore the house was haunted. I'd just laughed. But now I was having second thoughts. Hellfire, what was that *slithering* noise? Heart pounding, I switched on the table lamp – and found Ben creeping across the tiles towards the kitchen. Pulse rate dropping, I got up and gave him some juice which settled him. As I lit the fire, Nadine entered the lounge and he immediately kicked off. It was at that point that I experienced an epiphany! I'd formulated a new TV reality show titled, 'Help, I'm a Grandad, get me out of here.'

It was their final day and we set off for the Airport. Calling into Le Lude's Tabac, Nadine bought duty-free cigarettes. Then moving on to *Intermarché*, I fuelled up the car and we headed for Tours.

All went well until we encountered a cordon of police, security, and customs near the airport. What was this? Had they heard that Ben was headed their way? No, it was a film crew shooting a TV commercial, we heard later.

After check-in, we commandeered a restaurant table, ordered *frites* and drinks, then hogged the space until the flight was called. At eleven thirty the incoming plane roared in, landed and quickly disgorged its passengers.

Bing-bong! The outgoing flight was called, and we all stood up … and *that's* when Ben acted out his swan-song.

With the two kids, their buggies and hand luggage for Kay and herself to wrestle with, Nadine had attached a safety wrist-band and leash to Ben to prevent him running off. As they joined the customs queue he refused to walk, and sat on the floor crying. With a queue pushing behind and flat out of options by then, Nadine was forced to drag him kicking and screaming through customs on his backside. Then just as we wondered what else could possibly happen, he suddenly stood up and began waving cheerfully at everyone.

Smiling angelically, he shouted, 'Bye bye,' to the assembled crowd. Then turning back again, he disappeared into the departure lounge.

Oh my God! With everyone's eyes on us and feeling guilty by association, we watched them board the plane and take off, before slinking out of the concourse like whipped curs. Too stunned to speak, we drove home in total silence – except for the coughing that is. ... We'd both picked up Lewis's cold.

We arrived home utterly drained; and while Diane made a snack I tidied up robotically. Then totally wiped out, we fell asleep. Waking after an hour feeling worse if that were possible, we stayed awake until Nadine rang to say they'd arrived home safely. She then told Diane what'd happened in Tours departure lounge.

When they cleared customs, Ben lay down on the floor screaming. With people blatantly staring at them by then, she lost the plot, shouting, 'What's the matter? Has nobody seen a two year old throw a tantrum before?'

And, as no-one offered to help, she'd had to get him, the buggy and baggage to the plane. Following behind her, Kay pushed Lewis in the other buggy, while lugging shoulder and carrier bags. With their hand luggage finally stowed in the overhead lockers, she strapped Ben into his seat – where he slept throughout the whole flight home.

Chapter 7

Back to normality

It was ridiculously early when I came to. Unable to get back to sleep, I cradled a cup of hot milk while gazing vacantly at a video left in the VCR. Nodding off somewhere around four am, I woke three hours later, lit the fire, and slumped down in the lounge with a coffee. Sleepwalking into the situation, Diane flopped down listlessly next to me. Recognizing her need, I headed for the kettle. Within minutes, she too was clutching a coffee.We just sat there for ages too stunned to move, savouring the unusual quiet. Feeling shell-shocked, we took on our caffeine hit in silence.

Snapping out of our lethargy with great difficulty, we forced down breakfast then got on with our day. Within minutes, Diane had the guest bedding whirling in the washing machine, while I readied my saw for action. Behind the weathered *mouton* hut a pile of silver-birch trunks lay begging to be logged. And growing nearby, the flame tree displaying red candle-like seed pods needed pollarding. After all, winter was looming and could easily catch us out. Even though the wood was unseasoned, it would prove a valuable asset for the future.

Initially the saw performed well – that is until it decided to have a prima-donna tantrum and throw off its chain. Aware how dangerous that *could've* been I consulted the manual – a rare occurrence, Diane would say.With the problem fixed, the valley echoed to the Komatsu's staccato bark again. Amid a rain of sawdust, a pile of logs began to emerge.

Heading into the house after stacking a logpile, I found lunch almost ready. But after eating it, we wished we hadn't stopped working. We both felt too listless to start again. Struggling to fight off our colds, we decided to go easy on ourselves. After all, we'd tidied the house, bedding was drying on the line and I'd cut a stack of logs. We deserved a break. On the whole, we'd enjoyed the family visit, but we needed to pull ourselves together and get back to normality.

Needing a boost to our revival, we decided to cut each others hair. When I left school jobs were hard to find, and with few choices, I entered a hairdressing apprenticeship. After three years I moved into industry. But the cutting skills hadn't deserted me, and had served me well throughout my life. While tending to past girlfriends, my ex-wife and boys, I'd passed on my knowledge, ensuring that I also got *my* hair cut. With Diane as my latest student it was even more useful. She'd been cursed (she'd say) with long, thick, curly hair. She found it a nightmare to manage, and had rarely found a hairdresser who could tame it – though many had tried and failed. The final straw was her parent's joint 70th birthday party, when the salon appointment booked by her mum ended in disaster, putting a damper on her day. It was time to lay those ghosts. I mean, what had she to lose? Living in the boondocks with no UK visits planned, we'd only the locals and sheep to impress – so no pressure! She really needed a shorter, manageable style, more suitable to the French climate.

Determined to right a lifetime's wrongs, I experimented, by setting up three mirrors angled obliquely to one another. In them, she could see all aspects of her hair reflected, while I pointed out what I had in mind. After agreeing the style I cut it in stages; letting her see everything I did as it developed. Soon, a pile of hair covered the tiled floor.

'There's enough here to stuff a cushion,' she joked nervously.

Having removed the bulk. I stopped. I wanted to give her time to get used to the shorter length. If she wanted more cut the next day, then so be it. Swivelling her gaze between the mirrors she was excited. It was almost how she'd wanted it after a lifetime of disappointment.

The next day dawned; and with Diane suggesting just a little more shaping, the final cut took place. After she'd shampooed and styled it, the difference was remarkable.

'By George, I think we've got it,' I said, paraphrasing the late Rex Harrison.

Later, I received an extra special trim in appreciation. And with us both feeling so much better afterwards, it helped us on our road to recovery.

Despite still feeling dog rough on the Saturday, we decided to press ahead with a visit to Saumur. It was the beginning of December and a gloriously crisp winter's day. As we cruised along quiet country roads in brilliant sunshine, rich earthy smells blew in through the car windows lifting our spirits.

Parking under plane trees with the car sheltered from the glaring sun, we crossed the road to *Emmaus* which was buzzing with jostling humanity. Browsing leisurely, we snagged a couple of bargains then ducked out. A stroll along the riverside was much more beneficial. Absorbing the architecture and picturesque views refreshed us, and feeling much more alive, we left for home.

Driving back, we were once again diverted around Vernantes – after visiting the classic car showroom of course. Following *deviation* signs, I then drove through the pretty little village of Mouliherne, a feast for the eyes.

Feeling totally relaxed when we got back, I helped Diane unpack before ringing my ex-manager regarding my pension fund. Sprawled on the settee afterwards, we passed the late-afternoon and evening sampling a few glasses of *rosé* while discussing our day.

Reading a novel in bed the next morning was a chilly affair, so getting up, I lit the fire. I felt better than yesterday, but Diane was coughing hoarsely. Her problem was, despite trying hard to give up, she occasionally smoked. And the previous evening, while enjoying her wine, she definitely shouldn't have. I'd given up on Millenium eve, and doubtless she'd find *her* right time. But right then she was honking like a seal.Though neither of us had much of an appetite, we forced down breakfast believing it would set us up for the day. Now some people retire to a life of ease in the sun, but we had neither the time nor funds for such a sybaritic lifestyle. Of course we had the odd day out, but we had a plan in place to restore the farm, and with only Jane as competition, our house could be let out while we turned two of the outbuildings into holiday *gîtes*. With a set budget and a five year French mortgage there wasn't much time for leisure. So Diane's agenda, despite her cold, was to empty the kitchen cabinets and welsh- dressers, move them and paint the back wall. She reckoned the paint fumes would clear her lungs. What doesn't kill you makes you stronger, being her motto.

As it was drizzling, I donned waterproofs, and with the chainsaw, spare fuel, and tools in the barrow, I set off to find wood. I'd managed to discover quite a bit on our land, and by keeping busy, we burned less. Coming from 'up north,' we try to follow the axiom – there's no such thing as bad weather, you're just wearing the wrong clothes. In other words, keep busy and layer up.

I was busy in the woodshed that afternoon, when Diane shouted, 'Bertrand and Véronique are here.'

Downing tools, I went indoors. Entering the lounge, I found them admiring our latest changes.They'd just returned from visiting François, where they'd squeezed in a cross-border trip to Biarritz. They said the temperature was high and the cost of living low. Hearing my saw labouring when they arrived, Bertrand couldn't resist lecturing me on tooth sharpening. I'd intended filing them after cutting the last few logs, but they'd turned up before I finished. Knowing that he meant well, I gritted *my* teeth and let it pass.

After a short visit they left to meet friends; Bertrand nipping off to his *cave* first to decant *eau de vie* into an unlabelled bottle. With dusk approaching, I carried in two log baskets, banked up the fire and closed the shutters. It was just as well. I'd just finished, when a sudden squall ripped through the valley pushing a heavy rain front.

The weather worsened over the following week, and fighting wet and windy days our colds lingered on. Therefore, unless I had wood to cut or we needed to shop, we worked inside.

We began Monday by stripping and repainting the kitchen units, though, I was forced to leave Diane to it at one point. The saw was acting up, so driving to *Jaman*, he fixed it under warranty. While I was away, Diane had followed her instinct and begun painting a cabinet. Though I'd been against the idea initially, I had to admit it looked good, so grabbing a brush, I helped her finish.

Earlier that morning, I'd hitched up the small trailer and driven up to the woods. The recent storm had brutalized the trees, leaving broken branches strewn everywhere. I amassed quite a stash in the woodshed; and returning with my last load, I passed Bertrand sawing logs on a trestle. With Véronique assisting him, he made it look effortless. I envied the way his saw just eased through a stack of wood. Of course he had years of experience, owned a couple of expensive chainsaws, and his wood had been seasoned for three years. But our budget couldn't accommodate wood buying, so we'd just have to burn whatever I could lay my hands on.

49

With the trailer offloaded into the woodshed, I strolled over to borrow Bertrand's scaffolding as arranged. Catching sight of me, his routine sawing suddenly switched to a virtuoso master-class. He just couldn't help himself. However he went too far this time, as he topped off his performance by sawing one-handed. That was a big 'no-no' in the chainsaw manual, and I couldn't resist the opportunity to turn the tables on him. '*Non non,*' I said, wagging *my* finger from side to side; '*Il est dangereux.*'

Concurring whole-heartily, Véronique scolded him; and looking suitably chastened, he shrugged then shook my hand. After planting three kisses on Véronique then exchanging pleasantries, Bertrand and I carried the scaffolding and planks over to Le Ferronerie. Avoiding Diane, who was still painting, we rigged up the platform for the following morning. With good light and an early start, the job should go well.

With Bertrand gone, I helped Diane continue painting until eight pm before stopping for our meal. Afterwards, I was up for a night of wine and rock videos. But if I'd succumbed, we'd probably have lost the next day nursing a hangover. It was right what that retired nurse told me months before. Casual drinking could easily get out of control. That old chestnut, 'the Sun's over the yardarm *somewhere,*' had become our mantra recently. However, on this occasion it hadn't a chance to become a problem. Before Tina Turner could get into her stride, I was nodding off on the settee, my untouched glass on the tiled floor beside me.

Once the kitchen units had been fitted the next morning, I got ready to climb the scaffolding. I wasn't keen, though, as we both felt rough. We just couldn't shake off our coughs. At first we'd blamed our head-colds, then the smokey fire. But we couldn't detect any leakage or smell, so feeling chilled even when fully dressed, we had no choice. The fire had to continue burning.

With it banked up work began. But after an hour of feeling cold and miserable, we sloped back off to bed. Unfortunately it didn't help *me*, as almost immediately, Diane began snoring. Sighing, I got back up, stoked the fire into life and made coffee. Enlivened and a little warmer after my caffeine intake, I re-visited the scaffolding. Mustering a determined effort I patched the ceiling. *But that's me finished until it dries out*, I thought. Yeah – of course it was!

Climbing down, I noticed the empty log basket. Donning warmer clothes, I grabbed the chainsaw and headed for the woodshed. Though knackered, I cut wood until the fuel ran out, ending up with enough logs for a few days.

Heading back in, I found Diane had resurfaced and was looking worried. 'While you were in the woodshed, a white van pulled up and a scruffy looking guy climbed out. He had a quick look around then drove off again.'

We'd had trouble with these people before. Some were genuine '*Marchands de ferraille,*' or scrap-merchants, who'd doorstep you, asking if you had any scrap metal. But others were thieves casing your premises. The police had warned Bertrand to take care, so I mentioned our visitor to him – just in case.

Later, while Diane made a snack, I filled the log baskets. With the fire banked up and the heaters set on maximum I hoped to raise the room temperature. It was so cold that our hearts weren't into working, so we stopped and did an E.T. (phoned home.) Speaking to Stewie and Helen helped us feel better; and despite it being bitterly cold, we continued working for as long as we could. But with bed looking decidedly attractive, it was another early night.

When it's four degrees C in your bedroom, you know things are bad. But gritting her teeth, Diane continued painting throughout the morning, though, her breath was clearly visible despite all attempts to maximise the heating.

However cold it was inside the house, though, venturing outside was worse, as the wind-chill factor heightened the problem. Nonetheless, finding wood was vital, as the fire was devouring it an alarming rate. In desperation, I was forced to ignore François' warnings. In his absence, I dragged some silver-birch windfalls from the copse next to ours. They'd obviously lain there for years, and were moss-covered and mouldering. Cutting them into manageable lengths, I dragged them to the woodshed. Maybe it wasn't kosher, but sorry François, we're fighting to stay warm here.

Another wood source, though un-seasoned was one of three huge cherry trees. Overhanging the storm-ditch it was dangerous and needed pollarding. Cutting off the main branches would yield lots of logs – though none we could burn right then. Nonetheless, it needed doing.

Balanced above the ladder wedged in a tree-fork wasn't the *best* place for the saw chain to fly off – but it did. Climbing down, I re-fitted it in the workshop. But back up the ladder it flew off again. And this time, a locking-nut flew off into the long grass. I searched high and low for ages without success. Had I a magnet, or an old speaker I could cannabalise for one? No was the answer. So, asking Diane to come out in that deathly chill, we finger-searched the whole area. I could have kissed her when she eventually found it – if my lips hadn't been so numb that is.

Following re-assembly, though, I had another problem. The chain drive wouldn't turn. Oh great, just what I needed. Removing the chain, I noticed damage to the base of the drive bar. Oh-oh! I had to box clever here.

Back in my workshop, I stripped the saw down. After cleaning it scrupulously it *still* wouldn't turn, so re-assembling it, I took it to Jaman. Enquiring after his pregnant wife's health to get him onside, I then proceeded to give him a whitewashed version of what'd happened, hoping to get it fixed under warranty. Removing the guard, he grunted and pointed to the damaged bar. Peering over his shoulder I feigned surprise. I swore that I'd followed the handbook faithfully; even taking lessons from Bertrand before using it. He looked at me shrewdly. I returned his stare innocently. Cutting a new length of chain, he fitted it '*gratuit.*' After a thorough checkover, he pronounced the saw to be '*parfait.*'

I returned home a chastened man. By then it was twilight and bloody freezing. If I didn't warm up soon, the nuts on the saw wouldn't be the only ones dropping off.

My next experience with the saw was the following morning. Balanced precariously up the ladder once again, I attacked one of the two lower limbs – both as thick as a weightlifter's thigh. As each one fell there was an almighty 'thud'and the tree shuddered. Stepping back, I assessed the upper section still to be topped. After much thought, I came up with a brilliant solution (in my mind that is.) I'd tie myself to the tree before making the final cut. Noooooohhh!

When the saw finally chewed through its thick girth, a groaning noise emanated from the stricken tree. And like a drunken man, the top section keeled over. With a loud cracking noise, it parted company with the main trunk and crashed heavily to the ground.

Have you ever seen a tuning fork vibrate? Well that was that cherry tree as it was suddenly released from all that weight. It shook violently with me hanging on desperately. Jesus! I thought I'd lost my fillings. Climbing down after the shaking, I decided to leave the rest of *that* job for later.

Following a quick change of clothes, we hitched up 'The Hippo' and drove to La Flèche for insulating panels. With them stacked onboard, we headed home, keeping to side roads to avoid nosey *gendarmes*. It didn't help that the load stuck up above the trailer. Let's be honest, it even looked dangerous unloaded.

We began measuring and cutting early the next day, and by lunch-time the panels were fitted to the walls. But until we could afford central heating, we'd done all we could. The panelling had proved expensive, but before we fit it the room was like a walk-in freezer. With the bedroom door open, cold air had flooded into the kitchen. And wrapped up in our blankets at night, was what I imagined lying on a slab in the morgue would be like.

Chapter 8

Jobs, jobs – and more jobs

With the clock running down, we began dreaming about outstanding jobs. The kitchen with its colour-matched units was now finished; magnolia paint gracing the walls, and the ceiling emulsioned in white. It was time to tackle the lounge ceiling, and Bertrand's scaffolding stood there daring me to climb it. But first there was wood to cut.

I headed off to the woodshed after breakfast while Diane blitzed the kitchen; and with log-baskets filled, we covered the lounge furniture with dust-cloths prior to painting.

However, it was *Emmaus* day at Saumur and a rare sunny day into the bargain; a combination hard to resist. Downing tools, we ate lunch then set off through empty countryside, noting wood-stacks everywhere. Of course we could have our own stacks – if we were prepared to spend a sizeable chunk of our budget on them. But unless the 'wood fairy' left us some *gratuit,* we'd just have to muddle through.

Our visit to *Emmaus* yielded a quality tea service amongst other useful items. We also met a nice couple living in Mouliherne who owned *two* French houses; one bought jointly with their daughter who'd intended letting it as a *gîte.* However, she moved in with a Frenchman and lost interest so they'd bought her out. They also owned a cottage in England which they rented out. If only *we* had that much equity we sighed. We weren't jealous (honest.) They seemed like a hard working couple, so we wished them good luck in their endeavours.

Our new aquaintances left after exchanging contact details, and waving them off, we went to pay for our items. At the cashier's desk however, the operator couldn't process either of our bankcards. With a queue of impatient buyers building behind us, we had to use cash. Without cards we couldn't buy Christmas presents or food, and we daren't try the cards in an ATM in case it 'munched' them. The problem needed sorting quickly, as we were also running low on diesel for the car.

Deciding we'd best curtail our trip, we drove directly to Saumur's *Credit Agricole* to report the issue. After queuing for ages the teller tried the cards. They both worked just fine.With a wry smile, she implied that the guy at *Emmaus* could have inserted them incorrectly. Feeling relieved, I thanked her and we drove on to *Leclerc*, where Diane used our *'Carte de Fidelite'* points to buy Kay's Christmas present. Sadly, Chris lost out again, as we still couldn't find anything for him. After buying fuel and food, I called into *Brico* for a cooker hood.

'Avez vous ca Monsieur?' I asked the assistant, giving him the make and model number.

'Non,' was his abrupt response.

When I asked, again in French if they did sell them, he nodded. 'So when will new stock arrive?' I asked.

He shrugged his shoulders. 'Well thanks for your help pal,' I muttered.

Meeting Jane at Noyant's *Mairie* on the Thursday, she helped us with our *Carte Vitale's* and car registration enquiry. After a long wait, the clerk said, *'Beaucoup documentation'* was required by Baugé's tax office and produced a list. Paperwork was also required by Saumur's Prefecture of Police should we require a French licence plate. Thanking Jane for her help, we drove home for a re-think.

When we got back it was zero degrees C inside the house. More heat was essential. Even with a roaring fire and our superser belting out heat, our breath was still visible. But hang on, weren't we given *another* superser by Rob and Nicola? It was battle-scarred and dented, I think, but useful if I could find it. We'd forgotten about it after the move. If memory served, it should be at the back of the barn. Wrapped up against the chill, I trawled through remnants of an earlier load. And moving a tarpaulin aside there it was, dirty and unloved. Fantastic! It could become a vital link in our attack on the 'big freeze' – if it worked. On opening it, though, I found the gas bottle was empty. Damn!

When we first arrived, we'd had to buy a gas bottle and regulator costing fifty five euros. We could do without repeating the process right then. But we had no choice. English bottles were a different fit and couldn't be traded against their French counterparts. Even the *déchetterie* wouldn't take them, saying they must be taken to a special facility fifty kilometres away for dismantling. (Yeah right!)

After working half- heartedly in the Arctic atmosphere for a while, we bit the bullet. Driving to Le Lude, we bought another gas cylinder and regulator. Then utilizing the trip, we swung over to La Flèche seeking Christmas presents for the family, plus a cooker hood at their *Bricomarché*.

Our first stop at L Flèche was *Gifi*, where we found presents and some seasonal decorations. Jill and Dale's gifts were easy, but Chris was unlucky again, though we now knew *what* to buy him. We also struck out with the cooker hood at *Brico,* finding out at the checkout that we'd been given the wrong one. And the correct model (you've guessed it) wasn't in stock. However, one *might* arrive next week, the assistant said with a shrug. When asked if we could order one, '*Non,*'was his answer.

Furthermore, he added, I shouldn't ring to check if stock has arrived as no-one would tell us. *Excuse me!* Even allowing for errors in translation, that sounded a bit abrupt. It seems customer service wasn't his forté.

Back at Le Lude we posted Kay's Birthday present; then nipping into *their Brico* on the offchance, we found the cooker hood had been delivered soon after we left.

Back in Le Ferronnerie, I soon had the superser working. Then firing up *all* our available heat sources, we gradually began building a little warmth. Even so, we thought of going to bed early to save fuel. But before we could decide yeah or nay, though, the phone rang. It was Nadine. She'd taken Ben to the GP as his prescribed medication wasn't working. She wasn't a happy bunny I can tell you; especially when the doctor's only alternative was, he should join a toddler group. She said she'd already tried that but it didn't work. The intrepid medic *then* suggested she might be exaggerating the problem. Oh boy – a doctor with a death wish. I really had to meet this hero.

Months later, Ben finally got the correct treatment. However that was a long way off. In the meantime, at least they were warm. As I switched off the heaters, Diane headed for our freezing bed clutching our lonely hot water bottle.

It was more of the same the next day; Diane painting, me working on the lounge ceiling. I only left the job to cut more wood. Now I know many of you of you are thinking, 'Come on man, just give in and *order* a load.'

Unfortunately, with precious little insulation, a broken flue and no central heating whatsoever, buying logs would be like feeding an elephant on strawberries. Needing the money elsewhere, we decided to grin and bear it. Also, being stubborn, I actually believed I could keep us supplied with my chainsaw. I really thought other people's woodpiles were excessive. Oh foolish pride!

Strangely, our only light relief at that time was provided by Henri and Annette. Having not visited for a while, they were in raptures when they saw our decorating. Impressed by what they believed were new kitchen units, Henri insisted once again that we were millionaires. Where did we buy them? When told that we'd painted the old ones they couldn't believe it; or that the cookie dough and cream colour combo was Diane's idea. That is, until we showed them other detached cupboard doors laid out to dry on newspapers. Seeing the paint roller and tray lying nearby, they touched them in wide-eyed wonderment like children exploring. Annette said Diane must become her designer and decorate their house. *Not a bad gig to get into*, I mused!

She then went off on a completely different tack. Grabbing my arm, she warned me about police patrols taking video footage of cars in the area. Due to past linguistic misunderstandings, I thought I'd best check with Bertrand first, especially as we were visiting the Prefecture's office on Monday.

Shortly after Henri and Annette left, another car drove up, passed the house and stopped on the track.

'Look at this Diane,' I said, as an elderly guy emerged and opened the car boot. Pulling out a long-handled tool and a sack, he and his wife headed off to the woods.

'What the hell are *they* up to do you reckon?'

Getting ready to go shopping, Diane replied, 'God only knows. But if you find out tell me later.'

When she'd gone, I continued painting and missed the couple's return. I was just in time to see the car drive off. I thought, maybe they'd been collecting holly, mistletoe, or ivy for Christmas decorations. If so, I didn't see any harm in it. It could be an established tradition around here. If it was anything else, then what we didn't know wouldn't hurt us.

Finishing the kitchen panels, I laid them to dry while I tested the bathroom floor-tiles. The paint seemed ready for a second coat. But it was ferociously cold, even with a superser working flat-out nearby. Before painting, I removed slippers and socks as usual to avoid contamination. On my knees, I reversed towards the doorway, with my feet like ice-blocks and my ass in the air. Just then the door opened, and fresh from her shopping trip, Diane gave me a wolf whistle. Though she provided tea and sympathy, I'm sure I detected a wry smirk there.

After tidying up, we admired the gleaming ultramarine tiles before adjourning for a meal and entertainment. With the log fire crackling, the superser's spluttering, and the oil-filled radiators giving off that hot paint smell, one room was relatively warm – for now anyway.

It started early as we worked quietly inside. It should have been peaceful; after all it was Sunday, a day of rest. But silly me, I forgot the hunt didn't I?

A frenzied howling way off in the distance was followed soon after by the tooting of trumpets and shrieking whistles. As the bedlam grew nearer, we heard the occasional cry of 'Merde,' as boots slipped on frosted grass. Grinning at each other, we shook our heads before knuckling down again in the bitter cold.

Once the hunt had disappeared along the valley, it turned into a relaxing day spent tackling a few easy jobs. But jobs that made a lot of difference. I began by refitting the kitchen unit doors, then after fixing a ceiling lamp, I cried, 'Let there be light.' But flicking the switch, there wasn't.

Gutted, I unearthed another lamp, which I cannibalized to mend its friend. But the lamp *still* wouldn't work. After checking the wiring, I set them both aside and began fitting the extractor hood instead. However *that* didn't work either; though, after tracing the fault, I fixed it. Everything else went just fine. But that damned lamp really bugged me. I'd really liked it. Worse still, I couldn't buy a replacement for it, as Sunday trading was unheard of back then. But even if the shops *had* been open, I *still* couldn't buy one. I couldn't get out. Our drive was blocked by hunter's vehicles, while their owners ran across the fields chasing their damned dogs. Roll on Christmas!

Deteriorating rapidly over the next week, bad weather forced us to work indoors yet again. With our time concentrated on essentials, it was surprising what we accomplished. I rectified dodgy electrics then fitted curtain poles, allowing Diane to hang drapes in the dining room. Walls were 'prepped' and painted, and the lounge ceiling received its final coat; then with scaffolding dismantled, I returned it to Bertrand.

During this period the valley experienced regular power-cuts, with no warning or reason given. We just had to work around them. Life was anything but boring in our *commune*.

One of the few times we ventured out was to replace a gas cylinder, then take the overflowing trailer to the *déchetterie*. We'd checked opening days, and luckily for us our jovial little guy was on duty, as technically we should be using the facility near Noyant. Our farm was just inside area 49, Maine-et-Loire; but as our designated *déchetterie* was miles away, we used the one just along the road in area 72 Sarthe, Le Lude. The last two letters on vehicle number-plates denoted the '*area de habitation,*' so when we pulled up with our English-plated rig the first time he looked puzzled. Asking us if we were from area seventy two, I of course replied, '*Oui Monsieur.*'

He was happy enough with that, and came to know us well over the following months. He ran an immaculate site single handed, which we respected by always cleaning up after ourselves. Anyway, did it really matter which site we used. After all, rubbish is rubbish isn't it?

Unloading into the *monstre,* or general waste skip, we swept out the trailer before returning home to prepare for our next mission, picking up the furniture from Le Lavendu.

Bertrand had designated December the twentieth for the moving operation, the day their new furniture was being delivered. We too had a deadline. Jill and Dale were spending Christmas with us. With the house almost finished and fine weather promised, it was all systems go.

François called around before we left for the *déchetterie*, saying his 'fazzaire' would be ready around one thirty. Arriving on time, I paid him for the furniture then planned the lift. Driving over to Le Ferronerrie on his tractor we hitched up 'The Hippo.' Linked together, they were ideal for the job.

At Le Lavendu the dining table and six chairs were loaded for the first trip; then with François and I holding things steady inside the trailer, Bertrand set off.

The second trip involved the heavy oak *armoire*, which thankfully came apart in two sections. Though it was heavy, we delivered everything damage-free through the French windows. Then we all sat down to coffee laced with *eau de vie* to celebrate our success. After the strong spirit, I wasn't sure if I'd misheard him when Bertrand declared he was definitely building a vintage car. '*We'll see,*' I thought, shaking their hands as they left.

Well the dining-room was finally complete. Standing back, we took in the beamed ceiling with hanging vintage ships lanterns, the oak *armoire*, dining table and chairs. The effect was '*trés elegante.*' Being a long room, it also featured a large Spanish-oak bookcase and a glass-fronted cabinet. With silk drapes and tie-back swags gracing the French windows, we reckoned the room was *magnifique*.

Christmas – bring it on.

Chapter 9

Flying in for Christmas

Come mid-December, the already freezing temperatures plummeted to minus 25 degrees C. Apparently we were headed for the coldest winter in France since modern records began. And as the winds increased in ferocity, news spread that a freak storm in the north had killed six people. Serious times!

Trapped in our own arctic cocoon, we carried on with last minute preparations, including hanging decorations. Our faithful old faux Christmas tree was taken from the granary and assembled. Bought in a post Christmas sale in Hexham Northumberland long ago, it'd given years of loyal service. Assuming residence in a corner of the lounge, Diane took great delight in dressing it with baubles – though for some reason tinsel was a no-no. Garlands were then draped across the mantelpiece, augmented with holly, berries, and pine cones from our wood. And the dining table was a triumph. Lavishly laid out, it featured a silver-plated candelabrum bearing red candles as its centrepiece.

It was the morning of the 21st, and with Jill and Dale arriving the next afternoon, we did last minute jobs before a final tidy-up. Nipping into the lounge, I switched on the heaters, lit the fire, and scuttled back to bed until the house warmed up. Yeah, like *that* was going to happen. Bowing to the inevitable, we leapt out of bed, dressed warmly and faced the day.

Inside the house, the windows were rimed with ice as usual, while outside, rainwater had frozen into thick opaque slabs. Moving around in the lounge, our breath was clearly visible. What on earth did we think were we doing, inviting two septuagenarians to this frozen hell hole?

But it was too late now. We were meeting their plane the following afternoon, so the least we could do was make the house as warm and cozy as possible. 'The plan' was, I'd work through the rooms tackling last minute jobs, while Diane cleaned from top to bottom. During lunch, we'd tick finished jobs off the list, then divide up the remainder for the afternoon.

I began by fitting a new insulation jacket to the hot-water tank, and a new valve kit in the toilet cistern. Wearing her marigolds, Diane scrubbed the fire surround with Bertrand's acidic cleaner; then breaking off from her jobs, she drove to La Flèche for a complete food shop. Meanwhile, I stayed behind and hung two chandeliers, fitted a blind, then lagged the outside water-meter. After carrying in two baskets of logs, I was tidying up when she returned driving the heavily laden Peugeot. Once we'd unloaded the boot-full of goodies, we kind of collapsed in a stupor.

I lit the fire after dinner; and with the heaters sited around the lounge, and the settee and chairs moved to encircle the log fire, we relaxed. We'd done everything we could.

Up and breakfasted by seven thirty the following morning, we ran our eyes over the rooms. Perfect! All that remained was washing the car, which left us enough time to make a sign saying, 'Welcome Bos party,' to hold aloft at airport arrivals. Oh, how I wished I could've laid my hands on a chauffeur's cap. Never mind, we were ready. Swinging by the orchards, we dropped off Diane and Cecile's *panniers,* before heading out to the airport.

We set off early due to dense fog; though, with it clearing quickly, we arrived on time. Esconced in the restaurant sipping coffee, we watched the Ryanair flight land bang on schedule. Seeming to hang in the shimmering air for ages, its final descent came quickly; bouncing onto the runway with a puff of smoke from its tyres. Taxiing to the main building, brakes were applied and the throttled back engines were cut, as overall wearing ground-crew rolled steps up to the doors.

Though Jill and Dale led the charge from the plane, their luggage was the last to appear on the carousel. But that was a mere bagatelle for them, compared to emerging through the glass doors and seeing our banner. With handshakes and hugs exchanged, we made our way through the concourse to the car. Like others before them, they were amazed at the efficiency of such a small operation, and astonished that we could park opposite the entrance doors – for free.

With passengers and luggage safely aboard, I drove away from the airport. Filtering onto the busy highway, the urban sprawl disappeared behind us as we headed out into the countryside.

Pulling up at the house forty minutes later our guests seemed impressed, though, we left outside viewing for later. Our immediate priority was reviving the log fire and switching on the heaters. While I attended to that part of the operation, Diane made tea and sandwiches; after which the intrepid duo were given the grand tour. They said they loved what we'd done so far, and appreciated the difficulties we'd had to overcome. Of course our lavish Christmas decorations didn't go unnoticed; especially those gathered from the surrounding landscape.

In the dining room later, dinner was served by Chef Diane. Then after a joint washing up exercise, we adjourned to the lounge, where we spent the evening chatting and watching comedy videos. As some collective yawning was happening by then, we retired for the night; all of us worn out for different reasons. Feeling noble and selfless, we donated our lone water bottle to Jill and Dale. Smacking our foreheads, we then wondered why we didn't ask them to bring another over with them?

After the upstairs tour the next morning, I blocked off the stairwell. By using the downstairs rooms only, we hoped to contain as much heat as possible. Dressed warmly after breakfast, we then walked the land, gazing across the valley from the hilltop while planning our itinary for the days leading up to Christmas.

Snatching a brief window of good weather later, I drove us to Saumur, where we introduced them to its architecture and varied shops. Then, after a leisurely stroll up to the château's cliff-top gardens, we took in panoramic views of the city and river Loire far below. It wasn't the best day weather-wise, but our stimulating walk, followed by lunch at 'Le Bourse' restaurant made for a good trip out. Well fed and satisfied, we drove home along empty roads pointing out things of interest on the way.

Back at the farm, Dale and I swung into concerted action, attending to the fire and heaters while the ladies made tea and a snack. Then relaxed in our huddle, we discussed renovation plans. With a comprehensive roundup of gossip to end on, our beds called to us at eleven thirty pm.

Noyant market was first on the agenda the next morning; though, overcast and chilly it promised little. However, well wrapped up after a hearty breakfast, we set off anyway. As we feared, it didn't take long to stroll around it. Being Christmas Eve, most sellers hadn't turned up. Trooping from the market disappointed, we drove to the local *Intermarché*, where we bought comforting treats to take back with us.

Having enjoyed lunch, and with the weather improving greatly, a visit to Château-la-Vallier fit the bill. Following a brisk ten kilometre lakeside walk, we ended up with wet socks and leggings, but feeling totally invigorated.

Cruising back, we luxuriated in the soporific warmth from the car heater. After parking, we nipped inside quickly and changed into dry clothing. I lit the fire while the ladies prepared hot drinks, then warmed through, Diane and Jill decided to cook dinner *and* prepare the Christmas Day feast.

Needing preserves from the *cave*, we decided we'd all like to explore its hidden depths. Opening the creaking old door, it seemed eerier than I remembered. The ceiling, festooned with cobwebs housed huge scuttling spiders, giving the gloomy space a gothic look. Enhancing that look, a colony of huge snails had taken up residence on the door, leaving silvery trails across its gnarled old wood-grain.

Back inside, Dale and I thought '*too many cooks*' etc. So slipping away to read by the fire, we left Diane and Jill in charge of the kitchen. After the initial clamour of preparation, a cornucopia of goodies was soon cooking; the aroma of sweet-mince pies in particular making my taste-buds drool.

As a Grand Finale to the action, the humming ice cream maker whipped up Nigella Lawson's lime and lemon desert. Paying homage to the Domestic Goddess's recipe, Diane's concoction promised to be a *tour-de-force*.

Sitting down to table, our meal began with a starter of liver pate with buttered baguette, helped down by a chilled bottle of Chablis. The main course was roast pork with all the trimmings, accompanied by a bottle of cote-de-rhone. And for 'afters,' Diane served a portion of Nigella's delight to cleanse the palate; before coffee, brandy, and a cheese platter rounded off the feast.

Settle back in front of the fire, we chuckled along to Dale's favourite 'Fawlty Towers' episodes. We all agreed, it was a fitting end to a fine day.

Chapter 10

Ding dong merrily et cetera

Christmas Day and I was up early. Though brilliant sunshine streamed through the shutters, inside it was ferociously cold. Hastily igniting the heaters and fire, I induced a trickle of warmth into the room. With memories flooding back as I filled the kettle, I contemplated Christmas Day in our little slice of France.

Yester-year's Christmas morning's had been filled with the excited cries of children. Okay, that was a long time ago, but today it was deathly quiet. It just didn't seem right. The house should be filled with noise; whereas, here I was alone in a cold kitchen making coffee.

Hearing sounds of movement, I emerged from my reverie, and minutes later Diane sashayed into the lounge. With her tousled hair, she was a vision cocooned in fleecy dressing gown and fluffy bunny slippers. Grinning, I made her a cuppa. Accepting it gratefully, she sat near the fire. And pulling up a chair next to her, we planned our day.

In *my* past, the first order of business was calming over-excited kids, who'd be frenziedly tearing apart a mound of presents delivered by Santa Claus, (though, paid for by me.) However all that changed when the kids grew up. It'd become a more orderly exchange; first at home, then doing a round robin of family visits later.

Conversely, in Diane's family, the exchange of gifts took place in the afternoon; the practice stemming from Dale's time in the R.A.F military police, when Jill made them wait until he came off duty to open presents together.

This Christmas however was a *real* break from tradition. So, after handing out presents after breakfast, we began prepping for Christmas dinner. Looming large, though, was a promised visit from the Charpentiers later with the Grand Dame Anna in attendance. *This could be fun,* I thought. Could we witness a clash of the Titans, as the indomitable matriarchs Jill and Anna met for the first time?

However that was later, there was much to do first. With breakfast finished, Dale and I washed up while Diane and Jill tidied around. Then we fine-tuned the dining room for the impending visit. Laid out for Christmas dinner, the dining table looked both festive and elegant. Everything was ready for our guest's arrival, as we, the archetypal English family sat ready and waiting.

At ten forty five, a tentative knock rattled the door. Opening it, I found Bertrand dressed in his Sunday best, his arms full of goodies. Followed closely by Véronique, they entered exchanging kisses and handshakes. Then, as if to a trumpet voluntary, Anna swept through the doorway with a solicitous François in tow. Introductions were then made to Jill and Dale – and for a nano-second there seemed to be a mutual sizing-up by the two Grand Dames. Then Jill, ten years the younger stepped forward, addressed Anna in French and shook hands. And from that moment, it was as if they were old friends.

With everyone settled gifts were exchanged. Frankly, we weren't prepared for the family's largesse, as we received a boxed-set of wines, a *paté*, and *rillettes de canard*. We then handed over *our* humble offerings. A large christmas pudding, (a complete mystery to them all) a festive box of English goodies, some home made mince-pies to tempt

Bertrand's sweet tooth, and a large slab of cheddar cheese; something that Véronique loved to cook with.

The grand finale was Anna's offering, *Quarante-Quatre;* a home-made liquor comprised of *eau de vie,* coffee and oranges, which, as the name implies took forty four days to mature. Presented in a dignified manner, it belied her modest circumstances. In her demeanour, she reminded me of a Russian *émigré* from the Royal Court. But whatever her lineage, the lady brewed a mean potion. It almost blew Jill's socks off – figuratively speaking of course!

With glasses filled, a magical hour passed; Véronique admiring our lavish table decorations while Bertrand mounted a charm offensive on Jill. At the far end of the table, a dignified but attentive Dale beguiled Anna, bringing an extra blush to her already rouged cheeks.

Sadly, and all too soon, they rose to leave. We all had much to do. They were visiting family and friends, while we needed to catch up with ours by phone. We were running a little late I suppose – but hey, it was Christmas!

Waving them off, we began our preparations, and in record time, the turkey was carried to the table. Surrounding the bird were copious side dishes. Spoilt for choice we attacked it all, pulling crackers, and groaning at the corny jokes that fell from them. Then full to excess, waistlines straining and paper hats askew, we all collapsed. For once the room was actually warm – due mainly to the oven, I suspect. And at Diane's insistence, we wallowed in seasonal muzak, letting the Christmas spirit envelope us.

When we felt able to move again, we watched videos sent by Michael and Chris as presents, while throughout the evening, a string of phone calls drifted in from the UK. Greetings came from Michael, Stewie, and others who'd been visiting family earlier. However, Chris didn't call till much later. As a twenty one year old singleton, he had a hectic social life to maintain. He'd probably just returned home after the *previous* night's festivities. Following that exchange, an unexpected call came through from Jill's sister Judy, which was a pleasant surprise for us all.

Here we were then, ending our first Christmas night in France, and it'd proven to be as happy as any spent in the UK. Different it may have been, but it was a special time for us all.

Why shouldn't Boxing Day *also* be special then? Deciding to get some fresh air, we dressed warmly after a hearty breakfast and drove to Luché Pringé. We intended blowing away the cobwebs. And where better than strolling along the breezy riverbank on a bright winter's day.

Parked under plane trees near the church, it yet again amazed me. Whenever we came here the town was deserted. Where do they hide all the people?

Setting off along the river's edge, we walked carefully along the muddy track. The river, swollen and running fast, reached out towards rowing-boats dragged up above the waterline. As we drew level with the old mill on the opposite bank, a weak sun was breaking through scudding cloud. In high summer, a mere trickle of water would topple lazily over the weir. But in mid-winter, it was a tumbling mill-race.

Passing the barren fields, we swung inland away from the river. Cutting through the deserted town, plastic Santa's were noticeable everywhere, apparently climbing into windows and chimneys indiscriminately. Diane and I had seen it all before, but to Jill and Dale it was a whole new experience. On a more serious note, though, they were impressed by the care shown to war memorials, decorated lavishly with flowers and flags of the republic. Unfortunately, in Britain they can seem neglected in comparison.

Driving on from Luché, we entered La Flèche, dressed in its finest on that special morning. Parked on the riverfront, we joined locals promenading leaf-strewn streets, window shopping and shooting the breeze. Securing a table at a pavement café on the riverside, we watched the world go by while sipping hot coffees.

Heading home, we entered Le Lude through its back streets and parked in the *Place de Mairie*. Then, after a stretch of the legs around the impressive, but sadly closed château, it was time for lunch.

Driving back, we spotted Henri and Annette out walking. Pulling up, I introduced them to Jill and Dale. We all shook hands and murmured season's greetings, but considering the inevitable language minefield, maybe it was best not to visit them with our guests. Something for a future visit perhaps?

As afternoon waned into evening, I closed the shutters and we settled down for the night – or so we thought. With the fire crackling and the heaters hissing, we lolled back snug and warm. Then the phone rang! It was François inviting us over for aperitifs. Initially Jill wasn't keen, as like Diane, she socialized on *her* terms. But considering it only polite, I accepted.

We arrived at Le Lavendu for seven pm, and as often happens, a situation you weren't looking forward to turned into something special. With François interpreting when needed, we probed the cultural divide. Relaxed in each other's company we laughed a lot; Bertrand and I clowning around. While Dale, with steepled fingers looked on, finding Bertrand's mannerisms priceless. At ease by then and rising to the occasion, Jill coached François with his homework; outraged that his teacher had savaged his English project.

Then without warning, our happy evening was turned on its head. The TV, left flickering in the lounge, suddenly blurted out an emergency broadcast. François shushed us, as footage showed a huge volcanic eruption in the Indian Ocean. A gigantic tidal wave had hit both the Maldives and Sri Lanka. At eight point nine on the Richter scale, the eruption was reputedly the fifth largest for a century and was causing huge loss of life. There's never a good time for something like *that* to happen; but it was especially sad that it should happen at Christmas.

Returning home at eight thirty slightly subdued, we were relieved that the aperitifs we'd been invited for hadn't turned into one of Véronique's five course meals. Walking back along the track our torch wasn't necessary, as a full moon glowed in the star studded sky.

Entering the lounge, I was just in time to nurse the fire back to life; then while the ladies dissected the sacrificial turkey, I investigated the flashing light I'd spotted on the phone's messaging service. Chris had eventually surfaced and been trying to catch up with us. He'd since gone out with friends. Never mind, we'd touch base soon enough.

Visiting duty done, we relaxed watching videos, and didn't go to bed until midnight. Maybe we were worried that it would be too cold in our beds. Well, it might be for *some.* We'd donated our lone hot water bottle to Jill and Dale again. We weren't jealous – honest!

Up early lighting the fire, I was sad that our guests were leaving. Taking advantage of the brisk sunny morning, Dale wandered off with his camera, snapping a few last frames in the magical light. Meanwhile, loaded up with jars of Diane's preserves, Jill insisted she was still within her baggage allowance.

By ten thirty am, we'd set off for the airport. And despite the usual dicing with death that seems '*de rigeur*' on French roads, we arrived safely and in good time. Finding seats in the concourse, we sat detached watching the controlled bedlam of last minute check-ins. until a roar overhead signalled the arrival of the incoming Ryanair flight.

A sheep-like frenzy then ensued, as people rushed to passport control. Being old school British in attitude however, Jill and Dale took their time finishing their drinks; before, rising in a dignified manner, they gave goodbye hugs, and swept through customs into the departure lounge. With the arriving passengers disembarked, the last we saw of our guests, was them walking out to the plane, waving as they vainly tried catching our eyes through tinted windows.

Though it arrived late, the Boeing 737 was turned around quickly, and spot on time it taxied to the end of the runway. The engines were then revved to a high-pitched crescendo, the brakes released, and it surged forward. Gathering speed it hurtled along the runway, and with a deafening roar it passed us. Lifting effortlessly, it climbed steeply into low cloud and vanished from sight. Everyone, including us stood waving at the concourse window, as if their loved ones could see them way below. We drove home deep in thought. It'd certainly been a special Christmas. But sadly, it was over.

Chapter 11

The New Year – bring it on

With our visitors gone, life returned to normal. It'd been a great few days, but a substantial drain on our fuel reserves. It was time to fire up the chainsaw. Revving it lustily, I decided, anything that could burn and stood still long enough was fair game. Beginning in the woodshed, I sawed enough logs to fill both baskets and stacked a lot more. With saw-teeth freshly sharpened, I said goodbye to Diane and set off for the woods. Much later, after a long and fruitful day for us both, we discarded our jumpers and settled in for the night.We'd drunk sparingly during Jill and Dale's visit, so we decided we owed ourselves an *après* Christmas celebration. Nothing heavy mind you, as we had a busy schedule planned for the next day – just a glass or two while watching videos.

Following overnight rain, dawn brought a warming glow to the valley. With breakfast demolished, I'd just donned my work-clothes when Bertrand and François turned up on the tractor. They were heading up the field to cut back overhanging branches. Once they were removed, they'd ride around the perimeter re-seeding grass up to the fence lines, hoping new shoots would stifle weeds. It made sense if stock were to graze the pasture in the future. But first on the agenda, a sheepish-looking Bertrand hauled the Renault 6 out of the copse; his penance for dumping it there for

Monsieur Renard. With it removed, he began clearing scrub for burning. After the top field had been cleared, he intended dragging out two more wrecks from the lower meadow. As François described it, they were just a small part of Monsieur Renard's personal junkyard, hidden under huge swathes of gorse. I insisted on helping. After all, it was my land.

Carrying my saw up the field, I arrived to find Bertrand already hard at it, his tractor ripping out huge bushes using a long chain. François suggested I cut off the best branches for future firewood, and they'd burn the remaining brash later. They were always planning ahead; a concept lacking in much of today's instant gratification society.

After grafting hard all morning, Bertrand broke off to change for work. Yes – he was off to do his afternoon trucking shift. Shaking hands, he set off down the field, while François and I stacked logs into the loading bucket. Hiding the saw in a gulley, I followed François as he drove down the hill; arriving to see the load tipped outside our woodshed. In the kitchen, I saw Diane preparing lunch; so once I'd thrown the logs into the shed, I munched a cheese and ham baguette washed down with mugs of tea. Then it was time to walk back up the field. Nearing the edge of the wood, I found François replacing a broken chain shackle. After a quick repair, he continued clearing brush deep into the copse. By mid-afternoon, we'd stacked three huge piles of brush, and I'd cut a bucketful of logs. With the light failing rapidly, we gathered up our equipment and climbed wearily aboard the tractor. Lurching down the bumpy meadow sat on the mudguard wasn't the most comfortable experience, but I hadn't the energy left in me to walk. I thanked François for the lift; then after he'd tipped the logs, I stored my gear and walked stiffly into the house. That last load would have to wait until the morning.

Anticipating my need, Diane ran me a hot bath; and peeling off my grubby clothing, I climbed stiffly into it. As I slid gingerly below the surface, the steaming water lapped up to my chin. *Aagghh!* Cramped muscles slowly relaxed as the herbal additives worked their magic, and twenty minutes later, I climbed out before I fell asleep. With a hot meal inside me, I lay back content. Though the day hadn't turned out as planned, I'd gained precious fuel while tidying up the land. It'd been a good day.

In the aftermath of overnight rain, we woke to a promising morning. Still aching from yesterday, I sat down gingerly to breakfast. I was about to relax afterwards when I spotted Bertrand, on his way up our field. Sighing, I donned my work-gear, gathered my equipment and set off after him.
However, *this* time the car was carrying everything. I drove very carefully, though, as the track was deeply rutted in places. But as it wound past our work area, getting the Peugeot to do the heavy lifting made a lot of sense.

I arrived to find Bertrand, François, and his two cousins hard at it. Parked up, I piled my equipment over the fence. Then climbing over, I gathered it together and headed off to meet them. Shaking hands all around, I asked François what I could do. Pointing to Bertrand crashing into the thicket on his tractor, he said once *that* was cleared out, I'd have free reign with my chainsaw.

While fuelling the saw, François updated me on the Indian Ocean catastrophe. He said, gigantic waves, reputedly travelling at 500 mph had obliterated many islands, causing 40,000 deaths to date. India, Africa, Sri-Lanka, and the Maldives were all affected. It was unbelievable, and almost impossible to take in. He went on to confirm my suspicions, saying meteorologists had attributed Europe's recent storms to earthquake aftershocks. As we chatted, Bertrand, our resident pyromaniac lit the three bonfires we'd stacked, using waste oil as an accelerant. Within minutes, a dense pall of black smoke hung low over the valley, cancelling out any eco -credentials he might have. Upwind of the noxious cloud, I'd just begun sawing when François strolled over. Signalling me to stop, he said. 'My fazzaire, he thinks your saw needs sharpening.'

And at that, Bertrand arrived, whipped out a small file, and administered 'a light dressing' to the teeth. I held my tongue in check. But when he began lecturing me on how to saw correctly, and the others pitched in with *their* advice, I began inwardly seething. I believed they meant well, so breathing deeply and recovering the saw, I carried on.

With noon fast approaching, Bertrand left to prepare for work. And with the others due at the stables soon, they also left; dropping off the remaining logs at our woodshed while passing. Nursing a slightly bruised ego, I finished sawing; then forking brushwood onto the fires, I tidied the site. The lads had said they'd return later, and I wanted to show them I could hold my own alongside them. It was stupid of me really, as I was old enough to be their grandfather.

I left a couple of hours later, after finishing the burn and snuffing out all the embers. Arriving home, I found Diane had loaded all the wood into the woodshed. What a woman! After taking two baskets of logs inside, lunch was served. Then appetite assuaged, I waited. However, the tractor and crew didn't return. I didn't mind *at all*. They'd worked hard and deserved a break. But as Diane said – so did I.

It was as well we finished when we did. The next day was a washout. With gunmetal skies, squally rain, and plummeting temperatures to contend with, we couldn't get the fire and heaters lit quickly enough. It was hard trying to motivate ourselves; and lacking enthusiasm, we dragged out breakfast discussing the New Year. It wasn't New Year's Eve we were worried about, which promised to be quiet. It was the year stretching ahead and what it might bring.

Our discussion was interrupted by the tappety engine of the *Poste* van, followed by the squeaking mailbox flap.

'Let's hope its some good news,' I remarked.

Dashing out in heavy rain, I ran back clutching a letter franked EDF. Skimming it across the table to Diane, I went to dry myself and re-boil the kettle. After the ripping of paper, I heard, 'Bloody hell,' as I lit the hob.

Returning, I found Diane checking figures on the letter.

'What's up?' I asked, sitting down next to her.

'What's up? Look at this,' she groaned. 'It's an electricity bill for 300 euros. Good god, we must be subsidising the whole valley. It has to be a mistake.'

After she'd calmed down, I checked the meter readings. They were correct. Before now, we'd only received two small bills, which may have been under-estimated. Maybe this was catch-up time. Ringing EDF's English speaking helpline, I said '*Excusez moi Madame, parlez vous Anglais?*'

An abrupt, '*Non*' was the reply.

Breathing deeply, I asked if *anyone* in the office spoke English. Again, the answer was an emphatic, '*Non!*'

As this was EDF's dedicated English speaking helpline, I found that hard to believe!

Before visiting our bank the next day, we asked the long-suffering Jane if *she'd* ring EDF, and in her fluent French, ask if the bill was correct. If so, did we have the best tariff? It could be a mistake. But it was expensive if not corrected. Another explanation could be our water boiler, set on auto following Bertrand's advice. We may have to re-set it to demand only; but surely that shouldn't be necessary.

Anyway, while they were sorting it, I had other problems. Our wood stocks were dwindling fast. In my ongoing quest for fuel, I remembered the long poles from the dismantled chicken pens. I'd already burned some damaged ones, while storing the best for future use. After ruling out a career in ostrich breeding, or as a supplier to second rate pole-dancing clubs, firewood seemed the logical option. Hedging my bets, I cut up the warped ones; leaving the rest 'just in case.'

Stowing away my tools, I told Diane I was off to *Brico* for two-stroke and chain oils. Hitching a ride, she nipped into *Intermarché*. As tomorrow night was New Year's Eve, she thought it best to stock up on essentials.

Our final call was to *Intermarché's* garage, where I filled the car's tank and bought petrol for the chainsaw. Often, a French public holiday could stretch into a three or four day shutdown. *Best be safe*, I thought.

The morning's weather looked promising, and with nothing planned, a run to La Flèche seemed tempting. Sorry, I meant in the car. Jogging? – Are you *mad*? We strolled around the usual shops but returned empty-handed, which for Diane was quite worrying. I made a mental note to take her temperature when we got back.

Wandering aimlessly we filled in the day. In the UK, we'd have had New Year's Eve nailed down long ago. But knowing the Charpentiers, there could still be a last minute invitation to a family party. Meanwhile, we were wandering around town like 'Billy No Mates,' in a landscape populated by strangers.

We arrived home after deciding on a quiet New Year – as if we had a choice. We reckoned, if we'd featured in our neighbour's plans, we'd have known by then. Besides, we'd rather avoid a party where no-one spoke English, and we were the elephants in the room.

After our meal, we watched videos with the shutters closed. Then at midnight we listened. Nothing!

An hour later we switched off the phone, and lying in bed listening to BBC radio, we heard Big Ben ring in the New Year in the UK. After wishing each other all the best, I switched off the set. Then, turning over we tried to sleep.

Chapter 12

New Year, new problems

Well, it certainly didn't feel like New Year's Day. Not like any *I'd* ever experienced anyway. Waking extremely early, without a headache, dry mouth, or queasiness was weird. I didn't know whether to feel relieved or disappointed.

This *couldn't* be New Year's Day. It didn't feel right. Without a TV link to the outside world, we couldn't re-live celebrations in Trafalgar Square – or anywhere else in the world for that matter. We felt totally bewildered. Had the year really changed, or was this just a dream?

I opened the shutters to absolute silence. There wasn't even the usual birdsong. This was weird! With no signs of life from next door or antwhere in the valley, we felt like sole survivors of a Nuclear Armageddon. We needed to see people. Anyone really, just to know there were others out there. I checked the phone. There were no messages from the UK. And as it was too early to ring anyone there, we dressed and breakfasted, then jumped into the car. Pointing the bonnet towards Saumur, I drove off.

At first the roads were totally empty, with not a soul to be seen anywhere. But at long last, we spied a car heading towards us. I just hope they weren't too unnerved by the sight of an obviously deranged English couple waving at them, flashing their car's headlights and blaring the horn.

Realising we were, 'not alone', we drove on in a more sedate manner. However, it wasn't until we saw a news-hoarding saying *Le Jour de L'anne,* or New Year's Day, that we finally believed it was the first of January 2005. What a relief! We could finally relax, and take in the sights and sounds around us.

Actually, the city was quite busy when we arrived, as people strolled along empty streets enjoying the pallid winter sunshine. Maybe they were clearing their heads after New Year's celebrations. How could we tell? There weren't any signs of partying that *we* could see. Unlike in the UK, there were no bottles, cans, or food cartons anywhere. No vomit, no overturned waste-bins, no shop windows smashed, no car wing-mirrors, radio aerials or wiper blades snapped off. What was wrong with these people? Didn't they *know* how to celebrate?

Wandering along the boulevards, we peered into boutique shops, taking note of property prices in *Immobiliere's* windows. Crossing traffic-free streets at our leisure opened up new experiences to us; normally unavailable in the crowded summer season. On one graffiti-daubed wall, a tattered poster advertised a truffle market the following Saturday. We thought it might be worth a visit. It was that kind of day – surreal, and out of sync.with normality.

Driving back in the late afternoon, the sun had vanished and it'd begun raining. But we didn't care. We'd had a great day out, thoroughly enjoyed ourselves, and all without a hangover to overcome.

We called at a *boulangerie* on the way home, then armed with a baguette, a log from the woodshed, and a ten euro banknote, I did my own first-footing. Breaking with tradition, though, I wasn't carrying a bottle of whisky. The shops were all closed, and our newly purchased bottle was tucked away in the *armoire.* Would this kink in tradition mean an alcohol free year? Somehow, I doubted it.

Duty done, I lit the fire, while Diane made a cuppa and snack. Checking our phone messages, we returned calls, wishing family a Happy New Year.

Michael rang later. He'd been at work all day, fighting off rampaging customers during a sales promotion. After partying all night, he'd only managed four hours sleep. And Chris? Well he seemed to have two heads – neither of them working properly. Nadine was fine, but having issues with Nick. And Stewie, Helen and Kay were all in good spirits. So all in all, the year was starting off well.

With our phone-athon over, we downed a glass to celebrate our *own* New Year. While sat making plans for 2005, I fielded a call from Diane's sister Deborah. I passed the phone over and they were at it for ages, shrieking with laughter as always. New Year's Day ended for us around ten thirty. It'd been different, that's for sure.

Why does life have to be so difficult? We only wanted to browse around some shops. Today was Sunday, and with New Year's Day being yesterday, shops which were normally open on Saturday should open today instead, François insisted. But as it was Sunday, many, giving church-going as an excuse wouldn't turn in. Then there'd be the really awkward ones, who'd also take Monday off as if by right. Apparently, it was a lottery as to what you'd find open. It was far too complicated for us, so we decided to visit Château-la-Vallière instead.

While Diane finished in the kitchen, I brought in wood for later; then clothing changed, we headed out to the car – to be confronted by a flat tyre. Well thank you God!

'Never mind, give me ten minutes and I'll have it changed,' I said.

Actually it took less; and well pleased, I stowed away the tools and drove off. All went well until I increased speed and the car began to shudder. *What now*, I thought?

With the steering-wheel shaking violently in my hands, I pulled up, got out and checked the tyres for damage. They seemed okay. But whatever the problem was, it was too dangerous to continue. Reluctantly, I turned around and drove carefully home.

We'd barely gotten back when François turned up. He was returning to Bazaz and had called to say *au revoir*. He was followed by Véronique, and Bertrand who was carrying a bottle of *rosé* and his portable corkscrew. They'd come over earlier to toast in the New Year, and been mystified to see us drive off – only to return soon after. Explaining about the wheel-shudder, Bertrand said I should leave it for now. He'd pop over after work tomorrow, and we could jack the car up and inspect it together. If *we* couldn't fix it, he'd lead me to his local garage in his Xantia. His friend the *garagiste* would look after me at a reasonable cost. With our trip put on hold, François said goodbye and disappeared in a cloud of dust. Right now, where's that *rosé?*

As it was still a holiday, reprising the Riverdance video seemed like a good idea. With the performance over and the sound of tap-dancing still ringing in our ears, an enthusiastic Véronique shot off home to fetch a Spanish video they'd bought on holiday. It wouldn't play on their machine, she explained. Perhaps it would play on ours.

On her return, I inserted the video and pressed play. No problem! It played all right – but only in black and white. A Spanish video in black and white is as useful as an ashtray on a motorbike. But after the initial disappointment, they realized they could still point out their resort and other areas of interest. Three hours later they left to phone François, who they said should have arrived by then.

Doctor Atkins entered our lives on Monday January 3rd It was the first day of our diet, and Diane was kicking off the

New Year with a mini spring clean. And me? A morning in the woodshed, what else?

With a sizeable pile of logs cut, I decided to let Bertrand off the hook and inspect the car myself. I thought perhaps it was something simple, then I'd look pretty stupid. Jacking it up, I looked underneath. I'd found the problem. The brake assembly was damaged.

As promised, Bertrand turned up after lunch and I showed him my findings. He seemed pleased that I'd tried to fix it; but after a joint inspection, he suggested the garage was the best bet. With the steering and tracking appearing okay, I lowered the car, and we set off slowly with Bertrand leading.

Hazard lights flashing, we arrived at the garage to be met by the owner, Gilles, who gave me a welcoming handshake. While the car was being inspected, we had fun trying to hold a conversation in the cramped office. Within minutes, the mechanic summoned us to the Peugeot, raised high on a hydraulic ramp. Holding an inspection lamp, he pointed out more damage than I expected. But isn't it usually the case when your car goes in for repair? A track-rod was bent, possibly by a pothole, he mimed. There was also damage to the wheel-arch and brake assembly, plus a leaking hose. And I also needed a complete set of tyres, he threw in casually, as if it were an afterthought. By French law mine were illegal. What! *Oh the joys of motoring*, I thought; remembering the car tax was due on January 31st and the MOT test on February 6th. Besides the car bills, there was the upcoming ferry trip to the UK to factor in. Not to mention the cash I'd promised Michael for his wedding.

Well, Happy New Year!

I drove off with Bertrand, after sanctioning the repairs and promising to buy new tyres. Expensive or not they needed changing. It was a long drive back to the UK.

Walking into the office the next afternoon, I took out my overworked cheque book. The car was now driveable but the tyres needed changing '*toute suite,*' advised Gilles as I paid the bill. Arriving home in convoy, I thanked Bertrand for his help yet again. As he disappeared into the gloom, I went in to give Diane the glad tidings.

After the body-blow plans needed to be made, so I got in more wood; as by then the temperature had plummeted. While closing the shutters, I spotted five deer on the hillside. Though they were a beautiful sight, I saw Bertrand torching brushwood in his field and thought, '*run for your lives.*' Maybe they read my mind; who knows, but off they trotted. I wondered, should I go over and ask if he needed help? Nah! The next afternoon, we were tackling a huge area of hedging together. I'd had enough for today.

That night, Diane and I brooded over our latest financial hit, before going to bed early to conserve fuel. With snow forecast for the morning, I hoped the roads would be clear. A trip to La Flèche for tyres was a must.

The smudgy dawn broke with no sign of the 'white stuff.' And with the sun burning off a bank of fog, we breakfasted quickly. The Maximo lady was due later, and we couldn't afford to be sidetracked.

Slip-sliding over to the car with ice crackling underfoot, we scraped ice off the windows, defrosted the locks and climbed in. Then driving carefully, I headed towards the main road. *Sod the tail-gating French drivers*, I thought. Driving fast was out of the question. If I got pulled for speeding and my tyres were checked, I'd be in serious trouble. We crawled towards La Flèche, with hazard warning lights flashing and impatient drivers overtaking us. The most unnerving were monolithic trucks hogging our rear bumper, then swerving out unexpectedly to overtake us with no way to pull in again if they had to.

We arrived in La Fleche after a harrowing journey; finding a tyre company called *Robles Pneu.* Pulling into an inspection bay, I asked the receptionist if they sold *pneu rechape* or remoulds. I was told they did – but not for our model. We'd need to buy new ones. *Quelle surprise!*

The tyre fitter came out, checked the tyres, then handed the receptionist a list. She keyed it into her computer, and turning towards me with a smile, she quoted me 348 euros. Adam's apple bobbing, I queried the price, but was told that the fitter had noted some tyres were bald in places. '*Il est tres mal,*' she said, lips pouting.

'Ah,' I said embarrassed. It was my own fault. With a lot on my mind, I'd let tyre inspection slip. Out of options, I told her to go ahead. The order was processed, and it was then that I noticed the fitter struggling and sweating to get the wheel-nuts off. This didn't exactly fill me with confidence.

'*Non Monsieur,*' I said. '*Le voiture est Anglais – tournez a la gauche.*'

The car was made for the UK market, and he'd been trying to turn the wheel-nuts the wrong way. After that the job went fine – until the fitter approached the desk again and began whispering to the receptionist. Looking decidedly sick, she glanced furtively towards us sat in the corner.

'*Excusez mois, Monsieur,*' she said, plucking up courage. I walked over, and with a stricken look, she apologized. The bill was incorrect, she simpered. 'Ah, I *knew* it. We've been overcharged,' I called over to Diane.

Wincing at that, the girl *then* said the bill had risen to 440 euros. It seems the fitter had given his apprentice the job, and checking the spare wheel first, he'd fitted all four tyres to match. 'Okay,' I said, 'But why the price increase?'

When he'd taken off the worn tyres, the enthusiastic youngster had found they were incorrect. The fitter led me over and pointed to a small plate on the door. It stated that the car should be fitted with 185-65 tyres – not 175-60's as it had been. My car was a high performance model and should run on larger tyres, the girl translated. I had to agree that it made sense, though, wondered why it hadn't been noted on past tyre changes.

'Oh, and the mechanic has balanced the wheels *Monsieur,* is that okay?'

I recognized a *fait accompli* when it hit me. But cheesed off or not, the car drove better than it had for ages when we left. That then begged the question. Did the wheels still need tracking? The tyre fitter had pronounced, '*Le voiture est parfait,*' sticking his thumb up.

Deciding to cut our losses, I cancelled our garage appointment. Driving back to Le Lude feeling low, we called at *Intermarché* then Lidl on the way. Emerging from the store, we lingered to watch a spirited match at the local *boules* club. Sat on a bench watching the game in glorious sunshine, it was hard to stay peeved for long. With a Gallic shrug of the shoulders, and a *'Cest la vie,'* we walked back to the car.

Fixing a ceiling light after lunch, I planned what we could afford to do on our newly restricted budget. With a rueful grin, I said, 'Monsieur Renard's staircase has to be removed next. I'll be interested to see how it's fixed to the landing.'

Diane replied jokingly, 'Knowing *him*, I wouldn't be surprised if it wasn't fixed *at all.'*

And guess what? It wasn't. I couldn't believe it. He'd fitted two tiny angle brackets to the top of the stair-rails, and hooked them under the vinyl flooring. There was virtually nothing holding the stairs in place except gravity, and we'd been carrying materials and furniture up them. They could have collapsed under us at any time.

Choosing a bad time to visit later, Henri and Annette arrived during a shower. This could be awkward. We had to avoid mentioning Christmas, as they may have expected us to visit with Jill and Dale – which, let's face it would have been excruciating. But we didn't want to upset them. Also, where would we say we'd sourced our dining room furniture? It obviously wasn't new. But we couldn't tell them we'd gotten it from the Charpentiers. In the event, when they *did* ask, we said we'd bought it from friends who were modernising. It was true, and it didn't upset the balance between our neighbours.

As for Christmas, it wasn't even mentioned. They were *much more* interested in the puddle on the dining room table. We hadn't noticed, but rain was leaking in again. When they finally left, we set a bucket to catch the droplets, had our meal then went to bed.

In the cold light of day the next morning, we decided skimping on car maintenance probably wasn't a good idea. And as we needed a new hose anyway, having the tracking checked at the same time made sense. After all, look where cutting corners had gotten us so far.

Sat in the garage office, Gilles plied us with coffee during the tracking check. Then, following a test run, Alberte the mechanic pronounced it *'parfait.'* While fitting the new hose, though, another problem was diagnosed. The twin cooling fans weren't synchronized properly, he said. This would make the engine run hot and uneconomically. *Here we go again*, I thought. Off came the radiator shroud, and out came the testing equipment. It was beginning to look expensive, until he said it needed a new sender unit, but it would be okay over the winter. I said nothing. I just paid up and left before he found anything else.

Bertrand came over later to check on the car. Afterwards, we discussed changing to French registration, and how the *gendarmerie's* strictly enforced driving laws would then affect us. Mulling it over when he left, we decided that driving a Peugeot with French plates could mean regular stoppages by the police. We'd noted that spot checks didn't happen to English plated cars, which were routinely waved on. Maybe we should let sleeping dogs lie.

Chapter 13

Onwards and upwards

The *déchetterie* was open that morning, so we took in the trailer full of rubbish. After dumping the load – most of it *'monstre,'* or general waste, we nipped into *Brico* for ceiling boards and insulation. However, their materials were expensive. Even factoring in the extra fuel used for the return trip, La Flèche's *Brico* advertised substantially lower prices and would save us a fair bit of money.

On this occasion, Diane was driving, and we'd just left Le Lude when a van ahead of us braked abruptly. Whoops! As she edged out, I spotted a manned speed trap set up ahead in a lay by. It didn't worry us as we weren't speeding. We weren't in a hurry and it wasn't worth a 90 euro fine.

At La Fleche *Brico* our bill *was* a lot less; and heavily loaded, I drove back via the *Route de Sable*. Approaching the main road, we spotted a police cordon. They'd stopped a few cars, including one pulling a trailer in far better condition than ours. Knowing our wiring problems, I turned up a side street. Looking in the rearview mirror, I could swear I saw a *gendarme* laughing as we made our escape.

With the trailer unloaded, it was time for lunch then a nap. We were both experiencing side effects from the Atkins diet. Besides feeling tired and listless, Diane had hip joint pain, caused by a lack of magnesium and calcium according to the good doctor's hand-book. All this and headaches were common, though temporary it stated. Diane looked online for supplements. But with no propriatory outlets, they were expensive pharmacy items, so we decided to tough it out.

Our regular jaunt to *Emmaus* almost didn't happen that Saturday. Waking to heavy rainfall, I switched on the heaters, lit the fire, and nipped back to bed. By nine forty the rain had stopped; so with breakfast over and the skies clearing, we decided to go for it.

We arrived at two fifteen, to find *Emmaus* crowded and parking as hard to find as hen's teeth. Maybe people were looking for unwanted Christmas gifts. Who knew? Whatever the reason, the place was heaving. Fighting our way through the tightly-packed horde, we began scouting out bargains.

With the increasing influx of Brits, a shelf had recently been designated *Anglais* in the book section. Scouring it, I found a few decent paperbacks. But my best buy for ages, was a complete wheel and tyre for the Peugeot, which I unearthed in the salvage yard outside. Including the books, my total bill was a mere ten euros. Result!

One downside to the Brit influx was the increased difficulty in finding English newspapers, as shops stocked less once the tourist season ended. We weren't normally interested, but searching for one in a *tabac* one day, I noticed a poster abvertising a '*fete de truffe*' or truffle festival at Marigny Marmand. Writing down directions from it, we drove home footsore and weary; and with temperatures plummeting dramatically, I lit the fire.

As the room warmed up, we enjoyed hot drinks, food, and a steaming bath. When we finally went to bed after another abstemious evening, it was with our lonely hot water bottle warming our tootsies.

Noting rain running down the windows, I decided it was a good day for working in the woodshed. Leaving Diane to her own agenda, I headed out wrapped up – only to find a white van blocking the drive. The owner had left it parked between a telegraph pole on one side, and the storm ditch on the other. Then I heard it; a far off trumpeting and howling. Ah, *now* I get it. The hunt was headed our way, and the van belonged to a *chasseur*. As a breed, they were historically inconsiderate: accessing people's properties without thought or care. It seems today *we* were the chosen ones.

Soon other vehicles began to arrive; most of them parking more considerately, though, still spread across our field. I realized we were newcomers, and they'd probably been hunting on this land for decades. Maybe they'd had Monsieur Renard's permission, being a hunter himself. I was *also* aware that old maps showed a right of way through our land. But taking all things into consideration, they should still have the courtesy to leave us access to and from our home. As it was, we were virtually prisoners until they moved on.

Resigned, I was about to fire up the chainsaw when Diane shouted to me, pointing up the hillside. Coursing back and forth along the tree-line was a large brindle hound. Stopping abruptly, it lifted its head and bayed, before taking off at full pelt into the woods. Listening to its mournful howl echoing down to us, we were intrigued to see three other hounds appear and surge after it, pursued by an extremely fit dog handler. Minutes later, the four dogs re-appeared racing back down the track; the unfortunate guy running after them while trying to blow a battered old bugle. By then other hounds were arriving on the scene, and the noise level had reached a crescendo. With the howling dogs, the sound of trumpets, and the hunters shouting, it was pure theatre. As the saying goes, you just had to be there.

No sooner had the bugler disappeared, than the white van started up and headed towards me. Now how did I miss *him* returning? The vehicle drove slowly by, the driver sat upright in a dignified manner. As it passed, he swivelled his head slowly, waved politely and nodded. Then after a scary three point turn where he almost reversed into the storm ditch, he drove off. Soon, there was only a faint shout or bugle blast emanating from the next valley.

At last, I could begin woodcutting, stacking green wood for seasoning, while Diane, stimulated by the unexpected action tackled the housework with enthusiasm.

After lunch the weather improved, and it being Sunday a drive out seemed obligatory. Château-la-Valliére beckoned, and seduced by its natural beauty, we downed tools.

Arriving at the lake, I noted a few anglers, and a couple strolling along the woodland trail. With the car locked and our walk underway, the sonorous church-bells we'd become used to welcomed us to the lake.

We'd begun our day by weighing ourselves. I'd lost a kilogram the first week, but Diane had lost three and a half. Though it sounds excessive, some of this loss was due to us cutting out wine and exercising daily.

Our brisk walk took over an hour, and according to marker boards on the route, we'd covered nine kilometres. But who's counting? Well we were actually!

Though Monday was a gorgeous day, altering the *grenier* ceilings took precedence over outdoor work. We'd spent the previous evening planning and were raring to go. But first the panels needed cutting to size. We also had tracking rails, plates, fittings and fixtures – but no idea how to install it all. After much head scratching, we laid everything aside and had breakfast.

With the morning lost due to indecision, we were at *Brico* for two pm seeking advice. It was the manager who showed us the correct way to do it. Of course it wasn't the way Monsieur Renard had done his kid's rooms. *He'd* fixed wall panels to the ceiling – and badly at that. Armed with new information, we went home to reconfigure our plans.

On the way home an infuriating incident occurred. A French driver heading towards us, swerved deliberately into our lane to hit a pheasant, leaving it fluttering helplessly on the road. Reversing swiftly, he jumped out, wrung its neck, and slung it carelessly into his car boot. Having slammed on my brakes to avoid a smash, I veered around him waving angrily and blaring my horn. Did it bother him? Not a jot! Apart from being dangerous, it was cruel and unnecessary. It seems we still had much to learn about French country life.

Still angry at the incident, we found it hard to concentrate on our work. So packing in early, we celebrated our weight loss with a robust local wine. However, it was our first drink for ages, and our tolerance to alcohol seemed to have evaporated. Feeling light-headed after a couple of glasses, we re-corked the bottle. After ringing Michael to discuss his wedding plans and upcoming house move, it was time to call it a night.

Chapter 14

We carry on regardless

I couldn't wait to tackle the ceiling the next morning. Making a start after a light breakfast, I lugged materials up the newly connected stairs. And with the last of the old ceiling torn down, it disappeared through the *grenier* door to the garden below. Consulting my hand-drawn plan, I screwed plates to the beams. Then after some measuring and cutting, tracking rail was clipped to the plates.

Following Bertrand's advice, (now don't laugh) I tied lengths of fishing line across the tracks, unrolled fibreglass – then using a long handled broom and extension (I said don't laugh) I forced it under the fishing line. Now have you got all of this so far?

This feat of technical engineering was accomplished while balanced on the top step of a ladder, bent over backwards in some mystical yoga position in the roof apex.

With the insulation in place, I carried in a board cut to fit between the first two beams. And it was at this point that Diane came into play. While I balanced the board at the top of the ladder, she, stretching precariously on *another* ladder, passed me the drill and screws, as and when I needed them.

Finally our first board was up. Wonderful! Now for number two. Diane passed it up – and damn, it wouldn't line up with the first one. Because the hand-hewn beams were all different, this could mean a whole load of problems. Taking the first board down reluctantly, I unscrewed the tracking so I could modify it. Oh, this promised to be *hours* of fun.

With handmade packing pieces, I began re-fitting it. But the weight of the board and force of gravity began pulling the tracking loose, causing it to sag. Working with my head in the roof apex was awkward; and sweating and cursing, I was close to giving up. But it had to be right, or the ceiling could collapse onto sleeping visitors sometime in the future.

Thinking it through, and using a spirit level and more packing pieces, I finally fitted all the tracking to the ceiling. Calling it a day, we showered off the itching fibreglass, and with clothes changed, sat down to our meal completely demoralized.

It was eight thirty pm when the phone rang. It was Bertrand saying they had a *galette* cake they wanted to share with us. They were celebrating some saint's day or other. After asking him if we were visiting *them,* we changed again, grabbed a bottle of *rosé* and prepared to leave.

Tap tap! There was a knock at the door. Bottle of *rosé* in hand, I answered it – to be met by Bertrand *also* clutching a bottle of *rosé*. Following behind him, Véronique carried a huge cake. There was definitely room for improvement in our communication skills!

They stood there looking as confused as us, but entered when I ushered them in. Laughing at the mix-up, Diane and I valiantly squeezed cake into already full stomachs. We felt awful not troughing to our usual Olympic standards, but we were bursting. And what about Dr Atkins, I hear you ask? Hah, *that* ship sailed a *long* time ago.

Collapsing bloated onto the settee, we sipped *rosé* while discussing Monsieur Renard's D.I.Y nightmares and the problems he'd caused us. Heaving myself up, I showed them the materials we'd bought, pointing to the so-called ceiling boards we'd replaced. Bertrand agreed they were wall panels. Though the rolls of *line-de-verre* or fibreglass he'd spied in our hallway were correct, as were the *placa plaque* boards behind them. But I'd opened Pandora's Box now, hadn't I? He had to see upstairs.

I couldn't *believe* what happened next. Standing on the upstairs landing, he surveyed the ceiling. Pursing his lips, he examined my day's handiwork, then 'tut-tutting,' he pronounced it 'incorrect.' It should have been how I'd first done it, working from my own hand-drawn plan. I'd have to do it again, he said. And to get it absolutely right, I'd have to chisel out some of the A beam near the door. Fibreglass needs to expand and contract, he said, so space must be left behind the boards. With old farmhouses having metre thick walls, inadequate ventilation would cause condensation. I sighed, but for once, I was glad when he said he'd return the next morning to show me the 'correct' way to do it.

While discussing de-construction, I told him the staircase had been unattached, and how I'd had to fix it. He was aghast, knowing I'd spent a whole day lugging cement upstairs in a huge mason's bucket. He was shocked – but not surprised, saying Monsieur Renard was known as a bad worker, who conned people into helping him for little, or no reward. And since his death almost ten years before, nothing had been done in the house to his knowledge.

When the conversation switched to insulation and energy savings, we showed them our electricity bill. They reiterated, there were two tariffs, day and night-time. However, as with most French systems, it wasn't straightforward. The night-time rate was far cheaper, running from one thirty am until eight am. However there was also a cheap daytime rate from twelve thirty until two pm, as explained earlier. Therefore all heavy usage, like washing, slow cooking, bread making etc. was carried out during the night or at lunchtime, and was why married women workers rushed home at noon.

We'd have to adopt this system, as our bill was *three* times as much as theirs, despite them having central heating.

Even though we were already freezing due to poor insulation, Bertrand suggested we re-programme our hot water tank, setting it on auto for short periods only. If extra hot water was required it could be over-ridden. French electricity was extremely expensive, he stated, so usage should be strictly monitored.

The talk then veered to hunting, as Bertrand had just returned from a boy's weekend shooting party. He moaned that they'd only managed to kill three deer. One, a barely weaned fawn was brought down by hounds which ripped its throat out, he said with ghoulish relish. Seeing us grimace, he moved on, saying that Meteo had forecast warm weather for the next three days. In that case, I replied, we'd best round up more wood before it rained again.

Peering through fog and noting heavy frost when I woke, I thought it would serve no purpose trawling the fields. Instead, Diane would do better by going shopping, while I cut logs in the woodshed. With chainsaw teeth sharpened, I cut seasoned wood before attacking the cherry tree boughs; ending up with an impressive pile of logs, though, mostly 'green'. But added to the quince tree offcuts, it would come in handy in the future.

After barrowing the brash to the bonfire, I locked everything away. Looking towards the house, I noticed that Diane was back. It was easy to tell, because the car was parked in the barn – *with the lights left on*.

'Oh,' she said, when I told her in the kitchen.

'Oh what,' I asked?'

'Oh crap,' she said. She'd been back more than an hour.

Grabbing the keys, I headed out to the car. Noting the weak headlight beams, I wasn't hopeful. Switching off all the electrics, I tried the ignition. Nada! Sighing, I coupled up my battery charger, then closed the bonnet almost shut, mindful of the cables.

Never mind. No harm done. By then, the fog was lifting and the sun was peeping through. Going out to the terrace with a cuppa, we watched Meteo's forecast materialize.

Embarking on our cost-cutting regime later, Diane programmed the washing machine to run overnight. In a burst of energy, we then carried the *placa plaque* boards upstairs, ready for Bertrand the next day. Following that, in an obscene act of self indulgence, we read for an hour under the incandescent light cast by a sixty watt lightbulb. Gracious living or what?

I'd just made coffee the next morning when Bertrand appeared. While pouring him a cup, he said he'd given some thought to our electricity consumption. He thought our oil-filled radiators might be the problem. To check it out we must conduct an experiment.

First, we turned off everything electrical in the house. Then we checked the meter in the boiler room. Good – the drive-wheel was stationary. Next, beginning with one small lamp, item after item was switched on; each time checking the wheel as it revolved a little faster. It was a gradual and gentle increase – until we switched on the two radiators. Then the wheel almost took off.

It was ridiculous! Whilst entertaining both sets of visitors recently, those radiators had been running almost 24/7. No wonder our bills were huge. We decided not to mention it to our past guests. It was our problem and we'd solved it. Yes it was an expensive learning experience, but we'd just have to suck it up. We didn't want anyone feeling guilty and offering to help with our bill.

Anyone want to buy two oil filled radiators – almost new?

With *that* problem sorted, it was onward and upward as we tackled the panelling. Laying everything out first, Bertrand installed the spacer plates using packing pieces. Ten minutes later, after lining up the job *by eye,* the first track was on.

Aware by then how to continue, we sent him home to rest before going to his afternoon shift at work.

Being keen to try out cooking during the cheap lunchtime period, Diane left me to crack on upstairs, nipping down to prepare a casserole for the oven. Being curious, we went along to the boiler room at twelve twenty five pm. At twelve thirty exactly the meter clicked onto the cheap rate. Perfect! But hang on – instead of the wheel slowing down, it had sped up alarmingly. Ringing Bertrand, I apologized for disturbing him again and described this latest development. Ignoring my half hearted protests, he came back. Examining it, he agreed it was spinning even faster than before. Scratching his head, he could only suggest I stay up until one thirty am to see what happened *then*. When asked if I should I call out EDF, he whistled, blowing onto his fingers as if they were on fire. He said it'd be expensive, and knowing EDF, they'd probably suggest we buy a new meter. Yep, that sounded about right.

Chapter 15

Turning a corner

At long last the bedroom ceilings were finished. But before furnishing, we had a major decision to make. We had two bedrooms downstairs. If we also kept the two bedrooms *upstairs*, our plans to let out the house would be compromised. In French law, a three-bedroom house could be let without problems; any income generated being taxed at personal rates. But a four-bedroomed house would elevate us into the realm of business rates, which in France were very expensive according to Jane.

After much discussion, we settled on a master-bedroom upstairs, with the smaller room converted into an en-suite bathroom. We'd paint the ceilings white, the walls magnolia, and treat the oak beams against termites. That just left the uneven concrete floor. I planned levelling it with a skimming layer of concrete, then laying down laminate flooring. With the king-sized bed placed centrally under the apex and accented rugs laid on either side, it would look sumptuous.

While this layout avoided tax problems, we wanted the upstairs rooms to make a statement. This meant fitting a quality bathroom suite. Now I'm not that great a plumber, so we needed to find one quickly.

One bitterly cold day soon after, a knock rattled the door. Peering through the window, I saw a bedraggled, miserable looking little guy. Even heavily wrapped against the biting wind, he looked like a frozen mummy. He seemed harmless, so I answered the door. He was wearing an official badge, and selling calendars on behalf of the blood transfusion service, one of many charities and public services in France that sell them. Hearing that the house was occupied, he'd come to sell us one. He knew I'd worked at the *cave*, as it was *his* job I'd covered when I was there. When I invited him in out of the cold, he said he was now '*retraite*,' after fifty grinding years of hard work. So he'd retired eh? Not a minute too soon by the look of him. Feeling sorry for him, I commiserated, saying, '*Je retraite anticipée,*' or I'd retired early. This concept seemed alien to him, so with heartfelt respect, I bought a calendar. Then shaking his hand warmly, I wished him '*Bonne chance,*' and off he went.

As the weekend arrived the weather improved. Just right for a drive to Le Mans, we reckoned. Passing a pine forest en-route, our hearts lifted when we spied a young deer in a clearing. But while we were admiring its grace and form, a horn blared, hounds appeared, and in a split second it was running for its life. As we passed the area shots rang out. Let's hope it escaped.

Nearing Arnage, we joined the outer ring of the Le Mans 24 hour race track. On our first visit in 2000, we'd driven around the circuit in the old Peugeot 504 estate, trying to capture the thrill of being a F1 driver. Being more worldly-wise this time, I drove along it more sedately – though somehow, the speedometer seemed to creep up of its own volition.

We were headed for a retail park outside Arnage, seeking a superstore called *Leroy Merlin* (pronounced Laywah Mairlan, with a silent 'n.') Yes – we found it difficult too! After exploring its cavernous interior for some time, we moved on to a nearby *Super Gifi*. Gigantic compared to its

La Flèche counterpart, it provided excellent retail therapy for us both, and made for a grand day out.

Back at Le Ferronnerie H.Q, Diane was preparing dinner when the phone rang. It was always a lottery, but this time it was Véronique, inviting us to a meal she was cooking. As we always enjoyed their company, I said 'Beh oui.' And abandoning her prepping, Diane went off to change.

Arriving at *Le Lavendu*, I handed over the customary bottle of *rosé,* which disappeared into their fridge. After taking our seats, Bertrand handed us a chilled glass of theirs. With the first course served, the conversation centred on those damned hunting horns. As expected, Bertrand knew all about them, and proceeded to give us a master-class on the various toots and notes. The first toot signified a sighting, then different groups of toots indicated either deer or *sanglier,* and another meant a kill. Finally, he launched into his party piece, his imitation of an air raid siren. To some this was the most important of all, as it signalled lunch and often ended the hunt.

With our *entrée* finished, Bertrand began enthusing over his weekend's hunt; describing in intimate detail how he'd gutted a young deer. Nice! Then he told us its liver had been diseased, which in retrospect justified the kill to him. However, he could have picked a better time for this story, as Véronique had just put her home-made liver paté back in the fridge – after we'd eaten most of it.

During the main course, they asked what problems we'd encountered when moving to France. We told them, but when they recounted what *they'd* endured, both at work and building the farm, we felt like wimps in comparison. However, they'd been young back then, and we all go that extra mile when we first start out. The difference with these two was, they'd just kept on going.

The conversation then turned to the weather. The mercury was plummeting, and we were on track for the coldest period in twenty five years. Clear skies meant frost, and overnight temperatures way below zero. Snow was also forecast for three days starting on Tuesday. Well what a nice surprise!

As the day dawned bitterly cold, I remembered Bertrand's warnings and tackled the water meter immediately. Any leakages from the meter to the house were our responsibility, and exorbitantly expensive if Saur had to be called out. Also, if a leakage was fixed independently and they heard of it, they'd unearth it to inspect the workmanship then bill us. A lose, lose situation then!

I located the meter under a manhole type cover in the garden. It wasn't far down and I hadn't expected a problem – until I prised it open and found the hole flooded. A resident lizard wasn't too happy with my intrusion either! Baling out the freezing water and re-inserting the lizard, I wedged a brick under the meter to raise it above water level. Lagging and waterproofing it finished the job. It was a good fix – until someone came along to check the readings. To prevent future flooding, I dug a shallow trench around the cover to vent off water; then almost hyperthermic, I went back inside.

After a brief respite from the biting wind, though, I was out again. This time, Diane accompanied me, and we were dismantling the old greenhouse. It was a two-person job, as the huge structure had been over-engineered using three metre lengths cut from wooden telegraph poles. There were a lot of them, as the structure was about six metres long by three wide. It was the usual Heath Robinson affair that I'd come to expect by then. Attempting to make it rock solid, Monsieur had cemented the posts deep into the ground. Such was its strength, that in the event of a Nuclear Armageddon, it could very well be the only thing in the area left standing.

That afternoon proved to be one helluva work-out for us both. Treating it as an exercise in patience, we carefully dismantled the roof. We then began excavating the posts.

After hours spent smashing concrete with a sledgehammer and pickaxe, we'd managed to lever some of them out using large pry bars. With daylight waning by then, we surveyed the site. We'd made a good start, salvaging window frames, battens and struts; but with only a few posts unearthed, we had a long road ahead of us. At least there was no glass to worry about, though, Monsieur had used plastic sheeting.

It seemed such a waste thinking of the work involved in building it, but the monstrosity had to go. We had plans for a new greenhouse, but working carefully many items could be recycled. Glass panelled doors could serve as cold frames for example, and creosoted remnants would be handy for lighting unseasoned wood.

However, we had other things that also claimed our attention. Our UK visit had been brought forward due to a re-scheduled hospital appointment, plus, the car's MOT test was due the same week. Being registered in the UK, I couldn't take it to the local '*Controle Technique,*' but maybe it was just as well. François described the French test as being extremely difficult.

The temperature crashed *way* below zero the following week, but thankfully we had no snow. When François rang, he surprised us, saying they had snow in Bazaz. In such extremes, I ventured out rarely, mainly for wood. Though, on one occasion, I had to fix the *grenier* door, which had loosened and kept banging in the wind. Otherwise, after our modifications the house seemed noticeably warmer; one exception being the large downstairs bedroom which was still freezing.

With our work done, we'd settled down for the night – until a heater gas cylinder ran out. It seemed much too soon, but a replacement was needed as we had a busy day planned. I'd be insulating the *grenier* chimney breast in the morning, so, Diane offered to go into town for a replacement.

But first, we had an appointment with Doctor Atkins. We had to weigh ourselves. The scales stood there daring us to climb aboard. Happily, the combination of the diet and our hard graft seemed to be working. We'd both lost more weight, Diane, six and a half kilos in total. Mind you, it was bitterly cold, and I'd read somewhere that shivering burns up calories. So who needs Dr Atkins then? Couldn't we just freeze ourselves thin?

Heading out to chop wood, I remembered the old saying. You get warm three times from wood. Once when you chop down the tree, again when you saw it into logs; and finally when you burn them.

Though Diane brought back the gas cylinder, the house never reached an acceptable temperature that day. Oh how we envied Bertrand and Véronique, with their central heating set at a constant 20 degrees C, and their log fire crackling merrily. In the past, I'd wondered how people managed in these old farmhouses without central heating. Well now we were finding out– the hard way.

After eating our meal wrapped in fleeces (us, not the meal,) we tried watching TV. But it was just too damned cold. So switching it off, we slunk off to bed with our lone hot water bottle. Strange, but it was ages before we got around to buying another.

'*Le weekend,*' kicked off with a visit from François. Home from college and drawing on work experience with *Saur*, he'd come to inspect my meter lagging. Satisfied with the job, he left, and we shot off to La Flèche for the January sales – a rare treat to be enjoyed.

Venturing out with my saw after lunch, I espied Henri and Annette *promenading* their dog. They also saw *me* and waved. Sure enough, up the drive they came. Setting aside my saw, I reached for the coffee, while Diane automatically filled the kettle. When they arrived, we apologised for not visiting them lately, claiming a heavy workload as our excuse. But then of course, they had to be shown our latest improvements.

When they left, dragging their whining puppy behind them, I grabbed the chainsaw. Then well wrapped up, Diane and I attacked the shell of the greenhouse, piling up enough wood to last us a month.

Popping over later for a chat, Bertrand and François sniggered at my embryonic beard, grown during our forced incarceration. I intended raising a few eyebrows on our forthcoming UK visit, so I thought, *snigger away boys*.

They'd nipped over to ask what Bertrand could do in our absence, and for François to say goodbye. Commenting on the dismantled greenhouse, they said it was more useful as firewood; maybe we could erect a new poly-tunnel like theirs. It was apparent that Monsieur Renard's creation wouldn't be missed by *them*.

When they marched off, I gave it a few minutes in case they re-appeared to lecture me, then I began sawing while Diane barrowed the resulting logs to the woodshed. As twilight fell, we packed everything away and trudged inside.

It was unimaginably cold. And with ice riming the inside of the windows, I lit the fire and stoves pretty damned quickly. With our breath still clearly visible, we waited for the post. We were desperately hoping the car's tax disc would arrive. This was Monday and it expired at the weekend. The DVLC should have sent us the replacement before now. We were snookered if it didn't arrive today. We'd be entering the UK with an outdated tax disc.

Just before noon, I saw Jorge turn into Bertrand's drive. Leaving the dogs barking insanely, he turned and drove off to the next hamlet. Damn – no tax disc.

I rang the DVLA later but no-one could help. Checking our UK bank, Diane found the direct debit hadn't been taken by them. Great! While deep in thought the phone rang. It was Michael wanting to talk over his wedding plans. After discussing them, our project, and the freezing weather, I mentioned our car tax. There was a problem line to ring in Northumberland and he offered to try it. Maybe it'd be easier to sort out from within the UK. He rang back later saying the number was unobtainable. Out of options, we were driving off the next day untaxed.

The rest of the day was spent packing; checking the car and deciding which electrics to leave switched on while we were away. Building up the fire, we ate our meal while half-heartedly watching a video; then setting our alarm for three am, we turned in.

I woke before the alarm rang, and with the car loaded, we set off at three-thirty. Driving hard through the darkness, I pulled into Caen ferry-port at seven am. The ship sailed at nine am local time; and after a smooth crossing it docked at Dover Ferry-port ninety minutes later. Exiting the docks, we were absorbed into the manic A3 lane heading to London, proving to us that in our absence, British drivers had become as bad as the French.

Arriving in Burnham, I parked behind Nadine's flat. With the expired tax disc hidden from prying eyes we could relax, basking in unfamiliar central heating. Watching TV news after a snack soon had us yawning. So staggering upstairs early, Nadine's spare bed prepared us for the long journey north the next morning.

Chapter 16

Home and away

Setting off early from Nadine's after breakfast, I turned off the A1 for Durham mid-afternoon. Arriving in Burnhope soon after, Helen ushered us onto their drive, and the outdated tax disc was hidden from view. As we entered the house, Aaron ran to meet us. My God he'd grown. Stewie then emerged – just as I was unloading his duty free beer.

'Thanks Stew,' he said – taking it as if handling the Crown Jewels.

'No problem mate. Give us a hand with the rest of our stuff will you?'

Settled in with everything unpacked and stored away, we exchanged news with our hosts.

The next morning, I drove to Hexham Hospital for my appointment, while Diane took the car to Bellingham for its MOT test. Returning for me in a courtesy car, we shot off to Morpeth to sort out the road tax. Finding the office was easy, but the bad news was, the new disc had been issued eleven days after we'd applied for it and should be in our mailbox in France. The clerk said we couldn't have a photocopy, a covering letter, or any proof to show the police if stopped for any reason. We needed to go to Gosforth to sort *that* out.

We returned to pick up the Peugeot with its new MOT certificate. But heading back to Burnhope, we decided not to risk a fine by driving without a valid disc. And visiting

Gosforth could open up a can of worms best left alone. So parking up the Peugeot, we used Helen's car whenever we needed transport.

After transferring funds to France, we withdrew more cash to go shopping at Gateshead's Metro-Centre, where I bought a shirt for the wedding and a return ferry ticket. Then as arranged, Chris drove over to Burnhope where we spent the night partying at Alan and Pauline's.

Arriving at the church on the wedding day, Diane looked stunning in a black trouser suit, while I sported 'the beard.' Sadly, I wasn't looking forward to the day, as my ex-wife's family were attending en-masse. But as we pulled up in the car-park, Michael and Chris were there to meet us. Then to our surprise, some ex-family members came over and greeted us.

As the seating plan had been carefully co-ordinated to accommodate new partners in both families, the service went smoothly. Miranda looked radiant in an ivory dress, while Michael, suited and booted, looked 'the business.'

At the reception the speeches were a hoot; inevitable really with Chris as Best Man. And, though the situation was awkward, Diane behaved impeccably – not easy with past friends and family coming over to catch up. And as most of Chris's mates kep trying to get her up to dance, she thought it best to decline gracefully. As it was, they all ended up at our table anyway, and we had a high old time.

On balance it was a good day. But judging the right moment later, we said our goodbyes, arriving back in Burnhope in time for a quick change. Yes! It was Alan and Pauline's knockout pool competition.

One special visit the next day was to my sister Janis, who was justifiably upset at not being invited to the wedding. I felt awful, as no-one told me she wouldn't be there. Asking Michael at the church why she'd been omitted, he said his mother had arranged the guest list, and to keep numbers down she'd had to leave some family members out. I could understand that, as she had a large family. But surely, Michael's only aunt and uncle from my side of the family could have been squeezed in.

Tuesday found us setting off in the dark, the victims of another farewell party the previous night. Conscious of the tax disc situation, I parked behind Nadine's flat again when we arrived. We'd had to give Grantham a miss this time, as Diane needed to take Nadine to a hospital appointment.

During our two day stop-over at Burnham, we blitzed charity shops, hungry to buy books and videos for France. And on the last day, Jill and Dale met us at a halfway point for a pub lunch before saying their goodbyes.

Riding our luck again, I drove off at three-thirty the next morning. Flying under the radar, we arrived at Portsmouth well before boarding time. And, though an electronic bulletin board warned of force eight winds, the crossing wasn't bad. A little choppy perhaps, but we'd known worse.

We docked at three thirty pm local time, desperately tired and with colds picked up from the boys. But thanks to a smooth run down the French *autoroutes,* we arrived at Le Ferronerie at seven pm.

With the fire crackling away and heaters glowing, Diane poured hot toddies and we watched a new video. Then it was off to bed with our lonely hot water bottle, feeling like two slabs of frozen meat. Dammit, we forgot to buy a hot water bottle – *again!*

Venturing out in pallid sunshine the next morning, I spotted Bertrand out burning brash. Waving to him, I fired up *our* bonfire. With the shutters opened to air the house, Diane left me tending the blaze and drove off shopping. Returning with provisions from Le Lude, she pulled up just as Henri appeared. He'd been out walking and noticed our car.

Coming in out of the strengthening sun, he accepted a beer before mumbling the latest gossip. At long last Jacque's house had sold (thank the lord,) and Rosaline was now working part-time at the *cave* due to cutbacks.

Once Henri had gone, we pottered about doing jobs before enjoying a hot soak and late meal. Though tired, the restorative properties of a good red wine seemed ripe for testing. After trialing this treatment while watching another new video, we diagnosed bed rest as a wiser alternative.

Snow came to our valley on the Sunday, as temperatures crashed to an alarming low. Even with all our heating sources working overtime, it just wasn't enough. We needed more or we'd be virtually hibernating.

Though I'd blocked off the upstairs rooms, conditions downstairs were still arctic. So I fitted a curtain-rail and heavy drapes to partition off the dining room. After an hour, I checked the thermometer I'd placed in there. A difference of just two degrees C. Oh Lord, our freezer seemed warmer. Arriving just then to discuss shooting on our land, François asked; 'Why do you have the curtain?'

When I explained, he shook his head sadly and left. With dinner eaten and feeling like two frozen lollipops, an early night was on the cards. Wrapped up well, we entered the bedroom of hell..

Rising early, I planned my morning. First order of business was ringing my assurance company in the UK. But instead of the Scottish office I'd rung, my call was transferred to Mumbai India. Not a great start!

Next, I rang my building society manager, who returned my call later after slogging into work through a blizzard. Similar conditions had also trapped Stewie and Helen in Burnhope village, as a freak weather front ravaged Northern England.

But while we froze inside the farmhouse, Bertrand and François were out working. Spotting me carrying logs in from the woodshed, they hailed me to inspect a tree that might need felling. Diane ushered me out, saying we should stop being wusses. *They* weren't moaning about the weather.

After a hot lunch, we wrapped up and walked down to visit Henri and Annette. During our visit his brother Lauren arrived, and after introductions, wine and *eau de vie* flowed freely. But as snow began falling, we dashed back to build up the fire. With the logs crackling and heaters on full, the temperature crept up to a heady ten degrees C – but only in the lounge. Whereas in Henri's, it'd been twenty degrees throughout.

Though it snowed sporadically over the next week, it didn't stop Bertrand and François ripping out hedging one viciously cold day. When they went in for lunch, I took over; cutting up and storing useful wood, then burning the brash.

On their return, Bertrand offered to sharpen my saw. I'd just fuelled it and hadn't yet tightened the filler plug. Unaware of this, he grabbed it, yanked the cord to start it and got soaked in fuel. To cover his embarrassment and with misplaced bravado, he began leaping back and forth over the fire. *That's it*, I thought, *I'm outta here!*

Laughing heartily, he left to change for his afternoon shift, leaving François and myself to carry on. However, the weather-gods had other ideas; forcing us to call a halt because of hail soon after.

Snow fell steadily over the next few days; then a sudden thaw allowed the tractor driver to finish cutting the boundary hedge. And with Bertrand off shooting, François assumed command of the operation. It was also the final Sunday of the hunting season, and the *chasseurs* turned up en-masse. Diane's boss Dominic and his friends were amongst many who blocked our drive *that* day.

Retreating from the mayhem, I took in a basket of logs, then cleared out the large downstairs bedroom to assemble Bertrand's platform. If the weather stopped me working outside, I could now move inside. However, blessed with good weather for the time being, François and I continued hedgecutting.

Once the hedging was finished, I set off with Diane to do battle with the local matrons. It was 'meat week' at Lidl; and buying in bulk allowed her to freeze most of it, while cooking off some for upcoming meals. While she shopped, I looked for a foot-pump. *Intermarché's* garage had the only air-line in the district, and it'd been broken for two weeks. Guess who had two slowly leaking tyres?

When we fought our way to the meat section, everything that could be utilized from a pig except 'the oink' was on display. Apart from the normal pork products including the tail, there was a small toaster designed to crisp pig's ears, and half a pig's head split from brow to nose including one eye and half a set of teeth. Moving along the cabinets, I also spotted a tiny pack containing a round disc of meat with two holes, similar to a large button. When I asked what it was, the assistant gave a snort. It was the tip of a pig's snout.

Desperate to get out after the long spell of bad weather, I drove us to Luché Pringé to check out a house we'd seen for sale. It was being advertised by two agents, one being the local *Notaire*. As it was nearby, we called in to ask for information. Haltingly, the receptionist said details and keys were at their La Flèche office. As we were shopping there the following day, an appointment was made for then. Driving on to Le Lude's branch of *our* agency, we found it closed. But the window advertised some promising houses. So ringing Jane at home later, I made an appointment for ten thirty the next morning.

In the office early, we pored over property listings, arranging to visit four the coming Thursday. We weren't sure that we wanted to move, but the renovation work was taking its toll on us, and down-sizing would relieve our financial situation. We could reduce, or even pay off our mortgage. On the flipside, we had substantial space, a large acreage, and great neighbours to consider at Le Ferronerie. We'd have a better idea after Thursday.

Driving to La Flèche the next afternoon, a couple of other properties *A Vendre* caught our eyes. On closer inspection though, both were unsuitable, as was the house advertised with the *Notaire*. Thoroughly frustrated, we discussed the situation after dinner over a couple of whisky mixes.

At eight thirty there was a knock at the door. It was Bertrand and François inviting us for coffee and a chat. Unfortunately, we'd imbibed another couple of whiskies by then, and were ever so slightly inebriated. Nevertheless, we threw on coats, and set off after them along the track.

Though our progress was unsteady at first, everything was going just fine – until Diane slipped on some ice and landed on her ass. Luckily she was okay, and we arrived at Le Lavendu laughing like loons. When we told them *why* we were laughing, we *all* ended up in stitches. Thankfully it was only coffee we'd been asked over for. After an hour of fun, we went back to finish our video – and the whisky.

Saturday was a fair old day, but declining my offer of a drive out, Diane decided to finish her paintwork. In need of fresh air, I donned my boots and set off up the track to the woods. Scouring hedgerows and thickets, I found branches, old fence-posts, and some half buried logs left by Madame. By the time I'd finished, there were six sizeable piles stacked in the fields. Now all I had to do was get it all to the woodshed.

Hitching the small trailer to the Peugeot, I set off up the field gingerly. Without four-wheel drive and wary of my car's suspension, I took it easy. Parked at the top, I filled the trailer and boot. *'We're gonna need a bigger boot,'* I thought, remembering a scene from the film *Jaws.*

The drive back down was a little hairy, as the car kept sliding on the damp grass. But worse still, when the pile was unloaded it looked woeful. Using Bertrand's tractor would make much more sense, so I rang François, who said he'd speak to his father when he returned from work.

Diane was serving breakfast the next morning when Bertrand turned up on the tractor. As he was doing us a favour, I asked Diane to keep my plate warm while we set off to hitch up 'The Hippo.' We'd made inroads into the first woodpile when François arrived; getting stick from his dad for lazing in bed. With his help the work went faster, and soon there was a huge pile in the woodshed. François then suggested a trip around the *bottom* field, where wood lay after hedging, saying. 'We should take it before the *blé* is sown.'

Lurching around the barren field, Bertrand was driving, while François and I jumped off the tractor to throw anything burnable into the trailer. *That's everything,* I thought. But no! François suggested trawling the field violated by EDF. There were many shattered branches left to be gathered after their visit. 'That suits me,' I said. 'But are you sure?'

'But of course. It is logical,' François replied.

So off we went. By early afternoon, we'd scoured the property, and our wood-stocks were looking much healthier. We'd retrieved three huge trailer loads and were ready for lunch. Fetching my wallet, I offered Bertrand money for diesel, but he declined politely. So thanking them both warmly, I waved them off. When they'd gone, I went back to the woodshed. Wow! My chainsaw would be working flat out for days.

Kicking off my boots at the door, I entered the kitchen. Wiping her hands, Diane said, 'Your breakfast was spoiled, but how did the wood collecting go?'

'You won't be seeing much of *me* for a while,' I replied.

I was keen to crack on the next day, but before Diane could cook breakfast the gas ran out. This time it was down to carelessness, as we'd risked leaving it until we went shopping that afternoon. Never mind! After brewing a cuppa using the electric kettle, I grabbed the empty gas cylinder and a re-direction form for *La Poste,* and we visited town.

Dropping off a replacement cylinder on the way back, I drove on to *Super U's* sale at Château-la-Valliere. Finding nothing we wanted however breakfast called. And with the day still being young, we decided to cut wall-boards for the downstairs bedroom.

When I first tested the thickness of Monsieur R's insulation using a bradawl, I'd found it was a mere forty millimetres, whereas building regulations required ninety mills minimum. Bertrand said *he'd* fitted two hundred mills; and remembering the warmth of their house, we thought it best to do the same. Coating the panels with *plac*-a-*plaque*, I held them to the wall using planks and batons. And with help from my 'glamorous assistant,' Diane, the job was soon finished.

While relaxing after our meal the phone rang. It was Nadine. Lewis had contracted bronchitis and might need admitting to Hospital. Whatever next?

Chapter 17

We're staying put

After giving it some thought, going ahead with Thursday's viewings seemed a good idea. Though Le Ferronnerie had 'good bones,' it was turning into a money pit. To stay put and continue the renovations, we needed a cash injection. Without one, we'd have to shut down the house and return to the UK for the winter. Once there, we'd not only have to find work, but also somewhere to rent.When we mentioned our dilemma to Stewie and Helen, they suggested an alternative solution. Why not stay with *them* over the winter. I must admit, that hadn't crossed our minds. We said we'd give their generous offer serious consideration – but we'd insist on paying our share of everything; rent, food and other bills including the phone. We'd also help with housework, cooking, and of course baby sitting. However, we asked them to be absolutely sure before taking on such a big commitment.

That afternoon, Jane came up with another viewing. The property was near the village of St Jean le Motte, and the owner was another guy selling due to divorce. Unfortunately, nice as the house was, it was too small and reeked of dogs. And though the garden was impressive, it was generously littered with turds from his Great Dane!

On the drive home, Jane suggested she view *our* house; giving us a ballpark valuation for selling purposes. After a thorough inspection, she said we'd have no problem, either selling or renting it out.

We viewed three properties the next day. The first house was uninhabited, but rubbish was strewn everywhere and stale food had been left on the table. What *is* it with the French when they're selling houses?

It had its good points though – a great cellar and *cave* for instance. But it had little garden to speak of and was semi-detached. I'm afraid we'd been spoiled by the size of Le Ferronerie, so the next house was a *real* shock. It stood on a housing estate; and waiting for the owner to arrive gave us a ringside seat, to of all things a travelling circus. The big top, caravans and sideshows had been erected on a nearby plot, while behind them a paddock contained some very frisky emus. I couldn't believe it! Was this a regular occurrence? And did travellers also use the site?

The owner finally turned up, and we got to view the house. It was impressive enough, having masses of interior storage space, a wood-burning stove and central heating. Other positives were a huge cellar and separate *cave*. However the garden was miniscule, though it did have a terrace. Keen to sell, the owner gave us a bottle of home-made cider to help sweeten the deal.

The final property was a large old house needing lots of work, though it showed potential. Built on a large plot, it had out-buildings, a huge barn, veggie patch and greenhouse. It was the closest to satisfying our wish-list.

Leaving Jane, we drove home to mull over all three. We were tempted to make a cheeky offer on the last one, but hung back due to a late viewing Jane had arranged for the next day.

We arrived at the office at nine am to find she'd gone out with clients, so her boss gave us the keys and directions to the property. The three storey *maison de ville*, or town-house looked great on the listing, but that's where the embryonic love affair fizzled out. We arrived to find it'd been gutted, and needed a fortune spending on it.

Relaxing at home later, we reviewed our visits. All five properties had something to offer, but none came close to matching all our needs. After much deliberation it was no contest. We were better off where we were. We'd lose far too much by moving. With our minds now clear, we could forge ahead with our plans.

We popped into the agency with a little present for Jane the next day, thanking her for her help. Though she accepted it gratefully, she said it wasn't necessary,as she was just doing her job.

It was an absolutely gorgeous day, with an achingly blue sky and not a cloud to be seen. Busy as always, Bertrand was heading off to his woodshed, but stopped to comment on the weather. It would continue getting warmer over the next fortnight, he assured us, so we should plant out veggies at the start of April. He also suggested we sign on at the apple orchard on April 10th for the coming season. Though agreeing we would, I said a few weeks apple picking wouldn't solve our problems. We needed rental income from the house. If we didn't pull some in this season, our cash flow would diminish and we'd have to return to the UK for winter work.

It was mid-March, and we'd dived into *Intermarché's* sale to snap up some garden furniture. With it safely onboard the trailer, I anticipated my date with the lawnmower.

Unloading back at H.Q, the snarl of Bertrand's tractor alerted me. He'd driven over with a plan to enlarge the plot where the greenhouse once stood. However, due to Monsieur Renard's fly tipping, some of the terrain was in poor condition. Therefore, I should take my *brouette* to the upper fields, he said, where I would find lots of mature *merde de*

mouton (or shit of the sheep.) Shovelling it into my *brouette,*
I should barrow it down to my rapidly expanding garden.

Due to a series of stepped elevations leading up to the
fields, I had to construct three ramps before I could start.
Then the dirty, smelly job that was to take up my whole
morning began. In total, I delivered forty barrow-loads to the
garden. Yep, I counted them all!

After she'd finished wallpapering, Diane turned up to
help; and with fifteen loads already shifted, we began
working as a team. With her filling, me barrowing it down to
the garden, tipping it then returning for more, a series of
heaps materialized across the plot. We then walked the field,
forking and spreading the droppings far and wide. When it
was finished, we dragged ourselves in for lunch.

After he'd tilled and re-seeded his poultry enclosure,
Bertrand arrived with his tractor and plough, coaxing big
smiles from us when he praised our workload.

Before he began work on our plot, I asked if he'd level a
mound on the garden's edge which had bugged us for a
while. But on his first pass, a vein of assorted rubbish was
exposed – including a hibernating hedgehog!

As Bertrand continued down the garden, Diane and I
gathered up Monsieur Renard's crap as usual. The *good*
news was, the bewildered hedgehog was laid carefully under
a shade-giving tree to contemplate its future.

Toothache isn't fun, ask anyone. For a while now, Diane had
been suffering from a large abscess. Treatments she'd tried
included painkillers, whisky, and *eau de vie* – which gave
temporary relief at best. So off she went for a lie down.

Meanwhile, with ploughing finished, Bertrand suggested
we collect more wood from the bottom field. Maybe another
time, I suggested. After all, it was now mid-afternoon and
he'd been up since three-thirty for his early shift. 'No
problem,' he said; it was better now, as it would allow the
blé or wheat shoots to recover from tyre damage. Unable to

sleep, Diane came out to help, and between us, we collected three full trailer loads.

With the job done, we invited Bertrand in for coffee and a chat, but he said, unfortunately he had to go. He still had a crop of peas to plant out. Good god, the man was a machine.

Tidying up later, I spotted him walking down from the woods. Waving me over, he asked if I'd seen his *fouine* (pronounced fwine.) Not knowing what a *fouine* was, I said I wasn't sure; so he beckoned me to accompany him back up the track. Pointing to a cage-trap under a hedge, I spotted a brown and white creature resembling a polecat. Beautifully marked and with huge eyes, it snarled in fear as Bertrand poked it with a stick. He said he'd trapped it because they ate eggs and killed chickens. I asked what he intended doing with it. Without expression, he ran a finger across his throat.

When I described the creature to Diane, she said it sounded cute. After checking it out online, we established that it was a stone-marten. So at her insistence, I took her up to see it spitting and snarling in the trap.

We were given another chance to see it the next morning. Bertrand brought it down to show us – lying dead in the cage with two meat skewers forced through its body. Though I understood why he thought he *had* to kill it, I asked why do it in such a barbaric way. Why not just shoot it? Looking at me incredously, he said he didn't want to damage his trap.

In the granary bedroom, I was at peace with the world. Re-designing the chimney-breast was a pleasant job – until a plague of beetles swarmed in through the velux window. Dashing quickly downstairs, I grabbed the insect spray and swatter; then waving Diane off shopping, I resumed operations in my new position as joiner-cum pest controller.

Hearing a diesel engine later, I popped my head out of the window. Bertrand was passing by on his tractor pulling a heavy load of logs. Looking up, he waved and tooted his horn. As Diane was arriving behind him, I went downstairs. Helping her unload, I said I should give Bertrand a hand. She thought it was a good idea as she was about to start cooking.

When I arrived, he must have thought I needed his help again, so it was a pleasure to offer *him* a hand this time. Grinning, he said, '*merci Steward*,' so I climbed aboard the trailer.

The load took us half an hour to stack, after which we drove back to Le Lavendu for a beer. After one, he stood up, saying he was off for another load. Leaving with him, I told him to toot when he returned, and I'd help him again.

Unfortunately, when he *did* toot, we'd just sat down to dinner. Nevertheless, I'd made the offer, so Diane put dinner on hold until we finished.

Saturday the nineteenth was unusually hot for March. Though, at 35 degrees C, it was a great day to work outside. Wearing caps and sunscreen, Diane and I unearthed rubbish from the garden. All of it, including various animal skeletons went into the trailer destined for the *déchetterie*. After mixing cement, I hosed down the house wall and began rendering, while Diane went in to wallpaper.

Bertrand and Véronique drove by on the tractor later, pulling a trailer-load of field-stones for wall building. Seeing the rubbish in the trailer, he returned with the tractor and riddle to scour the garden. By then, Diane was raking her plot for veggie planting. Of course, Bertrand came over to inspect her handiwork, advising her – quite seriously that potatoes *must* be planted no later than ten thirty am. Where does he *get* all this crap from?

Anyway, with the planting done, we watered everything in. Unfortunately, Diane fell while raking and bruised her arm quite badly. But carrying on, her reward was a glass of wine on the patio as we watched a glorious sunset together.

As Sunday is supposedly a day of rest, we drove out to Château-la-Valliere. The Charpentier's seemed to have gone out early leaving Hermé barking non-stop. So why would *we* stay in?

Pulling up at the picnic area to the sound of distant church bells, we set off along the woodland track; exchanging greetings with families out strolling and anglers sat on the bankside.

Returning for lunch totally invigorated, we heard no barking; so we presumed Bertrand and Véronique were back, or Hermé had worn himself out and collapsed exhausted. Fired with enthusiasm, we burst into activity after our meal, as the forecast was for rain later.

The next couple of nights were weird. On both night's, my sleep was interrupted by an identical incident. I was woken around three am on *both* occasions by a loud *'bang'* right next to me. But, switching on the lamp, my heart pumping overtime, there was nothing to be seen!

As the days rolled by the weather changed constantly, inducing tiredness and irritability. After dinner during this uneasy period, we'd often nod off while watching a video. *Ah, to sleep, perchance to dream,* I thought. Paraphrasing Shakespeare, I had to agree with the bard. A proper night's sleep would be welcome.

The only bright spot that week was Nadine's call. Trying hard to control her temper, she read from a pamphlet she'd been given on child behaviour. The 'experts' advice was – and I quote, 'If your child misbehaves, they should be placed in a room with an egg timer set for ten minutes. You must then tell them, don't come out until it rings.'

Yeah, I can see that working. No wonder kids are so screwed up nowadays.

Chapter 18

New friends and a long journey

The end of March signed off with a storm. A blessing really, as it cleared the air, making it easier to sleep – though according to Diane, she didn't hear the thunder due to my snoring. She swore that I'd kept her awake until three am, which of course, I hotly denied. Joking apart though, sleeping had been a problem for us both lately. We had too much on our minds due to the mounting list of jobs. First on the agenda was the garden, which needed digging over and planting with vegetables urgently. All the public areas then required landscaping and terracing, while some of the outbuildings were overdue for repairs. It was all necessary work, but our main thrust must be getting the house ready for letting, otherwise it would all be for nothing as another season would be lost to us. Our biggest worry was the unexpected bills we'd incurred lately. With funds dwindling rapidly, we'd have to find a way to stem the flow – and fast.

After a heavy week's work and with our minds in turmoil, we considered Noyant's Good Friday market a must. We'd have an opportunity to buy some sturdy young plants, while swinging by Jane's holiday rental for a sneaky look. Unfortunately, a couple were sat outside on deck-chairs so we drove on by. The house still didn't look much to us, and the pool still looked small and uninviting. But it was generating cash so we couldn't argue with that.

Wandering in 'chill' mode through the market, we came across a real find. After visiting the 'chicken man' to see his fluffy new chicks, I spied a stall sporting a Union Jack selling English stock. The couple manning it were a friendly couple, who recognizing fellow Brits introduced themselves as Rob and Elaine, a Scots couple who'd lived nearby for three years. By the number of ex-pats who stopped to chat, it seemed they were well known. And when they suggested we visit them at their farmhouse, we agreed. We were happier still when Rob said they had a pool. They'd integrated well into the community, were on the internet, and drove a French plated car. Pleased to have made new friends, we drove home with our plants, looking forward to our upcoming visit. Motivation was hard to come by the following morning. It was raining heavily so I rang Rob; but getting no answer, I began cutting wood. He returned my call later, suggesting we visit at one pm on Monday. Replacing the phone, I glanced through the shutters and noticed storm clouds massing. Le Mans had been ravaged the previous day, and now I heard the unmistakeable rumble of thunder.

By mid-afternoon the sky was dark and angry, and with a crackling flash, lightning preceded a storm. In the lounge, we watched the high voltage display through opened French windows. Well you never know when a stray lightning ball might decide to pass through your house – now do you?

Easter Sunday was just another work-day for us, but being rainy and chilly it was a day for inside jobs. Lugging our equipment upstairs, I switched on the radio and we began. Seeing Jane's paying guests had galvanized us into action.

We found it hard to believe at the day's end. The insulation and panels were all fitted, joints taped, screws recessed, and holes filled and sanded. We were ready for papering. A coat of emulsion and it would be finished – well almost. There were still floor tiles to cut and fit, and skirting boards to paint, but otherwise the room was ready for furniture. Tidied up, we collapsed onto the settee.

Despite my insistence that she rest, Diane got up wearily, prepared a meal and poured wine. After the meal, though, I couldn't even think, never mind drink. Pouring it back into the bottle untouched, I followed Diane's example; having a hot soak before going to bed early.

After a restless night, with rattling shutters and rain drumming off the roof tiles, we lay in bed loathe to get up. Nevertheless, leaving at twelve thirty, (or so we thought,) I set off for Rob and Elaine's. On leaving Noyant, though, we couldn't find the turn-off they'd mentioned. Turning back towards the town, we decided I'd better contact Rob. Having forgotton Diane's cell-phone in our rush, we searched in vain for a phone-box. I could have tried a café or bar, I suppose, but it was easier to return home and ring from there.

When I finally got through to Rob I apologised, and this time wrote down *precise* instructions and a description of their *Longére,* or long farmhouse.

Setting off again, we passed through Noyant then Méon, before turning onto a side road outside town, where we found a rambling old building at the end of a track. After apologizing for being half an hour late, Rob said the clocks had gone forward overnight. So actually, we were an hour and a half late. Not the best way to kick off a new friendship.

Once seated, Rob said the house used to belong to Paula, the agent who'd handled our house buy, and with our *faux pas* forgiven, he gave us a rundown. Having been a dairy in the past, the house intrigued us. In keeping with the theme, troughs and stalls had been kept as features.

After a tour, conversation and wine flowed freely, and throughout the afternoon, we learned a lot. But all too soon it was time to leave. Our hosts had to change for a night out with some *other* friends. Apparently it was a social merry-go-round in Rob and Elaine's world.

We drove off slowly, skirting the pond carefully as we were over the limit. But driving carefully, and with cool evening air rushing through open windows, we arrived home intact. Lighting the fire, and seated with more wine, (yes, I know) we discussed our visit.

Disrupting my work plans, my assurance company gave me hours of fun over the next couple of days. Their outsourced office in Mumbai had messed up my pension annuity, and the UK headquarters had to sort it out. Having no fax facilities (remember fax?) Jane offered us the use of her office machine. The fiasco ended with fourteen sheets of paper spewing out across the agency floor. I apologised for this eco-outrage, but Jane's boss generously wrote it off to after sales service.

The following day was April Fools Day, and after pranking each other a few times, we set off for Noyant's market. Catching up with Rob and Elaine, we said we'd enjoyed our afternoon together and were up for a re-match. After a leisurely stroll around stalls heaped with fabrics and generic market ephemera, it was time for lunch. Then with stomachs satisfied, we followed Bertrand's tractor and trailer around our field. Three hours of backbreaking work gave us a large pile of fieldstones, and a full on work-out.

Jumping down from the tractor, Bertrand suggested I use his rotovator to break up our garden soil. But when I accepted, he said I must take it *immediately*. And when I then mentioned borrowing his long ladder sometime, he said, I should also take *that* immediately. With furrowed brow, I thought, *why the urgency*? It seemed strange, but I didn't ask why. I just humped the ladder over, following Bertrand pushing the rotavator. When we arrived, I was treated to a rigorous lesson on rotovator usage. Well what did I expect?

Spring had finally sprung. A deranged cuckoo woke me at dawn that morning to tell me. With the arrival of the new season, flowers began opening up, and a myriad lifeforms began hatching out. Life was joyful. But what really clinched it for me was, I'd finally caught Bertrand out in his immaculate weeding regime.

Arriving at his garden gate that morning, I was met by Lupé, who as usual seemed intent on eating me, but settled for barking at me dementedly. Spying a weed growing from a crack in his garden path, I challenged Bertrand triumphantly. At last I'd found a weakness. But no! I was told it was there to keep slugs out!

'What? *Your* slugs march up the front path, and that weed stops them does it?' I asked.

He didn't understand *everything* I said, but he got the gist of it. It was no use protesting, though. With a deadpan face, he just shrugged.

I'd called over to return his rotovator – after cleaning it to surgical standards of course. I found him loading his trailer before heading off to cut wood. All week he'd been up at three-thirty am for work, returning after lunch to toil in the garden until dusk. And here he was going out again. Oh my God, I was in the presence of greatness. The man never stopped.

Annoyingly, his work rate made me feel so guilty, that I returned home, dragged out the mower and began cutting the lawns, all the borders, the orchard, and anything else showing signs of grass. Six hours later, after strimming and edging, I put everything away. Utter madness!

A peeling wall-poster promoted a *brocante* in Vernante. It was happening today, so brimming with enthusiasm, we set off to check it out. On our arrival, though, a local told us it'd been cancelled. Pretty damned peeved, we drove on towards Saumur.

Serendipity then kicked in, as turning off a roundabout led us onto the '*Route-de-Vignerons*'– a wine trail hewn from a series of limestone caves. Each one was unique, offering tours and *dégustations,* or tastings from the barrel, but *all* ended with the sale of bottles and cartons. After taking a tour, we ambled off in blistering sunshine to the nearby riverbank. Sitting on a bench in the sun for a while, we then strolled on, past colourfully painted houseboats and barges, their reflections resembling stained-glass windows in the still water.

Picking up the route again brought us to the *Musée de Piere et Lumiére, or* Museum of stone and light. This fascinating building housed a collection of miniaturized villages carved from limestone. Entry was seven euros each, but twelve got you into both the museum, and a mushroom *cave* nearby. We enjoyed the museum but I passed on the *cave* – though with hindsight, Diane might have found my recent working habitat interesting. A little thoughtless of me, I suppose, but we could return in the future with visitors. We'd seen enough by then, so trundling off along country roads, I headed home.

Intermittent rain was the pattern over the next few days, but that didn't stop Bertrand trailering logs from Broc. On his second trip one day, he returned as a shower began. I'd planned to stop working and go over to help him, until the shower turned into a downpour. Nevertheless, soaked to the skin, he began unloading the logs. *To hell with that*, I thought. Working in shorts and singlet, he clambered over the slippery stack like a monkey. It was dangerous and unnecessary, as the weather front probably wouldn't last. But as I'd heard, 'You can't *make* a dog come in out of the rain.'

With everything drying out later, Bertrand and Véronique came over for coffee and to plan our Bazaz trip. After agreeing to pick us up at nine the following morning, they left. We both had lots to do. Driving off to the orchards, we filled in job application forms before returning to pack for the journey. But after a heavy day's gardening, it wasn't a night to drink. We needed clear heads for the next day. A four hour trip with just an English / French dictionary to rely on could prove interesting.

As expected, Bertrand picked us up at *exactly* nine o' clock the next morning. Communication on the journey was challenging, but fun; broken at noon precisely for a picnic. After laying a blanket out, Bertrand strode off and relieved himself against a tree in full sight of us all. It was a Frenchman's right to 'pee pee' wherever he liked, he proclaimed. I disagreed, having witnessed guys flagrantly abusing this supposed right, by flaunting their 'bits' openly. (I believe it's called flashing in the UK.) Only the other day, as Diane and I approached Le Lude roundabout, a man handed his wife a shopping bag, unzipped his fly, and proceeded to hose down a house wall as she waited patiently for him to finish.

Our next stop on the journey was the huge IKEA store on the outskirts of Bordeux, where I'm afraid, Bertrand and I misbehaved outrageously. However, Diane still managed to find her elusive *rideux,* or curtains; so despite our larking about, something was accomplished.

We arrived early at Bazaz, and since François wasn't expecting us until two-thirty, we called into a superstore entitled Michigan. The air-conditioning inside was a delicious shock, and after the searing heat of the town square, we made the most of it.

Following a good look around, we met up with François, who proudly showed us around his tiny apartment. After the ten second guided tour, Véronique made us a French ploughman's lunch while we chatted. But during the meal, Bertrand stated that a bottle of wine he'd bought earlier was corked. So off he trooped to the store, with François and I in tow. At the till an argument ensued, before the grumpy owner gave in reluctantly and changed it.

Leaving at nine pm after a pleasant visit, we followed François' directions to our pre-booked accommodation, a roadside coach house. In the darkened doorway, Bertrand located then pressed a large doorbell. The door opened to reveal our hostess – Mortitia from the Adams family! Following her inside and glancing at each other, it was hard not to grin.

After signing in at the desk, our hostess showed us into the impressive lounge, its walls and ceiling covered in rich brocade; while elsewhere, shelves displayed expensive *objéts d'art,* living happily alongside contemporary *bric-*a-*brac.*

Gliding ahead silently, Madame stopped and turned to face us. In the harshly lit room, with vivid red lipstick and pallid face, she resembled an older female version of Michael Jackson. Her long black hair with its broad parting of silvery roots resembled a badger's back. As she spoke to Veronique, I whispered this to Bertrand and he almost choked. Handing us our keys, Madame Jackson (as she'd be remembered forever) sort of hovered away. And left to our own devices, we chatted for a while before making our way to our rooms.

In the aftermath of an interesting night, we were sat at a dining table having a laugh. During the early hours the tailboard had fallen off our bed. And jumping up at the noise, I'd sent a glass of water flying from the bedside table. In the room below us, Bertrand thought I'd fallen out of bed.

We quickly stifled our laughter, as Madame wafted in to take our breakfast order. Swathed in a black silk kimono adorned with a dragon motif, a cigarette hung from her lips. When she'd sashayed out again, we all looked at each other open-mouthed, desperately trying to contain our laughter.

Breakfast was an unusual affair, cooked by the chain-smoking Madame as she chatted to us through the open kitchen door. While we ate, she slid languidly into the near empty dining room. Draping herself elegantly over the arm of a nearby *chaise-longue,* she opened up about herself. She was aged sixty five, she confided through a cloud of smoke. And since her husband died, she'd been struggling to keep the *auberge* afloat. Unfortunately, she had a wastrel of a son who spent all her money. I felt sorry for her, as she seemed desperately lonely. Though she resembled a Goth in some respects, she possessed an elegance and grace which spoke of better times; sadly, lost in the past.

Following our *'petit dejeuner,'* we drove back to Bazaz to meet up with François. It was market day, so we wandered around the stalls; many of which sold the famous local beef. François then took charge, directing Bertrand as he drove to the *Dune de Pyla,* supposedly the largest sand-dune in Europe at 107 metres high. Located near Arcachon high above the *Bassin* or lagoon, it's a large delta with islands of sand between it and the Atlantic. François insisted we climb to the top of the dune, which to us mature types, held all the appeal of mountaineering in the Sahara ladled with goose fat. At the top it would be extremely windy, he warned, saying that people had been blown off the ridge in the past and sent tumbling to the woods below.

Reaching the summit after a hard climb we were offered a stupendous sight. And because of its 360 degree overview, the position had been commandeered in WW2 for German gun emplacements. Now derelict, the pill-boxes gazed blindly across undulating wheat-fields, stretching off to the horizon.

Having regained our breath, we kind of lolloped down the far side of the dune to the car park, before driving on to Vivièrs, a wild beach accessible only through pine woods. All around us was evidence of the great storm of 1999, though, according to François, reclaimed land had recently been planted with trees following a government initiative.

Driving on, we rounded the headland, passing picturesque communities of Basque-style houses along the coastline. Arriving back at Bazaz worn out, Véronique and Diane prepared a meal, which we ate while watching Charles and Camilla's wedding on François' tiny TV. The colourful ceremony was followed almost immediately by the Pope's funeral, which seemed somewhat bizarre. Then leaving François at ten pm, we drove back to the *auberge* and bed.

Agreeing that we'd all miss the good lady, we said farewell to Madame Jackson at breakfast, before driving into town to meet François. Over coffee in his flat, we watched a Parisian bike race on TV. With rain shrouding the capital, numerous accidents occurred as riders slipped on the cobbled roads. On this occasion translation wasn't necessary.

Switching off the set, we headed over to the 13th century cathedral, the starting point of the *St Jean de Campostella* pilgrim's trail which winds across the Pyrenées into Spain. After lighting votive candles to past family members, François steered us to a local forest where he'd been involved in a cutting and re-planting project. Like a native tracker, he pointed out deer and *sanglier* tracks as we strolled along the track together.

Back at the apartment, we loaded the car with booze and tobacco: duty free buys from François' Spanish jaunt. Transported back by us, they'd be sold on to his friends when he next visited.

We set off at five pm, and after the long journey spent joking with each other, we arrived home just before ten pm.

On the drive home, numerous black cut-out silhouettes of motor-bikers marked the site of fatal accidents. Sad though they were, we shrugged off those morbid signs. We'd enjoyed a fantastic trip. It'd been a welcome change, re-charging our batteries before we cracked on with the house renovations again.

Chapter 19

Cementing friendships

As a change of pace, Bertrand decided to sow potatoes that day. Striding over to inform me of this decision, he said he'd help us plant ours, as he had a special machine which would make light work of it. What he neglected to tell us was, Maurice was ill so he was also sowing his.

He and Véronique arrived mid-afternoon. (Remember, it is *essential* that potatoes are planted before ten thirty am!) Doubled up on the tractor, they were towing a weird contraption which appeared to have been manufactured in the 19th century. Fitted with two rear facing seats, they were bolted to a frame, incorporating chain and belt-driven wheels with large metal spokes.

After studiously lining it up in the furrows, Diane was co-opted to sit alongside Véronique as it was towed along behind the tractor. Attached to the wheel-spokes were cups, which each received a seed potato from the girls as the wheels revolved. These then dropped at precise intervals into two adjoining furrows, and a blade at the rear turned soil back over them afterwards. It was ingenius!

Following behind with the barrow, I picked up the odd rogue potato plus any large fieldstones which were unearthed. Okay, it wasn't rocket science, but at the birth of the industrial revolution it must have been ground-breaking (no pun intended.) But like most of what Bertrand did, it was simple but effective.

We adjourned to the kitchen for a cooling drink after sowing the crop; then when they left, I tipped out the fieldstones before we headed in for our meal.

Shortly afterwards, I heard Bertrand on his ride-on mower, surgically trimming the grass around his house and garden. Does he *ever* stop?

The following Tuesday at two thirty pm, we sat waiting for Rob and Elaine to arrive. We'd tidied up after a morning's work, thrown rubbish into the trailer, and returned tools and materials to the shed.

Arriving bang on time, they expressed amazement at the size of the property as we adjourned to the terrace with drinks. Later, with a successful innaugeral visit concluded, techie Rob promised to return on Sunday to check our sluggish internet service. If the weather-gods were feeling benign, we'd promised them a BBQ and *degustation* in appreciation.

We were both feeling throaty for some reason the next morning. But when Jorge delivered a letter from our UK bank stating that £3,592 had been deposited into our account, our spirits soared. With no idea why it'd happened, I rang the branch to check out this unexpected windfall. But having mentally spent it, I was told it was an admin error and *we'd* be charged £60 to correct it. Excuse me! Ringing the manager, I demanded it was sorted out – without cost to us.

Going upstairs to calm down, I applied a coat of plaster to the walls as a sedative. With sanity restored, I came down to find Diane tackling a computer glitch. I'll say this for her, she won't be beaten. Otherwise, the day was a washout as we battled our cold symptoms.

In bed early dosed with medication, we were woken by a phone-call from Nadine. Once again, Diane doled out motherly advice, while barely able to keep her eyes open.

It was a hot humid morning, and Noyant's market was heaving as Rob and Elaine held court at their stall next to the toilets. After a quick skirt around, we collared Rob during a lull. He'd found a solution to our computer problem. While trawling the web, though, he'd chanced across a B+B booking site. He'd visited it out of curiosity, and after registering with the company, they'd already taken a booking for their house. We left while some tourists claimed Rob's attention, our minds racing.

Back home again, Diane shot off to La Flèche to buy quality food ingredients. She was hosting her first meal for Bertrand and Véronique in the evening. I offered to go with her but she declined, saying she liked to plan the menu in her head while driving.

Come seven-thirty our neighbours arrived, Véronique cradling two huge goose eggs. Setting them aside carefully, I poured drinks, as Diane our *Chef de soir* flitted between kitchen and lounge. Then disaster struck! The first course, *poirot-et-onione tartlette* had failed to rise. Improvising swiftly behind the scenes, Diane served up the liver paté we'd received as a gift from François. Thankfully, the rest of the meal went to plan, the crowning glory being Nigella's ice cream – a veritable *tour de force*.

Though the evening was a great success; by ten-thirty we were all fighting to stay awake. After handshakes and kisses, they set off along the track – both themselves and their torch beam weaving unsteadily in the darkness.

Carrying in a basket of logs the next morning, I found Diane wrestling with the goose eggs. As we'd earmarked the afternoon for a Saumur trip, we ate breakfast in the sun-dappled kitchen while making lists of things we needed.

Seeking a computer table at *Emmaus,* we drove to the city early, taking a stroll along the riverbank to pass the time.

The mighty river Loire certainly lived up to its description *that* afternoon, surging angrily against the bridge buttresses as it swept through the city. Carrying uprooted trees and scouring the weed beds, the tumbling water, gravy brown with sediment was higher than we'd ever seen it, lapping over the footpath on many sections.

Leaving the car park, we crossed the road and headed towards the *Mairie,* stopping to investigate two marquees we'd spotted on the drive in. Housing an *exposition-de-vin,* or wine sale, they offered good wine cheaply in volume. Having a full wine-rack by then, we carried on to the market, where we found it awash with crowds of early tourists.

As we sauntered along narrow streets of timbered old buildings, the intoxicating atmosphere entranced us. Eyes averted, we avoided the guy with a box of kittens on a shake-down table. On our last visit the box had contained a goat kid, but the principle was always the same. Entice children to pet some hapless little creatures, then sell parents overpriced titbits for their children to feed to them. It was a tough parent who could walk on by. Grabbing a vacated table at a pavement café, we watched a cross-section of humanity stroll by while drinking coffee in the sunshine.

When we left the market it was to call into *Gifi,* where Diane bought three pairs of *rideux,* or curtains. Then calling into Saumur's *Intermarché* on the outskirts of the city, we bumped into Rob and Elaine. Sitting down together for coffee in the precinct, we played catch-up; then with a meeting arranged, we went our separate ways.

Arriving home mid-afternoon, Véronique intercepted us, carrying two artichoke plants propagated in her poly-tunnel. Diane had agreed to plant them out of politeness, though we didn't particularly rate them. But they could wait until later. First, there was shopping to unload.

The bells rang out in the distance, calling the faithful of Broc to mass. It was a glorious Sunday, denying Bertrand's gloomy forecast of rain.

Knuckling down to work, Diane cleaned the house, while I cut all the grassed areas. Breaking off to nip into town for baguettes, Diane returned just before Rob and Elaine arrived. Adjourning to the terrace with our coffees, I lit the BBQ. As the aroma of sizzling chicken permeated the air I was handed a glass of the wine. We were off and running.

The afternoon was a great success; the weather staying sunny until late afternoon. When it finally clouded over we retired indoors, where Rob examined the computer. However he was unable to access the server on dial-up. (Yep, that's what I said, dial up.)

They left at seven thirty pm, having things to attend to. While, after clearing up, we half-heartedly watched a video before trudging off to bed.

The next few days slid by in a flurry of decorating. Curtains were hemmed, poles sourced cut and fitted, and rooms finished off. We only had one phone call all week. It was from the complaints manager at my assurance company. The error made by Mumbai staff had been rectified, and my pension annuity had now *doubled.* 'Please accept £100 in compensation,' he said.

And to cap it all, Diane finally got her artichokes planted.

Dropping off Rob's forgotten Raybans at Friday's market, we wished them a safe journey and a nice break in Paris. Moving on, we inspected the chicken man's stock; avoiding the guy with the now clinically obese kittens.

Arriving in Saumur, we found the River Loire in full spate again. We'd driven in for the half-price sale at *Gifi* and a browse around. Returning to the car, I jumped in, started it and selected reverse gear, but despite revving it furiously, it stubbornly refused to move. Climbing out, Diane saw that the front valance had caught on a protruding stone slab and was held fast. As the car-park was cobbled and sloped down to the river, she suggested she lift up the front end while I reversed. As the car broke free, the valance came loose and trapped her fingers. It must have hurt like hell. But after the initial shock, she just said, 'Come on let's go,' and with the panel secured with wire from the boot, I set off.

To make up for Diane's bruised fingers, I drove us to Tours the next day; somewhere we'd only shot through previously. After a long, hot drive, we crossed the river-bridge and found parking in the city.

Stretching our legs, our investigation began with the ruined old cathedral, and a twin-towered later structure. Then following a street map, we spent most of the day visiting churches, museums and art galleries. Wandering cobbled streets shaded by overhanging 12th century buildings, Saint Martin's church impressed us with its wonderful stained glass, and stone carvings. After a leisurely lunch, we perused antique shops, jewellers and clothing stores. Then passing the Grand Opera House, we crossed the *Pont de Fils* and entered a central square. Finding seats at an outside café, we enjoyed street entertainment for a while before moving on.

Leaving by the *Pont de Wilson,* we located the car easily, having parked it under a huge chromed sculpture resembling 'the incredible hulk.' After a wearying drive home, I made for the ringing phone as we entered. It was Chris, asking if we'd had a relaxing day.

Chapter 20

The fishing expedition

After losing a day to our Tours excursion, we were working flat out the next day trying to catch up, when Henri and Annette arrived. Observing social niceties, Diane served coffee, biscuits were offered, and we chatted. Getting up to leave later, Henri headed for the garden. Mumbling something incomprehensible, he pointed at the flower beds. As I obviously appeared mystified, he mimed opening his flies. With closed fist and protruding thumb, he swivelled from side to side, indicating crudely that my plants needed watering. I suppose we were lucky he used his *thumb* to point with!

In one of life's strange coincidences, François arrived shortly after with some plants from Véronique. And as he put them down, I could have sworn he said, 'Can I have a piss please.'

Taken aback, I said, '*Pardon?*'

Pointing at the kitchen roll, he said, 'Can I have a piece please? It is to wipe my hands.'

Moving on, he said both the goose and ducks were covering eggs, and a clutch of ducklings could be expected soon. 'But the goose, she does not know her eggs are not good,' he said mournfully.

It seems she'd gathered a clutch of eggs together, and attacked anyone who tried collecting them. Sadly, they hadn't been fertilized, but being broody she wouldn't leave them. 'Soon we will buy some baby geese. Then the goose, she too will have children,' he said.

Determined to fix our computer, Rob and Elaine popped over on the Tuesday afternoon. Once again, Rob couldn't find the problem – though it required the sampling of various wines before he reached this conclusion. *Much* later and well served by then, they left. Dignified in defeat, he drove off unsteadily down the road. After waving them off, we somehow cobbled together a snack – before heading for bed totally hammered.

Despite feeling rather fragile the next morning, we pulled out the staircase. After carrying it out to the barn, I began plastering the wall, while Diane, needing some air mowed the lawns. Heading out to catch up with her later, I spotted a viper in her work area. Following local advice, I found a stick and whacked it. Unsurprisingly it went rigid! But after telling Diane about it, I returned and found it'd vanished. Either a sharp-eyed buzzard had spotted it, or it was laid up somewhere with one helluva headache.

Unable to get a dialling tone on our phone at lunchtime, I consulted François, who rang *France Telecom* from Le Lavendu for us. He was told there was a fault on our line which could take days to fix. Anyone desperate to contact us could ring our mobile; but Rob was borrowing a modem to test our computer problem, and he didn't have our number. Unless they called by, we'd have to catch him later.

At Friday's market, I explained to Rob why I hadn't rung. But it wasn't a problem, as the modum's owner was on holiday in the UK. But when he said units were available locally for fourteen euros, we said forget it, we'd buy one. We left him 'spieling' to tourists as we set off to buy more plants. Finding some luscious scarlet geraniums and flowering lavender plants, we drove home, planted them, and watered them well in.

On a roll after lunch we re-fitted the staircase, then stretched a builder's plank from a stair tread to the ladder propped against the stairwell. Painting was my job the next day, but with prepping done, we went back to gardening.

Balanced precariously on the plank the next morning, I tackled the stairwell. I was interrupted when the telephone engineer arrived to fit a new junction box. He left around noon, and with it being freakishly hot by then, I finished off, showered, and we nipped off to bed for a *petit-somme*.

Mid- afternoon found me in the garden hoeing, while Diane had driven out to Le Lude. Passing by on his tractor, Bertrand paused to take the mickey because I'd shaved off my beard. Changing tack, he said he'd just unearthed an old petrol tank while ploughing. Peering inside he'd seen two snakes, he said – so being a concerned naturalist ... he'd set fire to it! Shortly after, it was François' turn to snigger at my beard; going on to say, he'd been fishing at the family lake and caught seventeen fish. He'd returned three carp and thrown fourteen sun-perch over the hedge, as he considered them vermin. As an animal born in this area, it seems life could be a fleeting thing.

The first of May was cooler than of late, and much more comfortable. After a morning spent gardening, we showered before visiting Rob and Elaine for lunch. On arrival, Rob directed us to cruise-ship style loungers near the pond. And relaxed under parasols, we assumed the persona of characters from an Edwardian travel brochure. In double quick time, the table overflowed with drinks and aperitifs; and with appetites sated, a game of *boules* was suggested, fuelled by more drinks to make the contest interesting.

Throughout the long, lazy afternoon, the neighbouring farmer trundled back and forth on his tractor. And after droning hypnotically overhead for quite some time, a light aircraft landed in a nearby field. Otherwise, the day was tranquility itself, broken only by the chirruping cicadas, the metallic 'clacking' of boules, and the sound of our raucous laughter.

It was a storybook afternoon – until Diane, stepping back from her shot tripped over an ornamental stone and fell heavily. The laughing stopped abruptly when we saw her knee and ankle which were swelling badly. She couldn't stand; and while trying to save herself, she'd landed awkwardly on her hand. Though we suspected a broken finger, we could only strap ice packs onto her knee and ankle, and a splint to her finger, as she couldn't take pain killers due to the alcohol. She really wasn't having much luck lately.

Game abandoned, we tried taking her mind off the pain by discussing the letting site and their booking. During our chat, they asked if we'd like to accompany them on their next Parisian trip. It sounded great. Then completely out of left field, they said they'd advertised their house for sale, and had already arranged a viewing. If it didn't sell quickly they intended wintering in Paris. If so, would we be their caretakers?

We sat there mouths agape. This was a body-blow. We hadn't known them long, and now they were thinking of moving. 'Was it something we said?' I joked.

Laughing, Rob said of course not. They'd moved here initially because they couldn't find anything suitable in Paris. Strange! Life here was a complete antithesis to the capital's teeming boulevards, I'd have thought.

Changing the subject, he said the modem we'd bought was incompatable with our computer, so our problem remained. As Diane was extremely uncomfortable by then, we left while I could still spot *gendarmes*. Passing through Noyant while driving back, I pointed out two huge American cars. Being a fan of U.S iron, spotting a Chevy Impala and a Buick Century made my day. Though, as she was in a lot of pain by then, Diane seemed less than enthusiastic!

On Ascension Day there was good news for once. Our UK bank manager confirmed that a substantial cheque had arrived in our account. Transferring funds to Credit Agricole, I bought the last ten lengths of skirting board at *Brico*, and placed seven more on order.

Back home, I was laying out the boards when Bertrand and François appeared at the door. Would we like to go fishing today at two thirty pm? Easily distracted right then, I replied, '*Beh oui.*'

Come three pm there was still no sign of the trio, so I rang them. They were waiting for *us* at *their* house. Confusion over, we set off from Le Lavendu.

Pulling up at 'the lake,' Bertrand realised he'd forgotten the bait, so, with whatever came to hand, we dug for worms. Unearthing the first one with a stick, Véronique baited up and cast in. Then finding another wriggler, she got me underway. On my first cast, my bait was taken almost immediately. I was into the first fish of the afternoon, a nice carp. Alas, it spit out the hook before I could land it.

After that, we *all* caught fish, Bertrand insisting that all perch were thrown over the hedge as vermin. By the end of the day, he was the only one who'd landed a carp, which he returned to bolster breeding stock.

We arrived back at Le Lavendu pleasantly tired, whereupon François proudly introduced us to his new money making enterprise – breeding rabbits. He and his dad had constructed cages in a shed, with additional pens outside on the grass. Rabbits, being rabbits would do the rest. We also got to see the goose sat stoically on her dodgy eggs, and a pheasant which was valiantly trying to cover a clutch of seventeen. Meanwhile, splashing around in the pond were Diane's favourites, a flock of fluffy yellow ducklings. We were impressed by the sheer amount of stock, but they said they needed more. They were off tomorrow to pick up thirty pullets, and possibly a dozen more ducklings.

Humming 'Hey big spender' to myself, I splashed out at Noyant's pulsating market, buying myself an eight euro watch, Diane a five euro bag, and a few things from Rob. He'd found us a modem for ten euros, and suggested they pop over the next day and he'd fit it.

Before they arrived on the Saturday, I nipped down to *Brico* for the boards. '*Pardon Monsieur*, your order, it has not arrived,' the assistant said. 'They must have forgotten to load it.'

'So when *will* it arrive?

'Maybe next week,' was his blasé reply.

'Well, could you ring La Flèche branch to check *their* stock?'

'I regret it is not possible. We do not speak to each other,' he said, shrugging.

I'd heard they were separate franchises – but come on! In high dudgeon by then, I got home to find Rob and Elaine had arrived, and it wasn't long before the modem was installed. Finally, we had internet access. '*Dah dah!*'

Setting up some web-sites to test it, Rob checked Jane's advert out of curiosity. He wasn't impressed at what she was offering, saying, 'If that's the best she can do, there's hope for us all.'

Well, there was no stopping Diane after that. When Rob and Elaine left, she went online sending our e-mail address to family and friends. Leaving her to it, I took my strimmer back to *Brico* under warranty. It could be away for three weeks, the guy said. Needing it desperately, I took it home, and flouting the warranty, I adjusted the carburettor. It helped a little, but as I was trying it out, Bertrand arrived with Maurice in tow. Was it possible to graze six horses for a few days? I owed Maurice a favour, so I agreed. Anyway, as

Bertrand was harvesting the grass soon anyway, did it matter? They'd also had an idea for installing solar powered electric fencing. It would be cheap, easy to install, and they'd pay for it, as it was to corral their horses. Encircling the top fields it would keep out large animals, especially *sanglier*. And when horses were grazed there in the future, they wouldn't try to escape. Well not after the initial shock anyway!

Trying the strimmer again, I found it was still acting up, so I put it away and went indoors. In the drawing room, Diane brought me up to speed on internet news from family. Nadine was talking of moving back to the North-East, which had left Nick feeling gutted. For once, I felt heartily sorry for him.

When *I* was finally allowed online, I visited some classic American car sites. Scrolling through one, I saw a Dodge Custom Royale for sale. Previously owned by John Travolta, it was a steal at only £13,500.

If only!

Chapter 21

Flaming June

It was scarcely believable but it was the end of May already. Time had flown by in a blur of work, broken only by the odd visit or phone-call. Our friendship with Rob and Elaine continued to blossom, visiting each other regularly and adding spice to our market days.

Recently they'd introduced us to Phil, a retired set designer for the film industry. Discussing our restoration, he agreed to build us a bespoke staircase and balustrade at a fair price. He suggested coming over to assess the job, then after measuring up, he'd order the materials. When the order was ready, I'd collect and stain all the pieces before assembly.

On our last visit to *Leclerc* I'd bought a digital camera. Along with our video camera, it would keep a record of ongoing improvements – including my latest project an elevated terrace. Once finished, it would give commanding views over the pool, gardens and lower field.

As we began laying out the foundations, Bertrand and Véronique arrived to dig post-holes for the electric fencing. Following closely behind, François called in with photos of our Bazaz visit, which of course put a stop to work. When he mentioned that Bertrand had hired an excavator to clear the storm drains, I suggested paying the operator to level our pool site. It would save us a helluva lot of work, and speed up the project enormously. He said he'd discuss it with his 'fazzaire' later, but first he had an errand to run. It was his young cousin's communion later that afternoon, followed by a family party lasting well into the evening.

Arriving after lunch to discuss my proposal, Bertrand said he was already imagining tomorrow's *mal de tete,* or bad head after the party. He'd just recovered from a wrestling match with the goose, who'd abandoned her sterile eggs and tried to kidnap newborn ducklings from their mother. Meanwhile, his pheasant was now struggling to cover twenty one eggs, so he intended donating some to a broody hen. Wouldn't it solve his goose problem if he gave *her* some to rear instead?

Driving down to C.A.P.L for weed-killer later, I spotted two 'Monster Trucks' parked on the *Place Gare de Ancien,* or old railway site. Posters slapped up nearby promised a spectacular display that evening; the dramatic artwork showing these gigantic vehicles jumping over cars. Maybe we could drive along for a look.

A knock on the door later revealed François dressed for the communion. He'd nipped over to tell me Monsieur Allande had died. Who? And what had his passing to do with us? He went on to explain. A parcel of woodland above their top field belonged to the late Monsieur – as did a strip along the top of one of *our* fields. He'd also owned a share in our wood, and a section of land on the next farm along.

In former times, parcels of land were often bought as an investment or for strip farming. Now, with his family feuding over his assets, those parcels could cause some headaches if his family decided to sell them. God knows what might be built on them when considering local planning regulations.

As I pondered this new development, François mentioned his latest chicken encounter. He'd gone to let the new pullets out of their coop for the first time – using a broom-shank to 'encourage' them – as you would. 'They will not stay out as required,' he sighed. 'They are not clever.'

I'd often found that to be an understatement when discussing the average chicken.

Following a bath and a meal, I drove down to see the monster truck show. Diane hadn't fancied it – but neither had anyone else apparently. It'd been cancelled. On the way back, my neighbours passed me heading off to their family celebration at Challone. Waving, I drove home brassed off.

We had a rare lie in on Sunday, anticipating our afternoon visit to Rob and Elaine. Pulling into their courtyard later, we found loungers set out next to the pond; and after reclining on two of them a lazy afternoon unfolded. As wine flowed freely, we loosened up. In fact, things became *so* loose at one stage, that Diane, who'd forgotten her cigarettes, accepted Rob's offer to try one of his cigars.

However, mid-afternoon a freak rainstorm forced us inside. A mere bagatelle, we decided, and partied on. Unable to stand the pace, though, party-pooper Elaine crashed out. And as Rob helped her to bed, we abandoned her to his tender mercies and left.

I drove home carefully, though the chances of seeing a police car in our area were remote. Nevertheless, we were pleased to get back safely. After incinerating a fry-up, I ate the charred remains while trying to watch a video through a veil of smoke. Meanwhile, *sous- chef* Diane had given up the ghost and wandered off to bed.

Being comatose really early, Diane was on the internet at two thirty am. We had breakfast at four thirty, followed by a trip back to bed again. Eight o'clock saw us up for the day; and not a moment too soon, as Bertrand, Maurice and Vincente turned up to string the electric fencing.

During a *second* breakfast there were two phone-calls. The first was from Stewie, who was laid up after pulling a tendon. The other was from Nadine the intrepid *voyageur,* who said she was booking flights for Stewie's family. We'd invited them to visit some time ago, and now they'd finally accepted. Oh oh, I'd have to fix the staircase quickly.

When the phone rang, we'd been discussing Diane's weed-killing saga – which putting it mildly had been a disaster. In fact the weeds seemed to be thriving on the attention. It served her right, as she'd once told me, 'Weeds are just plants in the wrong place.'

Totally frustrated with the garden, she'd focused on creating a website for the house. By taking photos of the *finished* areas in the house and garden, we could begin advertising. Desperate to catch some late bookings, I tackled the upstairs bedroom floor. After hand-mixing cement, I hauled it up in a builder's bucket using a block and tackle. I was taking no chances until the new staircase was in place.

While I laid the cement, Diane shot off to *Brico* for pipe fittings. The old piping from the bath to the *fosse-septique* needed replacing, which we hoped would get rid of the stagnant smell. Frusratingly, after I replacing the piping, the smell was still there. Checking out other possible causes, Diane noted that with the bath-plug in place, the smell seemed to vanish. This suggested a leak somewhere under the concrete floor. Great, that's all I needed!

Thank God we'd had a lie in. Feeling as fit as butcher's dogs, we readied for Rob and Elaine's visit. As it was, they arrived during a sudden shower, just in time to help rescue food from the terrace table. Getting everything in mob-handed, we dried out over a glass of wine. However, minutes later, the sun re-appeared; so determined to eat alfresco, we went out to re-set the table. We'd just finished re-laying it when the heavens opened again, and it was back inside with everything. Oh for the gazebo right then!

At the third attempt, I finally got the food barbequed and we began eating. Then BOOM! A thunder-clap rattled the

151

windows, as swollen clouds burst apart once more. Jumping up, we carried everything inside again. But that was the final straw, as during *this* outburst we were showered with huge hailstones!

Our guests left at six thirty pm after an eventful visit; while *we* settled down to send e-mails to family.

A frustrating exercise in laminate floor-laying tested us the next day. No matter what we tried, the expensive tongue and groove boards just wouldn't stay connected. We concluded that the floor couldn't be perfectly level; and stuck for time, we abandoned the idea. Instead, a trip to *Brico* was mooted to check out alternatives. Whilst rooting about, I bumped into Christopher Borelle, my nemesis from the *cave*. As we no longer worked together and my spoken French had improved a lot, we had the longest conversation we'd ever managed – which let's face it wasn't difficult. Back home again, I shelved the flooring project.

While excavating the ferret enclosure recently, I'd unearthed a pile of skulls and bones. Not being an archaeologist, palaeontologist, or in possession of an anthropology degree, I concluded they were part of Monsieur Renard's ongoing legacy and dumped them in the trailer. Seeing me digging up the area, Bertrand insisted on levelling the site with his plough. Unfortunately, his initial pass opened up yet another vein of rubbish. This farm had become the gift that keeps on giving.

On the lighter note, he regaled me with three stories. The first concerned the goose, who'd eventually managed to cover six *fertilized* eggs. Sadly three became addled, while the three newborn goslings were killed by jealous hens.

The second story concerned him despatching a drake, which kept trying to kill its partner's new brood. It's a fairly common occurrence apparently, as they try to 'encourage' their partners to mate again. Mother Nature's cruel version of foreplay perhaps?

But the third story contained some *good* news. François' enterprise had taken off big style, as cages overflowed with hairless pink baby rabbits.

With June fast approaching, another UK trip reared its head. This one was to celebrate Jill and Dale's renewal of their wedding vows, and as usual family were congregating from far and wide. Being cash strapped on our project, these UK visits were eating into our funds. But how could we miss it?

Flying in from Tours on Friday 27th May, we were met by Nadine and the boys at Stanstead airport. After staying a few days with them, we travelled North en-masse, meeting family at the Colsterworth Travel-Lodge. Jill and Dale drove over later for a family tea, and Diane and I returned with them to stay overnight.

We set off in convoy the next morning, headed for Judith and Chris's Manor house near Grantham. Our arrival swelled the already large group, and it was great playing catch up. It was also quite a surprise for Jill and Dale, when a previously hidden Joanne emerged from another room after secretly flying over from Canada.

With everyone gathered, the group strolled to the nearby church. After a moving celebration, everyone returned to the house for speeches and a buffet in the sun –dappled gardens. With Chris and Judith hosting proceedings, the festivities continued into the night.

Going our separate ways the next morning, Stewie and family headed north, while Diane and I returned with Nadine and the boys. We'd offered to help her move house, so, with the kids dropped off at Nick's, packing began.

At nine am on the Monday, Nadine picked up a hired Luton van; and after six hours of loading, we set off, arriving safely 'up north' at seven thirty pm. After a phone-call,

Stewie and Helen came over to help, followed by Kay who'd been driven over by her Dad.

Tuesday flew by, and with the unpacking done, our group slept over before setting off at seven am. Nadine as the hirer was driving the van again. Alas – an hour later we were broken down on the hard shoulder of the A1.

With no help forthcoming from the hire company, we sat high up on the embankment for three long hours until Stewie turned up to help after work. With a van sourced locally and the load transferred our journey continued. Getting underway again, Nadine drove hard, but making up the lost time was impossible and we missed our flight. The next one available was the following Sunday.

We arrived home a week later, to find a message from Rob inviting us for lunch. 'We've cleaned out the pool,' it said, 'so bring your cozzies.'

After the visit which turned into a splash-a-mania, I drove back at five thirty pm, allowing Diane to check our emails before we crashed out exhausted.

I ran into Bertrand the next morning (a metaphor, he's fine) and asking about the planned horse delivery, he said the timing was bad, as Maurice was fighting a messy divorce. His wife had walked out, leaving him with the three kids. It was a shame, as he seemed such a nice guy. But of course there are two sides to every story.

There was *some* good news though. It was François' birthday, and his prezzie from his doting parents was … a rescue horse. It had to be gentled by Maurice before he could ride it, but what a present! They said it was also a reward for doing well in his exams, so take note children.

We had other good news – well kind of. Diane was required at the apple orchards *toute-suite*. Topping up the coffers after our UK trip would be useful. But then there was some *great* news. It's said that every cloud has a silver lining. Well this time we were the recipients, as Halifax plc shares boomed. Brokering ours quickly, we banked most of the proceeds. The remainder was destined to fund Diane's upcoming birthday weekend at a hotel in La Rochelle.

There was no reply from the orchard when Diane tried ringing. She'd just cradled the phone when Véronique arrived, followed by Vincente and his wife driving a huge horsebox. Its passengers were two fine horses, with four more following later. While admiring the vehicle's air-sprayed panels depicting cowboys, knights, and other horse-borne heroes, his wife told me they did stunt riding displays.

With the animals offloaded, the transporter trundled off down the drive. As the dust settled, we invited Véronique to stay for coffee and a chat. Naturally, she was upset about Maurice's divorce, and was helping look after the children. Though our French was by no means perfect, she seemed to appreciate having someone to talk to.

Vincente returned mid-week with two more horses and two ponies. They got on well together, and looked magnificent cavorting up and down the fields with the others. Sadly, they were all a magnet for flies which infested their eyes, ears and nostrils; and tics which sucked blood like vampire bats.

By mid-June temperatures were hitting 35 degrees C, but we couldn't slacken. With our website up and running, we had to step up the pace, though, it would be harder once Diane began working at the orchards. Thankfully, our hotel was booked for the coming weekend, so she could relax before picking began.

We caught up with Rob and Elaine at Friday's market to make plans for later. Returning home, we found François removing tics from the horses while Maurice mowed the fields in return for the stabling. Everything was going well – until we received an email. The hotel we'd booked had cancelled our reservation due to overbooking. Gutted, we drove over to the *Longére,* where we found Rob in the pool.

Our mood soon lifted, and it wasn't long before we were all splashing about. The ladies left us to it, as Rob and I tried – with limited success, to mount an inflatable Homer Simpson chair fitted with drink holders. We had a lot of laughs in the process, but the wine definitely impaired our performance.

On the way home, Diane the designated driver passed through Noyant, where I spotted a huge Dodge Royale sedan parked up a side street. 'Alright, I give in. Where've you hidden John Travolta?' I called out.

Arriving home, Diane managed to make another hotel booking online. This hotel was '*Le Chêne verte,* or Green Oak, at the seaside resort of Les Sables d'Olonne. It looked great onscreen. Relieved and delighted, we celebrated with a few glasses of wine. It may come as no surprised that we ended up going to bed at three thirty am.

Chapter 22

A birthday treat

The heat was already unbearable when we woke at seven thirty am. Having packed last night, all we needed to do was shower, dress, and hit the road. While loading the car, Bertrand and Véronique popped over to check on the horses and pick up keys. And as Diane was working through her 'to do' list, I helped Bertrand install some fence-posts.

Underway at last, I headed to Noyant, before turning right towards Angers. Stopping for breakfast at nine thirty, we took on calories before the long haul to Nantes. Leaving the city behind us, we threaded our way through La Rochelle and on to Lés Sables d'Olonne.

Though we weren't expecting a tickertape welcome when we arrived, pulling up to our hotel at one thirty and finding it closed came as a surprise. A notice stating that check-in began at three pm was pasted on the door. Deciding we may as well get acquainted with the town until then, exploring its renowned beach and harbour seemed a good place to start.

After checking in at three fifteen, a cooling shower was sheer bliss. Towelled off afterwards, we closed the blinds against the fierce sunshine and crashed out.

Resurfacing at six pm, another shower was needed before stepping out into a stiflingly hot town square. Breaking out into a sweat almost immediately due to the humidity, we wandered off to check out local eateries, comparing menu's before the hotel restaurant opened at seven pm.

Strolling down to the seafront, we were offered a plethora of alternatives, mostly seafood joints. Confused by the variety, it seemed easier to plump for the hotel after all. But after tramping all the way back, we found the restaurant closed. In a glass fronted case containing a faded menu, it stated seven day opening only applied in high summer. Ah well! It was back down to the seafront and into Molly Malone's Irish bar, for a beer and some Celtic music. With our thirsts slaked, we moved on to a nearby restaurant, where a table was found for us immediately. Then from a varied menu, Diane ordered *Moules Mariniere,* while I chose *Tagliatani* with a seafood platter.

We rose from the table at ten thirty pm, well satisfied with our three course meal. Stepping outside, we were enveloped by a lighthearted crowd headed downtown; incuding families with buggies enjoying the balmy evening. Besides family groups there were teenagers aplenty; some riding 'tricked out' motorbikes, while others cruised in customized cars. Though high spirited they were well behaved, and their presence contributed to the ambience of the town.

Under a full-moon, wave crests glinted as they broke onto the beach; the sea reflecting coloured lighting strung along the promenade. Despite it being dark, people were body surfing in water retaining the sun's warmth. And thankfully, there wasn't a triangular fin to be seen anywhere!

With so much going on, it was just as well we had a key to the hotel door. We didn't get to bed until one thirty am.

We woke up feeling just great. I wished Diane Happy Birthday, and she wished *me* Happy Father's day. Then slipping downstairs to the restaurant, we enjoyed a cooked breakfast before going back up to pack.

Checked out, I cruised along the coastline towards Noirmoutier. Coming across a Sunday market on the roadside allowed us to stock up on bottled water, before we plunged into the swirling sea-fret blanketing the Isle d'Lonne. It stuck with us for miles, before finally lifting as we dropped down to sea level on the peninsular.

Finding an atmospheric snack-bar in the old town, we had a decent lunch sat on the terrace, then explored shops, the harbour and cliffs. Discovering a secluded cove, I laid out a blanket on the beach. Then later, dusting sand off ourselves, I drove back via a toll road. Okay, it cost a few euros, but it cut quite a chunk off the return journey, and we arrived home at seven thirty pm pleasantly tired. Opening the door, we threw everything onto a settee and collapsed; only to be jerked back into consciousness by a knock at the door. It was François, who'd seen us arrive and popped over to invite us to a party. We'd be celebrating Diane's birthday, Father's day twice and his belated birthday. How could we refuse?

At the gathering there was a major breakthrough, as Bertrand unwittingly asked why we didn't rent out our house to guests. 'Well what a good idea,' I replied.

We left at ten thirty pm, as Bertrand had a four thirty start the next morning, and as it was only nine forty in the UK, I rang Michael. He was driving down soon with his family for a few days, so I warned him about the Paris Périphérique. According to François, most insurance companies won't cover drivers on that dangerous stretch of motorway. With their visit looming it was best he was forewarned.

It was Diane's first day back at the orchards. And while I worked inside the house, François arrived with a detailed map showing the best route for Michael's journey. However, our chat ended abruptly when Diane returned for lunch. Crashing into the kitchen without noticing François, she groaned, 'Oh God, my bloody feet are killing me. 'Ah! Hi there François, *ca va?*'

After planting three kisses on Diane's blushing cheeks, Francois left. While I boiled the kettle, she struggled to prise off her workboots. Braced for tales of woe, I was surprised when she said she'd had a *great* morning. She was still working under Céline, but a new, chilled out and enlightened version. Dominic was also worryingly benevolent when she met *him*. *Hullo, what's this?* She'd thought, as she was placed alongside Pauline, Annette's English speaking granddaughter. The Gods were smiling on her. Life was suddenly good again.

Her first shift ended at four thirty; and after changing, we pottered around in the veggie patch for a while. After our meal and a glass of wine, she began yawning; and excusing herself, went off to bed. When Nadine rang at ten thirty, I took a message for my comatose wee apple picker.

The patinated old butter churn decended slowly attached to a thick rope. Swinging pendulum-like in front of the barn, it made a gentle landing. I'd repaired it after finding it in the granary broken; and surrounded by some flower tubs it would form an arrangement where the ferret pens once stood. It would be a pleasant surprise for Diane when she drove home at lunchtime. I'd removed some plants from the flower beds to fill the tubs, and once I'd arranged them, they'd look terrific.

She roared up the drive at twelve fifteen, and spotting my handiwork, she cried out, 'Oh lush,' before commenting on the newly-painted *cave* door. Oh yes, I'd been a busy boy!

Diane's morning had *also* gone well. She'd been teamed with Pauline again, and they'd had a great time chatting in English. Pauline was finding it difficult getting to work, so Diane offered her a regular lift. And as Céline and Dominic hadn't regressed to their old behaviour, it was a great start.

With Meteo forecasting extreme temperatures for the Wednesday, Diane was asked to start work at seven am, before the heat built up under the nets. After waving her off, I carried on preparing for Michael's visit. As they'd be using our downstairs bedroom, I assembled hanging rails in the granary bedroom for us. Apart from us sharing the kitchen, this gave them the downstairs to themselves; allowing for nightime issues with the kids, easy access to their own bathroom, and another bedroom if needed.

After stripping beds, I did the wash and hung it out under the increasingly fierce sun. Getting it dried was important, as we'd promised to visit Annette when Diane got in from work. She was going into hospital for a gall-bladder operation; and with Diane now working, I had lots to do before my family arrived.

Mid-afternoon, Vincente appeared to check on his horses; followed closely by Diane, who'd been sent home early due to the intense heat. The outside thermometer registered 34 degrees C, so God only *knew* what it'd been at noon trapped under those field-nets. After a quick change, she helped me move the desk from our guest bedroom. Having given everything a final tidy and polish, she took in the bedding from the line, ran the iron over it, and made up the beds.

While watering the flower beds under the kitchen window later, I heard the phone. It was Michael. They'd left Charles de Gaulle airport, and were approaching the Périphérique headed south out of Paris. Since this orbital route is notoriously dangerous, I left him to concentrate on driving. Knowing we'd plenty of time before they arrived, we finished our jobs, showered, then changed.

Their next call, made much later was from Le Lude, and as it was dark by then, I drove to Le Lude to meet them. Miranda was driving, and insisted the Périphérique had been a doddle. Having driven it before, I was surprised; but I had to admit they'd made good time.

Arriving behind me at the farm, they unloaded and settled in, while I entertained Lydia and Dylan before their bedtime. Then with the youngsters tucked up, it was chill-out time on the terrace with a bottle of wine. But it wasn't long before we also headed off for an early night.

Chapter 23

Special visitors

Sunlight slanted through the kitchen windows as I waved Diane off to work. And with no recognizable lifesigns coming from Michael and family, I took myself off for a coffee in the lounge. It was then that I heard a dull 'thud,' in the dining room.

Carefully setting down my cup, I went to investigate – and found a huge green lizard on the tiled floor. Using chair struts as a comparison, I estimated it to be about forty centimetres from nose to tail. Obviously it needed to be removed pretty sharpish. But before I could catch it, Michael walked into the room carrying Lydia. 'Bloody hell Dad, what's *that*?' he asked, stepping back quickly.

I asked him to put Lydia down and help me corner the bewildered creature. But, as if sensing my plan, it ran behind the long drapes then scuttled up them. On the green and gold material it was hard to spot, but I made a grab for it anyway. Oops! Its tail came off in my hand! Michael didn't look too happy, seeing the tail waggling about making bloody patterns on the tiles. I told him, lizards are well known for this defence mechanism, but he didn't seem convinced. Though Lydia, who'd re-appeared carrying her cereal bowl was fascinated by the reptile. However, this didn't resolve 'the dilemma of the lizard in the curtains.' Though it would make a good title for a Sherlock Holmes mystery, I mused.

Picking up the still wriggling tail, I went looking for its owner. 'Aha,' I cried, grabbing the unfortunate reptile again – only to find the *stump* of its tail in my hand. This was becoming ridiculous. I was catching it in instalments!

Thankfully, it was a case of third time lucky, and I carried the traumatized creature out to the flowerbeds to recover. First, though, Lydia had to examine it and stroke it. After some petting, it scurried away under some foliage to lick its wounds – technically difficult, but possible.

Hearing the commotion, everyone was soon up. And with breakfast underway, the size of the lizard increased with each telling of the tale (tail?)

After breakfast, we drove to *Intermarché* for essentials, giving us all a good stretch of the legs. Though Lydia's didn't need stretching, they were long enough. Those kids were growing up *soooh* quickly.

On our return, we inflated our specially purchased kiddie's pool, and left the water to warm in the sun. Then, when Diane returned for lunch, the adults dined alfresco as the kids splashed around in it. We were having a great time until reality struck. Diane had to return to work. There was no chance of time off now that picking was under way.

After we all waved her off, Michael and I erected the gazebo next to the terrace; then somehow, I lost track of him. Being a confirmed 'townie,' he was overawed by the size of the property. So ignoring the brutal temperature, he'd grabbed the extended garden hose and wandered off spraying everything, including the trees. Though he was keen to help, I had to curb his enthusiasm. If he emptied the well, both properties would be without water. In that eventuality, I could switch to the town supply; the transition wasn't difficult. But well water was free.

Once again, Diane finished work early due to the heat. So after she'd showered and changed, we took Dylan for a long walk in the shaded buggy, leaving Michael and Miranda to enjoy a little peace and quiet.

Following tea, we all strolled down to Annette's for a visit. Pauline was on hand to translate the tricky bits – which in Henri's case was everything really. But with kids being the same worldwide, and with Annette fascinated by Lydia and Dylan, it was no bother at all.

After the kids were given juice, Henri took them to see his ménagerie, comprised of chickens, ducks, geese and doves – not forgetting the dogs and cats. But we didn't outstay our welcome, as Henri had endured a minor operation to remove a growth from under his eye, leaving him with a 'shiner.' And with Annette's operation looming, it was better not to tire them. We wished her well for her op. and left, waving as we walked back up the road.

Getting in around eight o'clock, Diane made a snack; then with the kids fed and bathed, they were soon in bed. Flinging the French doors wide open, we adults sat up until late, putting the world to rights over some 'interesting' wines.

I slept in the next morning, waking at eight am as Lydia was being led to the toilet. Poor Diane had risen at six, and was *long* gone. Following breakfast, I pulled out some attractions leaflets we'd gathered, and very soon the family were in the car heading towards La Flèche. They were off to Holly Park or La Flèche zoo – whichever took their fancy.

Waving them off, I rang Halifax plc and heard they'd eventually received our cheque. Phew! My next call was to Rob, saying my family had arrived, and we might have to skip this week's market. Mid-call, Diane arrived for lunch.
As she sat down, I noticed skin peeling from her shoulders; a combination of sunburn and chafing from her basket straps. The work was hard at any time, but brutal in that heat.

After lunch and the application of antiseptic cream to the ugly weals, I watched helplessly as she went back. Feeling incredibly guilty, I worked in the garden until she trudged in at four pm; sent home due to the overwhelming temperature.

Michael and family got back around six pm. They'd had a great day exploring the château and gardens at Chambord – a surprise last minute choice. We all helped get tea ready, after which the exhausted kids were bathed and tucked into bed. Dragged down by the humidity, our evening was spent indoors with chilled drinks, and wide open French windows to dispel the heat. As the wine took hold, the mood became maudlin. Reminiscing about my late dad, I said he'd have loved it here. Sadly, that was a conversation I'd never have.

Refilling our glasses, our discussion centred on our own brief existence on the planet. Wallowing in melancholy (and wine,) evidence was then examined regarding an afterlife. (Oh come on now!)

As the night progressed, Miranda and Diane went into a girlie huddle, while in turn, Michael got quite emotional with *me*. In fact, we all opened up a lot that night. Those British stiff upper lips were looking decidedly wobbly for a while.

At two am, I locked up and followed the exodus heading for bed – my head full of sobering thoughts, and my body carried upwards on inebriated legs.

We awoke to another animal crisis. It was already stiflingly hot; and with the windows flung open, Lydia walked into the dining room and found a dead bird on the floor. It must have hit the open window and broken its neck.

'Ah! It's gone to heaven,' I said, getting ready quickly to drive off in convoy to Saumur market.

We arrived in the Peugeot, Miranda following driving the hire-car. Parked up, we were carried along slowly by the crowds. As we traversed the pulsating market, the kids stopped to pet all the raucous birds and animals in their baskets. It was a superb morning, made more interesting when we met a couple from Derby who were enjoying a nine week tour in a campervan. Now that's *some* holiday.

We split up on the way back, Michael and Miranda heading back to the house with the kids, while Diane and I nipped off to *Intermarché* for BBQ food and other shopping. Getting back, we found a note on the table. They'd gone to Le Lude to get a disposable BBQ for Miranda. Oops! I forgot. She's a vegetarian.

It was mid-afternoon, when Vincente drove up with his horse-box to pick up two 'steeds.' The family had just returned, and we trooped out to watch the animals being loaded. Everyone admired the artwork on the vehicle, and though I'd seen it before, it hadn't registered that the multi-costumed hero riding a variety of horses, was an air-brushed, younger version of Vincente. Open-mouthed and impressed, Lydia stared at him as if he was a superhero. And the god-likeVincente wasn't about to shatter her illusions.

With both BBQ's up and running, we enjoyed a great meal in the sunshine – until Diane turned on the tap for the kettle. That's when we found out that Michael's enthusiastic watering had emptied the well. As Bertrand could be unaware of this, I had to go over and apologise. It meant both of us turning our water off overnight to allow it to return to normal. What was worse, water restrictions had also come into force locally, and we hadn't known!

After finishing our BBQ, Michael and I took plastic water drums over to Le Lavendu; filling them from Bertrand's stand-pipe. Then it was bedtime for the the kids – but not until Lydia told Grandad France in great detail, how she'd hit her face on a shopping trolley earlier in the day.

Draining our wineglasses around ten thirty, we abandoned the chirruping cicadas to their leg rubbing; and with the thermometer reading 25 C, we went in and tried to sleep.

Chapter 24

The petting zoo

The animal theme continued the next morning when we spotted another large green lizard. Fortunately, this one was outside and came equipped with a tail. Then, on a conducted tour of the garden, the kids spotted more of its smaller cousins, some grasshoppers, and a praying mantis. 'It's like living in a wildlife park,' said Miranda, who'd just pointed out two red deer up near the woods.

We'd all slept well overnight, after a drop in temperature in the early hours. With breakfast finished, Miranda lathered the kids in high factor suncream before they went out to play. But by noon it was 30 degrees C, so we all just chilled in the shade. With both Michael and Miranda being fair-skinned, sunbathing wasn't their favourite pastime, so Diane and I offered to babysit while they drove to *Super U.* Oblivious to their departure, the kids played happily in a ball pool we'd set up.

After lunch, we headed off to La Touraint for a special treat. Reached by driving through pine woods, the *Auberge le Lac* is a renovated railway hotel overlooking a lake and man-made beach. Very much a local favourite, it was buzzing when we arrived, with some people sitting on the grass or at picnic tables while others enjoyed the beach and lake. Skirting the area we saw a small gauge railway track. For a few euros you could ride around the lake behind a miniature steam train, hopping off at the *auberge's* restaurant-cum ice cream parlour if desired.

Spreading the car rug in the shade thrown by pine trees, Diane and Miranda settled down with Dylan. Meanwhile, Michael, Lydia and I walked over the sand to the lake. And as Michael paddled with Lydia, I went in for a swim. It was much too hot to stay in the sun for long, though, so we left after a couple of hours.

Overall it was a great afternoon, and we returned home sunburned, and dusted with sand. The adults showered and the kids were bathed. Then still excited by their experience, they had to be calmed before we could get them off to bed.

Sat outside on the terrace later, a few wine bottles were opened and we loosened up. All well and good, until the ladies spotted François near their garden and shouted him over. Our young Gallic charmer was then fussed over by the duo, while Michael and I were ruthlessly cast aside.

Bertrand and Véronique arrived home around ten thirty, and hearing the hilarity they came over. Introductions were made, more seats were pulled up, then we were off again, laughing and having a great time.

They stayed as long as possible, but with an early start the next day, they headed off reluctantly gone midnight after inviting us over later. It was soon afterwards that we went in too. But I'd forgotten. Diane *also* had to be up for work at six-thirty. Oh-oh!

I was up with Diane five hours later, after hearing rain drumming against the windows. This didn't bode well for her in the orchards, so I dug out her waterproofs and wellies. Then at seven fifteen, she set off, my shattered Amazonian warrior. The storm didn't seem to have woken our guests though, so I made another coffee and had a little 'me' time.

By the time they got up, scudding clouds had cleared and weak sunshine was peeping through. With breakfast out of the way and a promising day unfolding, they decided to visit

168

the zoo at La Flèche. Digging out our cool-box, I packed lots of water, juice and ice, and off they went. With Lydia already on an adrenaline high, 'Are we there yet Daddy,' could become repetitive for Michael.

Left alone in an eerily empty house, I got out my mason's tools and tackled the outer wall. During a long, undisturbed morning, I worked non-stop. Then at lunchtime our Peugeot appeared on the bottom road. Pulling up at the kitchen door, Diane emerged drenched in sweat. The rain had evaporated under the nets, creating a sauna for those trapped inside. She showered and changed while I prepared lunch. But after eating it in the cool kitchen, she was gone again all too soon.

I continued plastering the long wall; working all afternoon until Michael and family returned. Diane had been in for about ten minutes by then, and was in the shower. Changing from my work-clothes, I followed her in. (separately of course!) Then *everyone* took a turn.

Apparently, the zoo had been a great success. Like walking through a safari park they said. But it wasn't over yet. Oh no! After a meal, the kids had *more* animals to see. Wide-eyed, they were shown hutches full of rabbits, and pens full of chickens, ducks, and geese. And for once, Lupé and Hermé were on their best behaviour – though I for one wouldn't be petting *either* of them.

We'd arrived just after six pm, and as Véronique was delayed by a rush order at work, Bertrand entertained us. When Véronique turned up, she changed quickly and joined us. Drinks and snacks were produced, the kids were fussed over, and Michael and Miranda were soon won over by our neighbours' courtesy and friendliness. Likewise, it was a treat for Véronique who doted on children. And Lydia, with her platinum-blonde hair and porcelain complexion was a *real* novelty.

Unfortunately, the visit had to be curtailed when a tired Dylan began crying. It'd been a long day at the zoo for a little boy. We made our apologies, kisses and hand-shakes were given and we left.

With the kids home again, it was a matter of minutes before they were tucked up in their beds. Re-energized, we adults settled on the terrace next to the kid's bedroom. And though we'd promised ourselves an early night, it was after midnight before it was cool enough to entertain sleeping.

It was their last day. Dylan had raised concerns during the night, due to him coughing and wheezing. But whatever the cause, he was okay at breakfast. Diane was at work, but the rest of us were having a relaxing day. I'd intended finishing my plasterwork after breakfast, but Lydia commandeered my wheelbarrow filled with sand to make sandcastles. So, being a kid at heart, I joined in. I was also roped in later to help her plant a special flower for 'Grandad France;' a primrose she'd picked from the flower bed to commemorate her visit. It was so touching, that Grandad, feeling like royalty had a tear in his eye.

Before it got too hot, they decided to visit *Gifi* at La Flèche. As they headed off, I prepared to start plastering. However, midway through the afternoon the water pressure began dropping. As it trickled to a stop, I rang Bertrand, who said *their* pressure was fine, but he'd pop over to take a look.

By the time he arrived, Michael and the family had returned, and kept out of the way as we inspected the system. Bertrad's worrying conclusion was, it could be the pump that was at fault. Damn, that sounded expensive. Returning to change for his afternoon shift, Bertrand asked Véronique to set up their stand-pipe for us again.

When Diane returned from the orchards, we discussed the problem, and contacting the insurance company, we made sure we were covered. On my first journey with a twenty five litre container, I told Véronique the insurance was good to go, so she arranged for a plumber to visit in the morning.

Unfortunately there were no showers for our guests on their last night. The kids were sponged down in the bath using a bowl of warmed water, while the adults made their own arrangements. And of course, the toilet cistern could be filled after each flush. Maybe it wasn't the best end to their holiday, but it was certainly memorable.

Making the best of the situation, we had a last BBQ; including the kids who'd been allowed to stay up late. We all went to bed at eleven thirty pm; Diane saying goodbyes all round, in case she missed them in the morning when she left for work.

As it happened, everyone was up together. Emotional goodbyes were said and cuddles given, before Diane shot off down the drive. Then, with my trusty sidekick Lydia sat in the barrow, I trundled over for more water to see us through the morning. After they'd done last minute packing, I helped them load; and after breakfast, they visited the paddock to say goodbye to the horses.

The weather forecast was for another scorcher. The threatened storm hadn't materialised, so just before nine am, the family set off ahead of an imminent weather front. With a few tears from them and a lump in the throat of 'Grandad France,' I waved them off.

As they drove away, Bertrand and a friend arrived to inspect the water system. Thankfully, the problem seemed to have been due to overwatering, not the pump. And after they bled the system, life returned to normal and the plumber's visit was cancelled.

Chapter 25

The problematic pump

The horse-box lurched to a standstill outside the paddock. Opening the rear doors, Uncle Maurice led François' horse carefully down the ramp. A seven year old mare named Hoppie, she was accompanied by her foal Célice, who was keeping her company until she settled in. Naturally, François couldn't wait to ride her – but unfortunately for my young neighbour, Hoppie had other ideas.

Once she'd settled in, he came over to take her out riding. However, seeing him carrying a saddle, she suddenly developed a limp. After examining her fetlock and whispering soothing words to her, he took the saddle back home in frustration. Seeing him disappear, she galloped up and down the field with Célice.

Shaking his head, a grinning Maurice drove off.

On July 23rd a terrific storm tore through the valley, causing damage to trees and buildings and our electrics to crash. After re-setting the trip switches, we fancied a cuppa. But, though the electricity was back on, we had no water. Scratching my head, I checked everything I could think of without success. Ringing Bertrand, I asked his advice, and of course he came straight over. Having no luck either, he had Véronique ring a plumber. But until he could get out to us, it was back to their stand pipe again.

The plumber rang Bertrand later, saying the problem could be storm related. As our water pump was operated electrically and 'lived' down the well, the electrician, who worked for the same company might also be needed.

Bright and early the following morning, the plumber pulled up in his van. We quickly nick-named him 'The Terminator,' as after inspecting the tank, he pursed his lips and growled, 'I'll be back,' before driving off again.

He returned after lunch, leading another van containing the electrician and his mate. The passenger emerged first, a barrel chested guy with a huge handlebar moustache. Whereas, when he unfolded himself, the electrician was almost seven feet tall and giraffe-like. After studiously inspecting the power circuits, he asked where the well was. After leading the team across to Le Lavendu, they peered down the shaft; and after a discussion, barrel chest went back for the van.

Véronique then appeared, dragging the demented dogs away as 'Giraffe-man' fastened on climbing-crampons. Donning a head-torch, he dropped a rope ladder down the shaft, climbed into the wellhead, and disappeared from view. His workmates then lowered equipment down on ropes, and stood chatting and smoking while occasionally shining a torch down the hole.

Five minutes later 'Giraffe-man' re-surfaced, carrying information copied from the pump casing. He said the pump was *'casse,'* or broken, and removing his crampons, he connected us up to the *'eau-de-ville.'* After speaking to Véronique, they set off to source us a replacement pump. Ah well, at least we had water. And if we were *really* lucky, they might just return in the morning.

That same afternoon, their boss arrived with a quote for the job. For the emergency call-out, removal of the old pump, sourcing and fitting a new one, it would be 1,000 euros. (Gulp!) He said, if we gave him our insurer's details, he'd ring them immediately to authorize the work. His guys would then collect the new pump in the morning and fit it. He'd expect payment from us on completion, but not to worry, the insurance would pay out soon after. '*Pas de problème,*' he said.

Oh, it wasn't a problem for *him*, but it was a body blow for us. And we could hardly ring around for other quotes, as Véronique had called him out and he'd responded '*toute suite.*' We'd already incurred a bill for the call-out, so I gave him the insurance policy details and he left.

The team returned with the new pump the next morning. Our lanky friend, who Véronique called '*le cigogne,*' or the stork – for obvious reasons, strapped on his crampons once more and vanished down the well. A disembodied voice then echoed up, and his mate passed down tools. Soon, a metal cutter could be heard screeching as smoke issued from the shaft. Nineteen metres of pipe were then hauled up in sections before the pump itself emerged. Tying the new pump and replacement piping to the rope, the process was repeated in reverse as everything disappeared down the well. Finally storkman re-appeared, the pump was switched on and tested, the pipes bled of air, then everything was tied off at the well-head.

After a tidy up and multiple handshakes, the two vans swayed off along the track. With Lupé yapping frenziedly, and Hermé wuffling away blindly in all directions, they vanished in a cloud of dust. We had water again.

There then began a period of puzzling power cuts. We quickly realised that with a few electrical items switched on at once, the trip-switches flipped. I had *many* joyful visits to the pump-house to re-set them. Noting my repeated trips back and forth, Bertrand came over, and using his circuit tester, he checked the system. But though it all seemed okay, the trip-switches 'clacked' with depressing regularity.

Having eliminated everything else, the conclusion was undeniable. The problem only began after the pump had been changed.

I rang the boss, who first tried the 'no speakie English' ploy, so Véronique rang and explained the problem. When he *still* refused to listen, Diane researched online and unearthed the *Societe de Plombiere* ombudsman, a very powerful association in Paris. Taking this information with me to 'Mr Big's' office, I 'convinced' him to send out his men to examine the pump.

When *le cigogne* finally brought it to the surface, I checked it against the old pump still lying in the barn. The old one was rated at 5,000psi, the replacement 3,500. Being far less powerful than the original, it was struggling to drag the water all that way up the well, then across the field to the house. When I pointed out that we'd been charged for the larger pump, the correct one was soon fitted *gratuit*. It was an honest mistake said 'Mr Big.' *Of course* it was.

Never mind, our problem was sorted – that is, until a letter arrived from the insurance company requesting a site visit by their assessor. An appointment was arranged, and the first thing he found on arrival was, the well was in next door's garden. Though shown on our deeds as jointly owned, he sucked in and pursed his lips. Then there was the small print in the contract. A claim for storm damage to electrics wasn't *normally* a problem, he explained. But in *this* case the damage wasn't inside the house itself. It was down the well – which was next door.

After a heated exchange, he said he must report back to his superior. But first, he'd like to measure all the rooms and out-buildings. '*Pourquois*, or why,' I asked?

Apparently, they hadn't realised the house was so large when they first insured us; nor that there were other rooms half-completed. 'Well why didn't you check before you insured us,' I asked?

The next morning, we received 'Mr Big's' bill, which along with taxes and extras had soared to 1,500 euros. Feeling guilty, Véronique involved herself, checking both the bill and the insurance policy. She said, once the insurance company received the damage report, she was sure we'd be okay.

Long story short, they refused to pay out. Not only that, but they said our next premium would be substantially higher following the re-assessment. When we expressed our outrage and threatened to change companies, they said we couldn't. Under French law, insurance is a legally binding contract. We'd have to give written notice by registered letter. But that option ends three months before the renewal date. If we'd passed that point – which we had, we were stuck with them for another year. Véronique said this sort of hassle was normal. It's no wonder, that according to François, the French are generally under-insured.

The squeal of brakes announced *le cigogne's* arrival after lunch. Two days had gone by, and Véronique was visiting us when he pulled up. Tumbling out of the van, he staggered into the pump house. Rolling her eyes, Véronique mimicked twisting her nose. Apparently this meant he was drunk. She didn't need to tell me. The sour smell and the way he was swaying said it all. After completing his inspection, he shook my hand. 'All is well? Pump is okay?' Right, he was off.

Oh, he was off alright! He reversed *off* the drive, hit a concrete flower planter then screeched *off* down the drive. It was a blessing that he didn't have to climb down the well. Véronique said he'd been sacked before for drinking while at work – but re-instated later. If I needed him in the future, I should *never* book an afternoon appointment, as there was a strong chance he'd arrive half- sozzled. That then begged the question. Why did she saddle us with these 'numpties' in the first place?

Due to the onset of torrential rain Diane was sent home early. She arrived just in time to help me rescue the gazebo, which had collapsed under the onslaught. It hadn't been one of her *best* days, but a cosy night in front of the roaring log fire sorted her out. Recovering later, we spent time on the 'Friends United' website checking out old schoolfriends. But the way things had been going lately, I didn't feel like comparing lifestyles with *anyone*.

Chapter 26

Let's rip off '*les Anglais*'

Trawling through Saumur's shops on the Saturday, we visited *Intermarché* and *Vive la Maison,* before buying twenty five square metres of floor tiles in a *Brico* sale. The return journey was hairy, as the overloaded car's suspension was way down and struggling. However, we got home okay; and with the tiles unloaded, Diane hung out washing before we set off for La Flèche. And that's when it happened.

Passing the orchards, the car suddenly veered off to one side, then with a 'bang,' the front end collapsed. After a fruitless roadside inspection, I locked the car and we walked back home. Cheesed off, I rang Le Lavendu. Véronique answered, saying Bertrand was working on his vintage car at Gilles' garage. But as François and Phillipe were doing nothing, she despatched them with the tractor to tow the stricken Peugeot back to our farm.

When Bertrand returned, we examined the car together, and decided it was a garage job. He'd tow it in on Monday. But without transport how would Diane get to work? It was a helluva long walk. Then Véronique had a brainwave. Diane could use her bike!

The machine she dragged out of the barn and dusted off, was a heavy old bone-shaker with only three gears. Quietly aghast, Diane pretended enthusiasm and thanked her. Then, after a Bertrand 'inspection,' he inflated the tyres and Diane wheeled it home. Deep in thought pondering her 'Tour-de-orchards,' she tried relaxing with a glass of wine. But totally distracted, she trapped her thumb while closing the kitchen door. Don't ask!

We couldn't understand the loud hissing noise coming from next door on Sunday morning. What the hell was Bertrand up to *now*? I sneaked over to peek through the hedge, concerned that he could be emptying the well by over-watering. I should have known better, though. I found both him and Véronique dressed in white Tyvek suits and goggles, sand-blasting car parts on a huge plastic sheet. Seeing me, she lifted her mask and asked, '*Pardon* Stewaard, did we wake you?'

After breakfast, I re-checked the bike, drenching it in releasing fluid before Diane gave it a test ride. It was cumbersome and heavy, but it was either that or she walked. She then rang Pauline to cancel her lift, explaining the problem with the car. In reply, Pauline said her dad used to own a Peugeot 405. Maybe he could help.

An hour later, she arrived with her father Pièrre, plus Henri of course. The problem was quickly diagnosed as a sheared bolt in the steering linkage. It wasn't a big job, Pauline translated. The broken bolt needed drilling out of the engine block, a new thread tapped into it, and a larger bolt fitted. The new bolt should cost a maximum of five euros, and there'd be an hour or two of labour charges. Meanwhile, he'd rigged it so we could tow it to the garage.

Following overnight rain, Diane set off at seven-thirty in waterproofs and wellingtons, wobbling down the drive on Véronique's bike. After witnessing her erratic departure, I spent the morning tiling the bedroom floor. By twelve twenty though, I was beginning to worry. Where was she?

I then became aware of strange squeeking and wheezing noises – and up the drive came Diane pushing the bike. Red-faced and sweating, she was almost on the verge of collapse.

'It was fine going downhill,'she gasped, 'but hard work on the level. Uphill, forget it.'

At one pm, she returned to work early – on foot.

With Diane gone, Bertrand and I towed the Peugeot to the garage using a rigid towbar. After an inspection on the ramp, Gilles agreed that a new bolt was required, but the job was more complicated than we thought. It could take maybe five hours, and he estimated the bill at 180 euros. I said I'd think it over and get back to him. After telling Pauline, she said her dad thought it was a rip off, but he hadn't the gear to do the job so we were trapped. With no other garage anywhere nearby and our car being undrivable, I reluctantly told Gilles to go ahead, while squeezing the loan of an old Citroën BX out of him to get Diane to and from work.

Diane set off in her banger the next day, while I sat deep in thought working out our finances. First there was the 1,500 euros for the pump, now this unexpected car-bill, and soon an inflated insurance premium. With all this extra outlay, we'd have to dial down our plans.

My calculations were interrupted by knocking on the kitchen door. I opened it to find Bertrand and Véronique looking mournful. It was bad news. Gilles had rung Bertrand, saying the Peugeot was beyond economical repair.

What? This was crazy. He drove me to the garage, where Gilles in 'Lingua Franca,' said, to fix the problem the engine had to come out. *'Pourquois?'* I asked.

Because the steering is on the right hand side, he mimed.

'No, the problem can easily be fixed on the ramp from *underneath* the engine,' I told Bertrand, relaying Pauline's dad's conclusion. He told Gilles, who dismissed it derisively, saying, due to the extra work, it *could* cost up to 600 euros – or even more. I felt like throttling him, as I *knew* I was being railroaded. With a smile that didn't reach his eyes, he then said he'd buy the car for scrap value, then sell me his wife's car, for a bargain price of 4,000 euros. Alternately, he'd look out for a replacement car for me. Choking up, I said I'd discuss it with Bertrand, and left before I lost my temper.

When Diane came in, I updated her. Out of ideas and held over a barrel, we discussed the situation, agreeing our choices were limited. We dismissed raiding our bank accounts, but there was another option; taking a mortgage holiday or payment free month. We were allowed three under our agreement. One a year for three years, then that was it. At least doing that would give us breathing space.

Devastated by continual rain, Bertrand was inconsolable. He desperately needed to gather in his harvest before taking a planned break in Bazaz. François was visiting friends in Angers, so they'd be using his apartment as a base. They could then cross the border into Spain for a while. But everything hinged on the weather. He then asked, what was happening with our car.

By then, the Peugeot had been pushed to the back of the garage compound; hemmed in by other cars while Gilles supposedly sourced cars for us. Bertrand asked if I'd seen Gilles' latest find, a VW Passat Brake. I said we'd look at it when Diane returned from work. Trapped in a catch 22 situation, we drove to the garage after she'd changed.

The Passat was an estate car, and being sold for a butcher. Though he may have been a serial killer for all I knew, as I found a bloodstained knife under the driving seat. And while everything seemed fine on the test drive, it was a year older than our Peugeot and very expensive. We said we'd consider it, then drove to *Intermarché's* garage for fuel.

At the pumps, we'd filled our tank, but couldn't leave because of a Frenchman's stalled car. So we went to help him push it off the forecourt. Behind us, an impatient French woman blared her horn imperiously. '*Oh, you shouldn't have done that*, I thought. She soon gave up when a furious Diane appeared at her window and gave her a tongue lashing.

Later, Pauline's parents turned up, thanking Diane for giving Pauline lifts to work. Pièrre said our garage hassle was outrageous. Offering to help, he gave us the address of a car breaker who sometimes had decent runners to sell.

We drove there the following morning, but he hadn't anything in our price range, saying French used cars were very expensive. He showed us trade catalogues and newspapers to substantiate his story, so Gilles wasn't screwing us in *that* regard anyway.

We received a message the next day. Gilles wanted his 'clunker' back. We needed a car and he'd offered us some expensive options. In chess parlance it was check-mate. Mulling everything over, we decided to have the Peugeot fixed – though we were positive it was highway robbery.

Actually, we'd grown attached to our faithful car. It'd been a loyal and trusted servant, and pulling 'The Hippo,' it'd seen us through thick and thin. Nicknamed by Stewie as 'Hugo' after Hugo Boss (Stewie's fragrance of choice,) it was aptly named, and didn't deserve being cast aside or scrapped, no matter what the cost. Besides, if we moved back to the UK in the future, we'd be stuck with a left hand drive car, registered in France, and with a French MOT.

Returning to the farm our spirits needed lifting, so we decided to cut each other's hair. Diane's ended up just fine, but *her* spirits must have been at rock bottom, as I ended up with a severe crew-cut. Unrepentant, my grinning stylist said, 'You look like a right thug.'

'Thanks a bunch,' I replied sourly.

But maybe the brutish style wasn't such a bad thing, as soon afterwards a car pulled up with three young guys in it. I opened the door, head freshly-shaved, a thunderous scowl on my face, and a hammer in my hand from the job I was working on. They turned and drove away quickly. Maybe they'd just taken a wrong turn. Who knows?

Chapter 27

One man's junk …

It was a day to do something different. Scanning some tourist leaflets, we decided to give Rochemeniére troglodyte village a whirl. Bypassing Saumur on a deserted road, we drove into an eerily quiet village of cave dwellings. Parked up, we entered a museum. This led to underground houses, workshops, farm buildings – even a church. In the past, a small community had lived there, grazing stock on land outside, and bringing everything in before nightfall. With gates closed to keep out marauders, the villagers would congregate in a community hall in the evenings. Chatting, knitting, crafting, and repairing things, they lived in a constant year-round temperature averaging thirteen degrees C. They must have been a hardy breed, judging by the old sepia photos on display. One showed a grim-faced old woman in traditional dress riding a bicycle. Uniquely, both she and the bike were cocooned inside a transparent plastic canopy.

Moving on, we ate our leisurely packed lunch sat by the nearby river, watching tourists board the cruise *bateaux*. Discussing our visit, we felt privileged to have witnessed this slice of local history.

With the weekend relegated to history, Diane drove off to work as I began tiling. Returning for lunch later, she said her job might be ending the next day. Ah well, it had to happen sometime, so it was no use moaning.

As she disappeared down the drive, Rob rang, asking if they could visit on the Wednesday. I said Diane could be jobless by then, in which case it would be yes. But they should ring on the morning to confirm.

Diane *was* laid off on Tuesday, and when Rob and Elaine arrived on Wednesday afternoon, we sat under the gazebo discussing their recent visit to Edinburgh. They'd flown back during the G8 summit protests, encountering heightened security following the London bombings. The uneasy atmosphere, plus the strain of staying with Elaine's parents for a fortnight, had re-affirmed their desire to stay in France.

Since their return, they'd found a buyer for their house and decided to move to Saumur. Enquiring about *our* news, we discussed our recent calamities, and Rob agreed that ex-pats were a soft target to many French people.

They left at six thirty pm, and feeling tired, Diane had an early night. I sat up reading, but around eleven pm, I was disturbed by a muffled banging outside. Switching off the lights, I slipped out to investigate carrying the pick-axe handle. Luckily it was only fireworks exploding across the valley. Ah well, Bastille-day began in an hour. Perhaps some revellers were making an early start.

July the 14th is a very important day to the French, of course. They lost their heads over it, you might say. (Sorry!) To us, however, with the shops closed it was just an inconvenience. In a bid to be productive, we cracked on in the garden, but it was just too damned hot. As we came in out of the sun the phone rang. It was Rob. His toilet was blocked. Had I any drain rods?

We drove over with our equipment to save the day; arriving to find our two hedonists floating on airbeds in the pool. They climbed out, dried off, and while Rob and I tackled the odious toilet, the ladies discussed property costs.

As the U-bend proved too acute for the rods, we tried clearing it from the outside. There was no blockage, so we went off to check the *fosse septique*. Phew! We'd found the problem. The tank was full to the brim.

Never mind, Rob knew a man …

The market was heaving that Friday. While Rob was selling, Elaine chatted to their friends Mark and Wanda. We got a cheerful hello from Wanda, but her husband totally blanked us as they left. With prospective punters interested, we said goodbye and left for *La Poste*. Opening the door, we bumped into Mark and Wanda again. Once again, she spoke, but again he ignored us. We didn't know or care why. Maybe he was jealous and wanted Rob all to himself, or then again, maybe he was just ignorant. Who knows?

We arrived home, to find Bertrand careering around the bottom field on his old combine harvester. As it was minus a cab, he was sporting a pair of vintage motorcycle goggles, his face covered by a bandana. He was cutting the wheat in a temperature of 35 degrees C. We knew it had to be done, but it was sad to see those golden stalks sprinkled with poppies and cornflowers topple before him.

While he decimated the crop, François was bouncing back and forth on the tractor, his little girl cousin hanging on excitedly behind him. She became even *more* excited when two guys arrived to collect the ponies for an event.

Emmaus was brim-ful as usual that Saturday, but I was unsuccessful in finding a watch for work. However, I did find two beach-mats with inflatable pillows. They'd be great for sunbathing – but absolutely useless at telling the time.

We returned home to begin work, anticipating Rob and Elaine's BBQ the next day, and the opportunity to cavort in their pool. Unfortunately, Rob rang in the morning to cancel, saying Elaine wasn't feeling well. But after working hard lately, we were desperate to get out.

Our thoughts turned to Cholét, but it was too late to drive out there. Grabbing our new beachmats and the cool-box, I made for La Tourant's lake instead, it being much closer. Lazing on the beach fronting the pine-woods, we spent the rest of the afternoon reading, people watching, and topping up our tans.

Returning at five pm, we met Bertrand and François. I told them the insurance company had refused to pay out for the new pump; and worse still, we'd received 'Mr Big's' bill. They suggested I visit him and try to get it reduced, using the premise of a quote for central heating as leverage. I wasn't hopeful. It was as if the gods were against us right then.

For example, we'd recently cashed in a savings ISA locked in for five years. After fees and charges were deducted, we received £270 less than our initial investment. If we'd left the money in our bank account, we'd have earned £1,000 in interest.

Then Gilles rang from the garage. The car was ready, but the bill was even higher than expected at 668 euros (about £450 at the time.) With my arm draped in a friendly way across his shoulders, I gave his neck a damned hard squeeze as I handed over the 'ransom' payment; though, I had to admit, it felt good to get 'Hugo' back.

But we couldn't continue like this. Our savings were dwindling rapidly, and we were lurching from one crisis to another. I'd try leaning on 'Mr B' regarding the pump, but I wasn't very hopeful.

You know what it's like when you can't sleep for worrying? To take our minds off our problems, I sorted out the tool-shed while Diane topped and tailed blackcurrants for jam-making. Besides making her own, she'd decided to give some to Annette to cheer her up after her operation.

François arrived in the afternoon to move the hay bales before ploughing. And when he'd gone, we visited Annette, carrying the jams, and some empty jars. We picked up Henri on the way down. He'd just finished supervising the work on Jean's extension; a relief to Jean, I suspect.

When we arrived at the millhouse, Annette, who should have been resting was busy in the kitchen. She was pleased we'd brought the jars; but hogging centre stage, Henri whipped out a similar jar to ours. However *his* contained Annette's gallstone! It was the size and colour of a large plum, preserved for posterity in formaldahyde. How sweet!

Sunday 24th July was Le Lude's *Vide Greniére* day, and the sun was blistering as we set off. When we arrived, we were reduced to 'window shopping' as once again there wasn't a working ATM to be found. But maybe it was for the best in our reduced circumstances.

When we returned, Bertrand and François had turned up to dig post-holes for the electric fencing. Feeling restless, I burned off some tension helping them. Adjourned for coffee, François kept trying to pin me down with grandiose plans for our farm. To forestall him, I brought him down to earth with a bump, saying, with no bookings, work still to finish and a series of large bills to pay, he could forget his plans. Okay, the house was *almost* ready, terraces were laid out and the foundations dug for a pool. But as we hadn't the cash to even *buy* the pool it was time for a reality check. Let's face it; things had more or less ground to a halt. We could continue to scrape by for a while, but we needed a lot more cash to finish our project.

One money-making venture we got into was buying items at *brocantes,* which took place regularly throughout the area.They were a great day out, and we found some fantastic things. Two ex-pat friends, Pete and Shauna had introduced us to selling them on e/bay, and we had loads of friendly rivalry chasing bargains. Back in my workshop, I'd restore them, we'd photograph them, and Diane put them online.

187

But even though we were good at it, any profits we made were quickly swallowed up.

Once again, I offered to sell Bertrand some land; and with it being cheap, he could enlarge his farm. The money would have helped us a lot right then, but he declined. I mean, why *would* he buy it? He had the use of the land without paying for it.

It seemed we'd have to take up Stewie and Helen's offer. We didn't intend borrowing money, either from financial institutions or family; so barring a miracle, our winter might be spent working in the UK.

But before making any decisions there was one huge job to tackle. After tripartite discussions, Maurice borrowed a tractor-cum dozer, and arranged for a *ferronier* in Alencon to drive down with his truck. Then with Bertrand on *his* tractor, they'd attack the rubbish-filled pasture together.

Come the Monday, François, his cousins and I were all roped in to help, and the job began. The two tractors worked all day; engines roaring and cleated tyres spinning, as their chains dragged out gorse-bushes exposing a wasteland of scrap. The hoard included two Renault 6 cars, a Citroën 2cv, a Moblyette, a plough, two broken trailers, a large grass-cutter, a seeding machine and various engines. Domestic items like washing machines, fridges etcetera were also unearthed, and taken away as part of two huge truckloads. However, the sheer amount eventually defeated us, and as the *ferronier* had no intention of making a *third* trip, huge pits were dug to take the remaining junk.

During the excavation, a couple of snakes surfaced which had François panicking. But never fear! Bertrand the brave ran over and whacked them with his spade. Chopping them up, he fed them to his chickens.

With the rubbish buried and the land reinstated our group dispersed, leaving huge piles of brush to be burned at the end of autumn.

After Bertrand and Maurice trundled off on their tractors, François returned with some money from the *ferronier*. I told him to give his dad and Maurice some for fuel, and share the rest with his cousins. Well, that was one big problem solved!

Meanwhile, some things never changed. Hoppie had settled in, but she still refused to be ridden. She eventually had to be re-gentled by Philippe. Standing no nonsense, he rode her hard, holding a rope tied to her tail and yanking it if she misbehaved. She got her own back though. Just when he thought he'd mastered her, she bucked him off onto a bed of horse-chestnuts which badly scratched his back. Broken but unbowed, she eventually let François ride her. But it was a daily battle and always on *her* terms.

Chapter 28

A fearsome haircut

After following the Tour-de-France for a week towing his caravan, Phil turned up on his bike dressed in Lycra, to measure up for the staircase. Still fresh after an 85 kilometre ride, he measured up and set off to source materials from *Espace Verte,* a nearby builder's merchant. Picking up the finished pieces when they were ready, I stained them before we scratch-built the staircase and landing together.

With the job finished, I borrowed his almost new trailer for a trip to IKEA Nante, where we bought wardrobes, bedside units, a double bedframe and mattress.

We'd just finished assembling all the flat-packed items, when I took a call from Kevin, our building society manager. He was touring in France with his family. Could they visit the next day? Of course they could. Where would we be without *his* help in the past? It would be nice to show him what we'd accomplished. Inviting them to stay over, I helped Diane get the en-suite bedroom ready. Then, while she worked inside, I removed a hornet's nest complete with its angry occupants from below the Velux window.

During its removal, François turned up, saying Hoppie had been suffering lately. And with the vet unable to diagnose the problem, he'd tried enlisting the help of an 'animal whisperer.' This old man apparently worked by the laying on of hands or studying a photo of the animal, then by examining hair or hoof clippings, he'd cure the problem. It sounded weird, but who knows? Sadly, when they rang, his wife said he was suffering from terminal cancer and was unable to help.

After relating this tale, François asked if he could stable Hoppie in the old *mouton* shed over the winter. When I agreed, he cleaned out the building, then used the tractor to level the paddock behind it.

With Hoppie's stabling sorted it was all go, as Diane and I began harvesting our potatoes for winter storage. Looking up from our backbreaking task, I watched Bertrand sowing rape seed in the bottom field. He'd explained earlier that it *must* be fifty seeds per square metre. This was critical to my anal neighbour. Grinning to myself, I returned to 'spud' picking, then showered and changed later, we awaited Kevin's call.

At four pm a car pulled up outside. It was our guests, who'd asked directions at the local *Mairie*. The irrepressible Kevin climbed out and we shook hands. Then he introduced his wife, Paula and the kids, Bethany and little Mathew. Diane and Paula hit it off immediately, and Bethany got *my* vote when she asked if they'd checked into a hotel,

The size and scope of our investment impressed Kevin, who realised its potential after seeing it first hand. However, they'd had trouble finding our online advert. He apologised as we'd gone to so much trouble, but due to a change of plans, they couldn't sleep over. Nonetheless it was a great visit, spoiled for a crying Bethany when they had to leave at ten thirty pm for the long run home.

While picking tomatoes the following afternoon, I heard a shout. 'Stewart, are you able to kill a snake for me?'

It was François. He'd climbed up on the trailer to escape the unwelcome attentions of a viper.

'My father and I, we do not like snakes, but we kill them if we have to,' he said.

'*Yeah right,*' I thought shaking my head; and walking over, I decapitated it with my spade. He went on to say, we'd missed Maurice shoeing Hoppie yesterday while we entertained our guests. Damn! I'd wanted to watch him at work. Ah well, another time maybe.

I'd just finished in the garden, when Rob and Elaine drove up, trailer in tow. Tied on it was an old door destined for my newly-finished workshop, while clutched in Elaine's hand was a bottle of wine for our planned BBQ.

The weather was warm and sultry, but lacked a breeze to help fire up the charcoal. No problem. Iimprovising a home-made bellows, we were soon underway.

The ladies decided to forgo alcohol this time, but Rob and I drank too much, matching each other as usual. Sweating over the Barbie, I bitched about the extreme temperature, to which Rob replied that my hair was too long. And well served by then, he dared me to let him shave my head. Equally inebriated, I said, 'Okay, go for it.'

God only knows why, but Diane handed him my clippers. And against the odds all was going nicely – until half-way through the operation the clippers died. So there I was, with one side of my head ruthlessly shaved, and the other side swept back and bushy. Not the best look! Never mind, said Rob, he had *his* clippers at home. So with Elaine driving, we shot off to finish the job. I raised a few eyebrows, I can tell you; as driving through town, I turned back and forth to chat. Completely shorn, I was then driven home again. Seated on the terrace, my cohorts assured me that it looked just fine. Really! Why the sniggering then?

The next few days were scorching. And after François ploughed up our 'tattie' patch on the Monday, he invited Diane and I over to see his dad's new extension. Earmarked as Véronique's new abbatoir, it would soon be put to use. He then asked if we'd like to join them and Véronique's parents, who were eating in the shaded courtyard. We'd missed the earlier courses, but, Véronique was about to slice a wine and pear tart. Seated next to his grandparents who'd just returned from a trip to England, I had François ask if they'd enjoyed it. They said they had, but they'd found London to be dirty, and the streets strewn with rubbish. (Sorry Londoners, don't shoot the messenger.)

After our desert, François treated his two little girl cousins to a ride on Hoppie, before everyone was roped in for a stint of potato picking.

With the weekend over, we began cementing and fabricating. We saw no-one until Wednesday, when Bertrand and Véronique brought over a box containing melons, peaches, pears, and grapes. They were much appreciated, but from past experience, Diane would be expected to produce preserves, to be shown at our next visit. Normally this wouldn't be a problem, but right then work was piling up. We had a lot to do before Monday. It was the Prow family's long awaited visit.

Despite Stewie's mum Pauline's dislike of flying, she'd asked Nadine to book connecting flights, Newcastle – Stanstead – Tours, to avoid leaving her car at Stanstead airport. They were picking up a hire-car at Tours airport, but as, Adam, Stewie's brother sometimes needed a wheelchair, we took our trailer along for it and any extra baggage.

On the Friday evening, François visited, saying the orchard's *secretaire* had tried ringing Diane without success. There must be a fault. Actually Diane had unplugged the phone so they couldn't reach her. She needed to be at the airport on Monday to help out. Unable to get through to us, Madame had then rung François, saying, could he ask Diane to start work on Tuesday.

Why not? It's not as if she had anything else to do.

Chapter 29

Our near death experience

It was Sunday 4th September, and according to François, our area had the highest temperature in the whole of France. I believed him, as Diane and I sweated buckets getting the house ready for our guests.

Unfortunately, despite humidity, we awoke to ominous grey skies on the Monday and a poor forecast for the next few days. Then to make matters worse, Diane checked the family's flight before we left, and found they'd been delayed at Stanstead for three hours. That's *all* we needed!

Setting off anyway, Diane received a text from Helen *en-route,* saying she was demented trying to keep a lid on everything. But finally, after yet another delay, they arrived at Tours to find us waving a 'Prows on tour' banner.

After greetings and hugs, they went to pick up their hire vehicle, and found to their delight that they'd been upgraded to a Lancia SUV. With everyone and their luggage shoe-horned in, they followed us out of the airport car park – arriving an hour later to oohs and aaghs all round.

Once rooms had been allocated and luggage dumped, the stresses of the day were soon forgotten. Unpacked and showered, they couldn't wait to have the grand tour. Sadly, Diane had to keep a clear head while welcome drinks flowed. She had to be up for work at six am.

Surprisingly, everyone was up really early the next morning, and we all breakfasted together; Helen cooking while Diane got ready for work.

After our resident apple picker left, we tidied the kitchen then drove off to visit *Intermarché* – with the exception of Helen, who was happy just to chill out at the farmhouse.

We returned to find that François had visited, introduced himself to Helen, and asked her to tell us that Uncle Maurice had broken his ankle. Furthermore, his aunt had tried taking the kids. On no account should she be allowed to drive past us and get to Le Lavendu, as Véronique had assumed parental control. Whoah hang on there!

After taking turns all afternoon watching out for Maurice's wife, Diane returned early, saying there'd been a walkout by the pickers. As she couldn't find out what was happening, she'd followed the team off site. We weren't complaining as we'd been preparing a BBQ. So with Diane changed and balmy weather thrown into the mix, we had a great night.

With Diane off to work the next morning, we guys began dismantling the dog pens. Finding it heavy going, I borrowed Bertrand's angle grinder for Stewie and I to cut rebar in the concrete, making life a lot easier. After coming over to feed Hoppie, I introduced François to Alan and Pauline, who chatted to him as he groomed her in the paddock.

Arriving for lunch, Diane found the demolition well under way. Breaking off to clean up, we ate lunch alfresco, before I returned her to work in the Lancia. With the family onboard for the ride, we explored the far reaching terraces of apples before returning to our work.

Loading the trailer with rubble later, Stewie and I made two trips to the *déchetterie,* before picking Diane up in the Lancia. Climbing in, she said yesterday's walkout was because Dominic had demoted Sylvia the factory supervisor to picking on the terraces. She still didn't know why.

To make life interesting there was a mini-nightmare later when the computer crashed. Thankfully, Diane and Helen soon fixed it. It was such a relief, that drinks flowed like water as we chilled out on the terrace. With everyone cracking jokes, the evening became *really* funny when Pauline leaned back laughing and her chair collapsed. Like a slow-motion movie shot, she grabbed the tablecloth as she fell, pulling the drinks and snacks after her. Trying to avoid the avalanche, I tripped over an awning peg, ripped my trouser leg and fell flat on my back. Yes, it was a good night – though a bruising experience for some. Unfortunately; having 'retired' to their beds after sampling too much *eau de vie*, Alan and Stewie missed all the action.

Getting up the next morning, I surveyed the damage. Not bad considering. After a quick breakfast, Alan and Pauline began tidying up, while I took Diane to work. I needed the car, as we were driving in convoy later to Le Lude market.

Tidied up and dressed, the group set off. I led in 'Hugo,' Helen followed driving the Lancia. And after an uneventful drive, Adam was settled in his wheelchair and we hit the streets as the temperature rocketed.

Sprawling throughout the town, the enormous market seemed more colourful and diverse than usual. As we wandered around experiencing the gentle pace of it, the sights and smells seemed to intoxicate our guests. Exhilarated by our morning, we rescued Diane from the orchards. Then back home, lunch was taken next to the rose-beds on the terrace.

After a pleasant meal, it seemed sinful taking Diane back to work. Even worse, we'd planned a trip to Lac-de-Brielle. But gritting her teeth behind a smile, she wished us a pleasant afternoon, as we dropped her back at work.

Arriving at the lakeside was a surprise. It was almost deserted, and we enjoyed ourselves, swimming, sunbathing, and just relaxing on the sand. Drowsy after our exertions at the beach, we returned just in time to collect Diane.

While she showered and changed, I set the BBQ away. But I kept it simple; just chicken-legs, sausages and salad. Even so, after the food and a few beers, we were all flagging. So an early night was in order – especially for my weary apple-picker.

Friday was overcast, therefore a good day to work. After Diane left, we guys tore down the dog enclosure, and when she returned for lunch, I commandeered 'Hugo.' I took two trailer-loads to the *déchetterie* after returning her to the orchards, where the team were still up in arms on the terraces. Making my getaway, I returned home and abused poor 'Hugo,' by using him to pull down a section of wall.

After collecting Diane at five thirty pm, we had an early meal. We intended to have a party later to celebrate our demolition, but before we could, bad news struck. We received a call from Stewie's sister Sharon. Alan's mother had been rushed into hospital. Feeling helpless, the family went into panic mode as they planned how to get home. Trying to instill calm, Diane went online to check for flights, knowing there were few options from Tours, and other airports were hundreds of miles away. Also, connecting flights in the UK had to be considered. Maybe we should find out more from the hospital first?

That night, Diane spent hours on the computer, enduring three power-cuts caused by a freak storm which sprang up from nowhere. Eventually, she was locked out of the internet. In the wee small hours of the morning, after no further news from Sharon or the hospital, everyone crashed out exhausted.

As dawn broke, everyone woke physically and emotionally drained. We'd heard from Sharon, that Alan's mother was stable after tests and a good night's rest. There was nothing we could do; and as Alan, Pauline and Adam were only staying for a week, they'd be flying back in two days anyway. Therefore, with the weather being decent, we decided to get out and clear our heads.

We drove off in convoy to Saumur, where by then it was fiendishly hot. It was hard work for Alan pushing the wheelchair through the market, but he wouldn't hear of anyone else taking over.

After trudging around all morning, the temperature had rocketed to over 40 degrees C. Worn out after our sleep starved night, Diane drove the hire-car back, calling into *Leclerc on* the way. By then, shattered and living on our nerves, I lagged behind in 'Hugo' after stopping for fuel.

Setting off again, I drove through Noyant, opening the windows as it was like a sauna inside the car. Next to me, Alan was nodding, while Pauline and Adam were fast asleep on the back seat. Desperately needing someone to talk to, I was trying hard to stay awake.

'BANG,' I came to with a start, seeing the grass verge rushing at me. Too late, I swung the wheel, shouting 'Look out,' as we skidded sideways into a deep storm ditch. Clinging tightly to the wheel, I tried stopping the car as it careered along the channel tilted at a crazy angle. As we came to a stop, all four of us were sat rigid. Locked in our seat-belts, we were unnaturally quiet and probably in shock. Let's face it, a minute ago we'd all been asleep!

Snapping out of it, I urged Alan to get Pauline and Adam out of the car and up onto the verge. I didn't think there was a risk of fire – but who knew for sure? Then it all turned surreal, as a car pulled up driven by an off duty *Pompier*. Climbing down into the ditch, he insisted on checking me over for head and neck injuries. But, despite feeling fine, he wouldn't let me move. Pauline's mobile had a signal so she rang Helen, who returned in the Lancia with the family.

Meanwhile, Pauline had risen to the occasion and gone into overdrive. Waving 'rubbernecking' motorists past, she kept traffic flowing while Diane ran to a nearby farm to get help. I wanted to be out of that ditch before someone got the *gendarmes* involved.

Within minutes, a farmer arrived with a rope. And with the Lancia hitched to the Peugeot, I was soon out of there. I quickly checked both myself and the car over, pulled a dented wing away from a wheel and fired up the engine. Thanking our Good Samaritans and giving the farmer his rope back, I crammed everyone into the car and set off slowly down the road – the Lancia following closely behind.

Fortunately, no real damage was done, though Pauline re-lived her near death experience on the way home – quite understandable given the circumstances. Miraculously no-one was hurt, possibly because we were all relaxed at the point of impact. The poor car didn't get off quite so lightly, though, but the damage was superficial. I fettled it by knocking out the odd dent and ripple later.

And though none of us are excessively religious; back home safely, we decided there must be a God.

Chapter 30

They miss the rodeo

A sombre mood hung over everyone the next morning. The aftermath of the accident had left us with mixed emotions, and with his mother still in hospital, Alan just couldn't relax. As Aaron hadn't slept well either, it wasn't a great start to the day.

While the girls fixed breakfast, Stewie and I worked on the car, straightening the wing and checking the wheels and undercarriage. We found some minor damage which I'd have fixed at the garage later, but all in all, we'd been lucky.

It being Sunday, there was nothing that could be done anyway, so we just enjoyed our day together as best we could. And as it was their last night, we wanted it to go with a bang. However, though it started well, it ended up being a damp squib, as no-one could drum up any real enthusiasm.

Monday dawned and Aaron had slept badly again, leaving Stewie and Helen shattered. Saying her goodbyes, Diane donned her waterproofs. I felt incredibly guilty driving her to work in the Lancia as rain drummed off the car roof. Wishing her luck for the morning, I headed off to *Intermarché* to top up the fuel tank.

In my absence the family had packed; and when I returned, Helen drove them in the Lancia to the car-hire agency, while Stewie sat with Aaron who still wasn't well.

We set off in convoy, arriving at Tours just before eleven; and with the car handed back, the trio were checked in. After hanging around until take off, Helen and I watched the plane disappear into the clouds. Then leaving the concourse, I drove her to the pharmacy to buy Aaron's medicine. Calling into the garage, Alberte made minor repairs to the steering before we hurried back to the farm. After worrying about Aaron while we were gone, though, we found both him and Stewie fast asleep on the settee when we tip-toed into the lounge.

For the rest of their holiday, Stewie helped me with jobs on the farm. And when not caring for Aaron, Helen did housework while her mum picked apples.

As Aaron's condition improved they had the odd trip out, but his Gran's illness and parent's return home had left Stewie on edge, putting a damper on their holiday. Discussing family, health and finances, they said what'd happened only reinforced the importance of family, and insisted we stay with them over the winter. Though reluctant, we agreed that it made sense, as we needed to earn enough to carry on again next year.

Dispelling our gloomy mood, a much needed tonic arrived in the form of François, who turned up unexpectedly one evening. He'd only been back to college for two days when the tutors walked out on strike. He'd come over to ask my advice. Sighing, he said, Hoppie keeps throwing him. Moreover, when he approaches her with the saddle, she seems to develop a limp. He didn't understand it. What did I think? It was desperately hard trying to keep a straight face.

Visiting Noyant market with the family, we introduced them to Rob and Elaine at their stall. Then after shopping at the town's *Intermarché*, I drove to Henri and Annette's. Unfortunately they weren't in, so after a sightseeing drive, noon found us picking up Diane for lunch. By then the heavens had opened; and with no signs of the rain abating, she drove herself back to the orchards after her meal. We then had to keep Aaron occupied indoors. Difficult though that was, it beat picking apples in torrential rain.

Returning at a quarter to five, rained off, cheesed off, and bedraggled, Diane had a long hot soak before our meal.

Meanwhile, François had turned up to disinfect 'the house of Hoppie;' and ringing later, he invited us over for a visit. (To the house, not the stable.) Though it was a kind gesture, we had to decline gracefully. It was a miserable night, and Aaron had just begun improving. On the upside, Michael rang later and we all had a catch up, Then with Aaron snuggled up in bed, we had a few drinks sat around the roaring fire.

We woke early hearing Aaron's hacking cough. It was another cold damp day. And when François came over to work on Hoppie's stable, Stewie and I gave him a hand while the ladies made breakfast.

As it was Saturday and Diane wasn't working, we all trooped off to Saumur together. The family were leaving on the Monday so they had presents to buy. While they sought them out, Diane and I bought the weekly food, plus meat for a farewell BBQ the following evening.

Having visited Emmaus and shopped till we dropped, we arrived home to find Véronique had christened her new abbatoir. She'd culled fifteen cockerels in a mass slaughter.

'Would you like to inspect them?' François asked.

'Maybe another time,' I suggested hastily.

We'd wondered why they hadn't crowed this morning!

After an afternoon spent topping up their tans, Helen fed Aaron, bathed him and put him to bed. Then after *our* meal and a few drinks on the patio, we called it a day.

Sunday was their last day, and a day to remember on all accounts. The weather was glorious, which boded well for our BBQ later. The bad news – packing had to be done. But with that attended to, there was a feeling of excitement in the air. It was 'rodeo day.' Yep, that's what I said!

The relationship between Hoppie and François had come to a head, as she stubbornly resisted being ridden. Pretending to be lame had tested François' patience to breaking point – as had being thrown off when he'd actually dared to mount her. Therefore, the family were congregating en-masse at 'the 'house of Hoppie' later, where Philippe the master horseman intended breaking her once and for all.

Before the event, though, Stewie and Helen needed to buy last minute gifts at *Gifi,* so Diane acted as their guide while I sorted out the Barbie.

Unfortunately, Bertrand and his cohort turned up early while my family were out shopping. The group consisted of, François, Véronique, Anna, Philippe, and his young brother Edmond. Bringing up the rear was Maurice on crutches, his leg encased in plaster. Damn! The rodeo was to have been a finale to Stewie and Helen's holiday, with the BBQ following afterwards.

Mind you, I wasn't the only one upset. Hoppie didn't look too keen either. With ears laid back, nostrils flaring and eyes rolling, she watched Philippe approach her carrying a muzzle, saddle, and ropes. He was standing no nonsense. Slotting the bit between her teeth, he threw the saddle over her quivering haunches, cinched her in and prepared to mount. She immediately began to buck, whereupon Maurice whacked her hard across the rump with his crutch. As she froze in shock, Philippe leapt into the saddle – then rearing up, Hoppie took off. Wow! Where were my group? This was priceless.

Whinnying shrilly, Hoppie galloped off across the field, Philippe digging his heels into her flanks brutally. He rode her hard, while she bucked and twisted, but she was getting nowhere with the fine young horseman. Sensing her tiring a little, he reined her in next to Maurice, who quickly looped a rope around her tail and threw it up to Philippe. Startled, she shot off again bucking wildly, only to have her tail yanked hard. Round and round the field they went, with Philippe repeating the manoeuvre until she finally got the message. Philippe was in control.

Eventually, foam-flecked, head bowed and dejected, Hoppie walked docilely up the field, obeying voice commands and light touches on the reins and stirrups. Backwards and forwards Philippe guided her, talking to her softly but firmly.

Now François would have the horse he'd always wanted.

After a collective back-slapping for Philippe, the family wandered off, leaving François to gently wipe down the dispirited Hoppie. Talking quietly to her, he began forging their new relationship.

Hearing a car approaching, I turned. The family were back. Would you believe it? Lighting the BBQ, I brought the disappointed group up to speed with details of the rodeo, while, in turn they showed me their purchases. Then, it was on with the Barbie which we all enjoyed immensely □– unlike the unfortunate lizard that fell off a branch into it.

When a brisk wind sprung up from nowhere, we carried everything from the table indoors. And after collectively washing up, the evening was spent playing games on Stewie's phone, which was very much a novelty at that time. Much later, full-bellied and well-served, our final night together came to a resounding end.

Chapter 31

Almost there

Creeping out early the next morning while everyone slept, I checked the car over before setting off, then hitched up the small trailer for Aaron's buggie, cot, and extra luggage. With breakfast over and locked and loaded, we set off for the airport at ten forty five.

Racing into the car-park at eleven thirty after fighting heavy traffic, we just beat the incoming flight which was touching down as we screeched to a halt. After a flurry of hugs and goodbyes, a quick turnaround saw the plane take off on time. As usual, passengers waved to loved ones through the tinted windows. But once again, there was no earthly chance of anyone seeing us.

Back home again lunch took precedence, before driving into town for food and to post mail. More importantly, we filled 'Hugo's' tank. Last week, the UK had experienced fuel shortages which caused panic- buying at the pumps. It could spread to here, so *best be safe*, we thought.

Tanked up and back at the farm, it felt good to take back our lives. It'd been a great visit, but tonight, our only dinner guest was Billy Connolly. We shared a bottle of wine as he commanded the stage, but following a heavy day, bed called out to us before ten.

Well that was the last of our visitors for the season – family included. Diane still had her contract to fulfil at the orchards, but after that, there was nothing to hold us in France. We'd made plans for our stay with Helen and Stewie, but until the apple harvest ended, I continued prepping the house for winter. The Indian summer was fast drawing to a close, and though temperatures still hit 25 C occasionally, mornings and evenings were much colder. Change was happening all around us; however one constant was our neighbours, who provided a rich source of entertainment as always. Hearing an outraged squawking one day as I worked, I downed tools and walked over to Le Lavendu. Peering around the fence, I witnessed Véronique catch, then kill a huge white cockerel. She didn't notice me, so I quietly backed away. When she came over to feed Hoppie later, I mentioned seeing her in action. She said she'd killed, plucked, and dressed five large birds that morning. They were stored away in the freezer. Out of thirty reared, only two survived the cut.

It was a train wreck waiting to happen. Céline had blown her stack – but not with the pickers. She'd finally lost the plot with Dominic, who'd imposed ridiculous targets on the teams. Diane and Chantel swore she'd been fiddling their figures to appease him. But unable to do anything about it, they just soldiered on in the simmering atmosphere.

Meanwhile, I continued the never-ending land clearance; taking three 'Hippo' loads of assorted rubbish to the dump one day. After offloading it all, I lugged sand from the quarry, paid for on my new account.

I was busy building a stone wall around the planned pool area when Diane came in for lunch. Visibly wilting, she said she and Chantel had filled seven balloxes that morning in humid conditions. The norm was five in a full shift. Also, some of the girls had complained to Dominic about figure tampering, which seemed to validate her earlier story.

I had my own problems after Diane drove back. I saw Véronique shooing a flock of mallard ducks into her abbatoir. Hearing distressed squawking soon afterwards, I sneaked over to have a look out of morbid curiosity. Spotting me watching through the fence, Véronique waved me over. Stepping into the relative gloom of the building, I noticed a cartwheel hanging from a beam. From its spokes hung ropes, tied to the feet of sixteen of the doomed creatures. Hanging in a circle, they passively awaited their fate, suspended above a barrel filled with bloodstained sawdust.

Stepping forward, she asked me to hold the wings of her next victim; then casually slitting its throat, she held its head at an angle, bleeding it out while she spoke to me. She then swung the next one around and passed *me* the knife! Let's just say it wasn't my finest hour. I botched the cut, leaving the poor creature squawking desperately. Saying in French, 'Never mind, it's your first time,' she finished the bird off, while I headed back to my cementing feeling like a murderer.

After a Saturday morning shopping in Le Flèche, unexpected rainfall prevented outside work. So with Rob and Elaine on the cusp of moving, we decided to pay them a visit. We found them packing and grateful to take a break. Noticing that the pool had been covered and the pump disconnected, I said, 'What a shame. We could have bought it off you.'

Rob said they were having enough hassle with the French buyers as it was, and with the pool being part of the deal, it wouldn't have been possible. 'But you can take anything in the barn,' he said. 'I'm leaving nothing. They've been a pain in the arse to deal with.'

From that point the afternoon descended into anarchy, as Rob and I ravaged the barn; ending with a wine tasting session *par-excellence*. Much, *much* later, an abstemious Diane drove us back. It'd felt good to let off steam, though, as we hadn't seen them for ages.

Home safely and still in a great mood, I suggested we put on a video, giving Diane the chance to relax with a glass or two herself. However, in the bathroom later, I heard a panicked shout. 'Stewart, there's a bat in the bedroom.'

Actually, it was a bird that'd flown in through the skylight. The terrified creature kept us up till two-thirty, before it flew back out, allowing us to clean up the crap it'd splattered all over the room.

We awoke to a text on Tuesday. Aaron had just taken his first steps last night. Ah sweet! Otherwise, for Diane it was business as usual at the orchards; though, as if reacting to Helen's good news, the sun made a rare appearance.

I spent my morning collecting stones for a wall, while half expecting a visit from two rogue UK builders Rob had warned me about. They'd been visiting ex-pats, trying to bully them into giving them work. His friend, a retired cop, had come to blows with them in *Chez Jaques,* he'd told me. Rumour had it that they'd set up a phoney 'Association of British builders;' and were collaborating with an English estate agent operating a form of protection racket. Oh great!

While sorting through Rob's gifts later, Bertrand arrived. Would I like to accompany him to the quarry for sand? We could split the load and cost. Off he went, with me perched high on the mudguard, weaving between flower-filled planters on the main street. And with the trailer loaded and paid for on his account, we returned to base.

Settling up with him after we'd unloaded, I was putting my shovel away when Diane arrived, saying Céline was furious. She'd finally twigged that she and Chantel were taking the mickey out of her in English.

'Ah well,' I said, 'You were playing with fire. It was bound to happen sometime.'

To cheer her up, I showed her my treasure trove from Rob's barn. It came as no surprise to her, that it included the Homer Simpson pool chair with fitted drinks holders.

Though it was raining and too dark to *see* apples never mind pick them, Diane set off the next morning in her waterproofs. Changed into work-wear, I drilled holes in the fieldstone walls, allowing winter rains to run off the fields in our absence without collapsing them.

At lunchtime, Diane came in brimming with excitement. Dominic had promised everyone the next day off if they worked flat-out that afternoon. Off she went full of beans, while I went to cut up a fallen tree. I was putting my saw away later when the Peugeot roared up. 'The swine's cancelled the day off,' she cried. Dominic I presume?

After a bad night's sleep, both of us were shattered the next morning. Needing the car to collect cement later, I dropped Diane off at work in twilight. Unfortunately, ready to set off, I couldn't find my wallet. Calming down and using logic, I unearthed it – in the last place I'd normally look for it. 'Wake up matey boy,' I said, rubbing my eyes. And off I went to C.A.P.L for Baticem.

After breakfast, I began moving breeze-blocks. Autumn had arrived with a vengeance, and vicious winds were stripping the trees bare. Hearing a tractor engine, I saw Bertrand approaching with a load of wood. Before he could notice me, I whipped off my tee-shirt, and began wiping my brow as if hot. As he saw me his jaw dropped; *he* was wrapped in a heavy jumper and gillét. I couldn't help winding him up. It was so easy.

Driving into the orchards to collect Diane at lunchtime, I parked at the end of her terrace. Striding past me, Céline stared, nodded, and grinned hideously. Forcing a smile in return, my blood ran cold.

Arriving home, Véronique spotted us and hurried over. She said Maurice's divorce has been finalised, and the court had restricted his ex-wife to one day a month supervised access to the kids. It seemed rough, but due to her violent behaviour, the children's safety had to be the priority.

Chapter 32

The alternative en-suite

We were into October, and as the picking season was drawing to an end, we'd soon be leaving for the UK. With the days turning bleak and cold, it was as if a switch had been thrown on the weather.

One day around eleven am, the light turned really eerily pearlescent; and when Diane drove in for lunch, she said, there'd been a partial eclipse of the sun. It may have been more evident on the terraces, but unaware of the cause, I'd found it spooky out there in the fields.

That morning, Diane had been picking a strain of apple that, according to her team-mates ripens by the light of the moon. She thought it was a joke, but after research, I learned that some fruit retains more flavour and sustains less damage when grown and picked in moonlight, Go figure, as they'd say in the U.S!

Needing the car, I dropped her off at work after lunch, before posting Lydia's birthday card and present in Le Lude. Calling on Phil at Meon, I caught him tackling a plague of fieldmice. Well, not a plague in the biblical sense exactly – but lots anyway. We chatted about his time working in the film industry, his travels abroad and the stars he'd met. It was a fascinating half hour spent over a cup of coffee.

Mid-conversation, two guys returned his trailer, borrowed to collect material for a shower block. They'd been constructing a campsite for motor-bikers, Phil said, but they seemed clueless; spending 400 euros on grass seed amongst other follies. They were now having second thoughts and considering selling up.

Picking Diane up later, she came out with a real gem, 'One of the girls said she's married to a drunk whose family are into black magic. She asked what she should do.'

What? Diane had asked her if she'd considered getting divorced. But she said she was a Catholic, so it was out of the question. What a strange life some people have eh?

Driving Diane to work another morning, I continued on to the surgery at Mouliherne. Due to unexpected visitors, I was running late. Two Frenchmen had driven up in a white van as I worked on the barn weather-boards. They offered to paint my galvanised roofing for 500 euros, which I politely declined. I could do it for a fraction of that myself.

Picking Diane up at 5-00pm, she said Céline had acted outrageously towards the men on site; being crude and offensive after a liquid lunchbreak. Changing tack, she admired my latest project. Over the last week, I'd collected and cemented stone cladding onto the *cave* frontage, and built extended walls on either side. It was finished, and improved the view from the kitchen immensely. Véronique, who was grooming Hoppie, also expressed *her* admiration, then said, I should see *Bertrand's* latest project. He'd built two gate-posts out of stone at the head of his drive; then fitted large electrically operated wrought iron gates. *Touché* Bertrand!

I rang Lydia after dinner, asking if she'd enjoyed her birthday; only to hear she hadn't received her card and present. Now which postal service was to blame *this* time?

Friday's market was dismal. Dropping Diane off at work, I'd swung by to catch up with Rob and Elaine. I found a dispirited Elaine nursing a broken wrist, sustained in their recent house move. On the plus side, I met two ex-pat English couples, one of whom told me about a Sky deal worth following up. Then as I was leaving, Phil rode up on his racing bike. Dressed in Lycra, he looked set to compete in the Tour de France. After a chat, he agreed a meet-up to discuss a project I had in mind.

After a hurried lunch together, Diane took the car, leaving me to carry on with jobs. But later that evening there was a break from our usual routine. Le Lude's *Mairie* was hosting an art exhibition. Great! It was dress to impress at the *soiree*, as the local elite turned out in force for drinks and nibbles.

Dave Wilcock, a Leeds ex-pat artist was exhibiting his work. Invited to his home-cum studio after the show, we discussed painting and the sale of artwork. We'd also bumped into Chantel at the exhibition, who introduced us to two of her French friends. It seems things were opening up on the social scene.

Arriving home on a high, Diane went online to chat with family – and of course the computer crashed. How many more times can I say, *C'est la vie*?

As it wasn't late, I rang Rob, explaining the recurring problem. He suggested we drive to their apartment the following afternoon, and take the modem with us.

Nearing Saumur mid-afternoon, Diane realised we'd mislaid Rob's address. With no other option, we decided to wing it. Driving to Rue-St-Jean which we'd remembered, we found the street was pedestrianized, so we parked nearby. Then, carrying the modem and a bottle of red, we walked the length of the street hoping for divine intervention. In one quiet section, I even shouted their name out in desperation. When *that* didn't work, I began checking nameplates on apartment doors along the *very* long street. We finally spotted a crisp new card with their surname on it. Phew! We rang the bell, and a moment later a voice floated down from a balcony above.

'I've pressed the door release. Come on up, we're on the third floor.'

The apartment was huge, light and airy; consisting of three floors with a balcony overlooking the busy street. Nice as it was though, I preferred their farmhouse.

After the obligatory conducted tour carrying a house-warming drink, Rob stripped the modem. He diagnosed that one of its two cooling fans wasn't working. Not a problem, he said. We could run it with the side cover removed. Being unsure of parking regulations, I drove back to the farm at six thirty, mission accomplished.

With Diane at work, I emptied the upstairs rear bedroom. Phil was due soon to measure up for the en-suite bathroom. He arrived to find the room stripped and skirting boards numbered for refitting. With everything stored in the barn, he had a blank canvas to work with. Between us, we planned the lay-out of toilet, shower and pedestal sink unit, and after working out materials needed, he left to order them.

Waving him off, I went to gather the twenty giant pumpkins we'd grown. Yes, twenty! Diane planned making jam and preserves with some, others we'd share with friends and neighbours. We also intended storing some over the winter, after checking online to see if it was viable.

While pondering the mysteries of pumpkin husbandry, Bertrand collared me. He'd found fencing, wire, and concrete in the top field. We drove up, dug it all out and loaded it into 'The Hippo'. The wood I'd burn, but the rest would feed the *dechetterie*. My industrious neighbour then left to help Maurice pick up some furniture, as his estranged wife had taken theirs. Oh the sadness of soured relationships. Nobody wins – except the lawyers of course.

Over the next few days, Phil and I installed the en-suite; chiselling and drilling walls to accept pipes and wiring. The original walls were heavy going, being metre thick granite. I helped with the heavy drilling and lifting, in deference to Phil's age and to keep the cost down. But like any craftsman, he had his own way of working, so I was often his 'gofer' sourcing materials for him.

One morning, I set off to find pipes and fittings at a company named '*Maine Plastiques*.' Returning with them, he said he could manage alone for a while, so leaving him to it, Diane and I set off for La Flèche.

We found a shower stall at *Brico* that we liked, then on our way back, Diane bought a birthday card and an apple tart for Bertrand. Home again, I opened the large packing box, and Diane translated the instructions, which began with, *When fitting your telephone cubicle ...*

As you can imagine, they left a bit to be desired, but between us, Phil and I managed to assemble it and plumb it in. Now all that remained was the large-bore outside piping. But with his wife and granddaughter to take to the airport, and him feeling under the weather, he decided to take a couple of days off. With plenty of other jobs to get on with, I re-installed skirting-boards and we fitted cushion flooring in the en-suite. After decorating throughout, I re-stained the oak beams to enhance the room's rustic charm.

We'd just finished when Bertrand and Véronique arrived, carrying a bottle of wine and some snacks. Tomorrow was my birthday, so with it being Saturday night, it made more sense to have our double celebration now. No hangovers on the Monday!

The 16th dawned, but with heavy rain overnight, our planned birthday painting jaunt was shelved. However, we'd learned last night that Philippe was coming over later. Hoppie had been giving François a hard time again, so she was going to receive a 'refresher course.' Could this be another rodeo? I was about to get up, when Diane insisted I have breakfast in bed. I wasn't about to argue. With birthday cards opened, and better weather forecast for later, we gambled on our field trip. Having already packed our equipment, Diane set off. Despite having a stiff neck, she'd insisted on driving. 'It's your birthday treat,' she said.

Meandering through pretty little hamlets at random, we followed a minor road leading to Vaas, a pleasant little village with a picture postcard river frontage and quaint bridge. Some of its houses were half-timbered, and had landscaped gardens stretching down to the river bank; while others possessed their own moorings and a boat.

Setting out our equipment on a municipal picnic bench, we began initial sketches. Thankfully, only the odd passer-by stopped to watch us working.

Mid afternoon, with our future masterpieces laid along the rear seat, we drove home, arriving just in time to see Philippe showing François how to handle Hoppie. That is, until she dumped him unceremoniously on his backside and raced off across the paddock. Whoops!

After a restless night, I slept in and missed Diane leaving for work. When she came in at lunchtime, she said the next shift might be her last, as Dominic was pressurising everyone to get the pick finished. A more immediate worry however, was the car's cooling system. Diane said the gauge had been redlining and steam was belching from under the bonnet. Not good with a long trip to the UK imminent.

Leaving the engine bay to dry out, I examined the cooling system and spotted a tiny leak in the radiator Ahah! Using old school methods, I could have cracked an egg into it, but having some Radweld (other brands are available) the problem was fixed properly. Diane could test it on her drive back after lunch. Ideally, the radiator should've been removed, the core soldered and pressure tested, but no-one could do it in time for our trip. Fingers crossed for our journey home then.

Chapter 33

☐

Plumbing nightmares

As Diane's job wound down, over-wintering the house before leaving took on more importance. And of course, a stack of seasoned wood would be nice to come back to next year; so getting out the chainsaw, I fired it up. As if sensing our departure, it threw a hissy-fit and began acting up.
'Come on, you're only a machine,' I snarled, but after trying everything I knew, I sighed fatalistically and took it to *Jaman*.

When I arrived, I realised how quickly time flies when he said his wife was due to give birth within days. On my last visit, she'd just announced her pregnancy. After sorting out my saw's problem, which he waved away as *'gratuit,'* I thanked him, conveyed my best wishes to his wife, then returned to cut logs.

Strangely, now that her workload had eased, Diane began having aches and pains. But feeling better after a massage from 'Doctor Stewart – he of the magic fingers,' we set off the next day to Château-la-Valliére with our art equipment. As a weak sun wrestled to overcome lingering mist, we set everything up. We were enjoying the peace and quiet until two old guys sat next to us and began yakking. It would have looked churlish to up sticks and move, but with our concentration broken, Diane did the smart thing by drawing a brief *vignette* then packing up. Whereas, I persevered with my full-sized picture, but ended up regretting it as it turned out badly.

With our materials stashed away, we decided a visit to Henri and Annette was overdue. Taking two pumpkins and some mixed preserves with us eased our guilt feelings; and seated with coffee and cake, local gossip was trotted out. During a coffee top-up, they suggested we sign on for unemployment pay like other laid off workers. Even if that were possible, we'd be in the UK soon, but it was thoughtful of them to suggest it. It was also kind of François, who arranged for *Carte Vital* application forms to be posted out to us later.

It was a rare 30 degrees C on the 27th of October. Diane was suffering back pain, but she still battled on with jobs around the house. Actually, when I thought about it, we'd both been healthier when we had heavy manual jobs!

After tackling the breakfast dishes, I strolled out to meet François, who'd appeared carrying a saddle. Dressed 'to the nines,' he intended riding out with his friends. He thought the other horses might steady Hoppie. Making a sign of the cross, I promised I'd visit him in hospital after she'd thrown him off yet again.

'Non,' he said firmly. 'There will be no rodeo today.'

Returning later, he said Hoppie had behaved well for a change; so while his back was turned, Diane slipped her a slice of bread. Showing us the whites of her eyes, she took it daintily between her teeth. Then curling her upper lip, she seemed to grin at us. Unnerved by this apparition, I emptied the post box and went inside. Opening an official brown envelope, I read that our '*attestations*' had been received and our *Carte Vital's* would follow shortly.

Hearing a knock mid-afternoon, I opened the door to François, who asked if he could use our printer. His was malfunctioning, and he needed to print off a booking form. He was arranging a surprise holiday for his grandparent's golden wedding anniversary. Not a problem, said Diane. After all, one hand washes the other.

We'd just finished turning all the house-clocks back an hour. It was Sunday 30th and we'd been up since five thirty am. While lighting the fire, I noticed a message on the phone. Nadine said Lewis had been rushed into Hospital with viral pneumonia. He was burning up, had a temperature of 108 degrees Fahrenheit, and had blisters on his chest.

After waiting all morning for news, she rang saying his condition had stabilised, though, he *was* wearing an oxygen mask. Relieved, we asked to be kept informed of progress.

With the immediate crisis over, I went out to the garden and found François out ploughing. Pulling the tractor up beside me, he said, 'Do not forget, tomorrow is '*Toussantes*' day so all shops will be closed.'

'*Toussantes?*' I enquired.

'All Saints,' he replied.

Diane was working the day after the holiday as part of a tidying up operation. This gave me the chance to crack on with the upstairs undisturbed. Time was rushing by, and the loft conversion needed finishing soon. It was unfortunate that the apple harvest was running late, but on the other hand, every penny it brought us counted.

After overnight rain it'd turned into a pleasant day. And waking early, I was working on the roof gable when Phil arrived. He'd hoped to fit piping, electrics, the toilet and shower. Unfortunately the day started badly when he knocked over the shower door. And though it didn't break, it was scratched. Not the best start!

Leaving at five thirty pm, he said he'd finish off after the festival. With the shops all closed, the day would be wasted if we needed anything for the job.

Though Diane had been plagued by a really painful hip on Tuesday, she still went to work on Wednesday morning.

With painkillers swallowed and anti- inflamatory cream applied, she drove off. She returned at lunchtime, soaked to the skin after heavy rain; but changed, she had lunch and went back.

When Phil had arrived at nine, the weather was appalling, so we began working inside. After a long day, the plumbing was finished around five pm; but testing it brought problems. I spotted a leak coming from the shower base, and the water pressure was dangerously low. Worst of all, the pump was behaving erratically. We stood scratching our heads wondering what to do. Then Diane arrived, soaked to the skin and needing a hot bath. After giving it some thought, Phil rang a plumber friend who suggested purging the system by turning all the taps on full. At first there was a hissing noise, then a loud *Bang!* With an airlock vented, the pump kicked in and the pressure climbed sharply. Within minutes, Diane was climbing into a steaming hot bath.

Meanwhile, after settling up with Phil, he pocketed the cash and said leakage behind the shower had slowed to a drip. We should leave it as leaks often settled themselves. If it didn't, he'd return and fix it.

Unfortunately, numerous joints were weeping the next day. I tightened some, but the tank pressure was dropping alarmingly. After ringing Phil, he returned and checked out the whole system.

While he was busy, I dealt with a white van man who tried selling me chairs – then an upholstery re-covering service. Not having any luck with either, he then tried me with pots, pans, pillowcases, bed-linen and mattresses. Totally gutted, he then produced a guitar. Was I supposed to buy it, listen to him play it – or pay him not to?

With Friday's weather off to a dismal start, I drove Diane to work then returned home to write letters. (Remember doing that?) With Phil due around eleven, I nipped along to *Intermarché* before calling into *La Poste* with my mail.

Driving over to Noyant's market, I caught up with Rob and Elaine before shooting back home again. I was finishing off some jobs outside when it began raining. Watching rivulets cascade down the windows, I imagined poor Diane working under the nets out on the terraces.

Lunchtime saw me collecting my bedraggled apple-picker. As we sat down to lunch, Phil turned up, so Diane asked if he was hungry. After sharing our meal, he began working. It'd stopped raining by then, so, as Diane drove off, I began working on the roof. Mid-afternoon, with snagging jobs sorted, Phil headed home.

Diane returned at four-forty drenched, having sat on the car-rug to keep the seat dry. As she changed, I ran her a hot bath. While she toasted near the crackling fire afterwards, I took a call from Chris thanking us for his birthday card and cheque. He was off out 'on the lash,' he said. That boy sure has a way with words.

The rain continued overnight, but come morning the sky brightened, the sun peeped through, and it turned into quite a pleasant day. After breakfast, a tooled up Bertrand arrived to inspect our water supply. It'd been rumbling and gurgling ominously which signified an air lock; and when I'd mentioned it to him, he said he knew this type of system well. So stepping into the boiler room, he checked out the tank pressure switch, then drained and purged the tank. However, nothing helped. So temporarily defeated, he left for work, saying he'd look at it later. Just don't call out an expensive plumber, he pleaded.

Chapter 34

Getting ready for winter

The crackle of gunfire across the valley signified, that once again the hunters were out in force. It was a bleary Sunday and too drizzly to work outside; so with horns tooting and dogs howling, I left them to it. Phil was due soon to inspect the water system again. A few more leaks had materialised, and the pump pressure problem was worse than ever. And as Bertrand had *also* tried unsuccessfully to rectify it, there was no alternative. We switched the system off.

Rob and Elaine were due around three pm, and having burned a few *steres* of logs lately, I went out to chop more. It was still a bit nippy when they arrived, but the fire soon warmed us through. As the conversation flowed, I asked how they were enjoying life in Saumur. I sensed a certain reserve. Maybe it wasn't all they'd hoped for.

Three o'clock the next morning, and we were both awake; Diane with a stabbing pain in her leg. Doling out painkillers and filling the hot water bottle, I suggested she try to sleep. We both managed to nod back off, but just before the alarm clock was due to ring, rain rattling against the windows woke us. I wished for Diane's sake that the picking was finished. I felt so guilty helping her into her waterproofs and waving her off in the car. But whatever I said, she refused to take time off.

Expecting a call from Phil, I worked with the cellphone in my pocket. As no call materialized, I began lagging the boiler. I was finishing it when Diane drove up. Her hip was throbbing, and I was angry that she insisted on returning to work after lunch. But gritting her teeth, she went anyway.

As she drove off, I spotted Bertrand feeding Hoppie. I apologised for not returning his ramps sooner, saying I'd just finished cleaning them. Could he help me carry them back to his shed? I then felt awful when he showed me his newly electrified barn – which he'd struggled to work on while I had his ramps. The building was ready to receive his Citroën C4 vintage car, which would be complete once Véronique had re-upholstered the seats. Oh my god, was there *nothing* these two couldn't turn their hands to?

Opening the kitchen door to another bitterly cold morning, Diane set off for work. Waving her off, I began working on the terracing. Stopping around noon, I offered to help Bertrand who'd gashed his hand on a rock shard, but he said it wasn't necessary. He'd been out trucking since three thirty am, and now, sat on his tractor, he was about to treat the fields with nutrient pellets – a full afternoon's work.

The morning had flown by, and I'd lost all track of time, until Diane pulled up saying the pick was almost finished. With lunch quickly scoffed, she returned again.

Working on the terrace, I cemented blocks until she returned at five thirty. Kicking off her boots, she said, Dominic had begun paying off his temporary workers. As she was included in that merry band, she could soon relax.

Clothing changed, she rang Stewie and Helen with our travel plans. Then raising a glass, we celebrated the upcoming end to her very hard season

The ninth of November brought mixed news. Amongst several messages was a letting enquiry for the house next year. Nervous and excited, Diane replied quickly, confirming availability for the date required. But checking our website, afterwards, it stated we had four bedrooms, Sky TV and a swimming pool. The ad had been cocked up; and worse still, the high season price had been omitted. And of course the enquiry *was* for high season.

What a shambles! With the top end listing and low season price, no wonder they were keen to book up. Diane spent most of the morning sorting out the mess. Wisely, I kept out of the way, attending to other letters and phone calls.

Chatting to Helen after sorting out the booking problem, Diane promised we'd take over some of Alan's favourite cigars. But any shopping would have to be done before Armistice Day on Friday. I'm sure *we all* know by now, that it's a public holiday in both France *and* the UK

We spent the evening downing a curry and a couple of drinks while watching old comedy videos. We needed to go home – if only to buy some new videos.

A thick hoar frost coated the windows the next morning, a sign that winter was headed our way. Setting off for the woodshed, I glanced up the field, seeing Hoppie looking down at me like a ghostly statue in the mist.

Returning with a basket of logs, I met a yawning Diane checking the computer. As expected, there was no follow up regarding the booking enquiry once the caller had received the *correct* details.

'Oh, while I remember; Kay's thinking of having a small tattoo,' said Diane casually, while tapping away at the keyboard.

'Why?' I asked.

'How should *I* know? Why does anybody do *anything?'*

And after *that* profound reply, she added, 'By the way; when we go to the UK, Nadine wondered if we could do babysitting for Ben and Lewis.'

Messages offloaded, Diane went ahead and booked the ferry for Sunday. With the die cast and three days to go, she willed her leg to improve. It'd been a problem for a week, and unless it improved quickly, it meant a long solo drive for me. But, as I did most of the driving anyway, it wasn't a big deal.

Leaving Diane amending our online advert, I lagged all pipes inside and out; especially those from the underground meter. Later, with a bank appointment, a visit to *La Poste,* then last minute shopping at *Intermarché* lined up, it was turning into a busy day.

At the bank, we found ourselves double-booked to see the manager. The other couple sat waiting were Americans, and I was amazed when they said they were Newcastle United fans. It's certainly a small world. With the manager tied up, (metaphorically – it wasn't a hold-up) we were seen instead by a seemingly pregnant Anne Sophie. She didn't mention her condition, so neither did we. She may have just gained a few kilos. With our business concluded, we returned home.

Despite regular massages and s cocktail of painkillers, Diane's leg was still painful when we arrived at Rob and Elaine's on Friday. We entered the apartment, to find Elaine cursing whoever had torn off their car wing-mirrors and caused other damage. Apparently, quite a few cars in the street had been targeted – a disturbing spin-off from riots taking place across France at the time.

Once she'd calmed down the visit went well; listening as they extolled the benefits of Saumur's café society lifestyle. But aware of parking restrictions, we said our goodbyes early, promising to return early next year. Then it was on to *Intermarche* to change a gas bottle before returning home. We needed to fortify the house against everything winter could throw at it. And, remembering some of our more unsavoury visitors in the past, security also needed to be a major consideration.

Driving back past the desolate orchards, our day was made as we stopped for a herd of nine red deer, which crashed out of a thicket and trotted across the road into a field. Now *that* was special!

Cresting the head of the drive, we met François riding Hoppie. Alongside him, Philippe sat astride a chestnut gelding. They knew we were leaving the next morning, so we exchanged goodbyes. Later, Bertrand and Véronique arrived to give advice on security and overwintering, saying they'd look after everything in our absence.

Alone once more, we emptied the freezer contents into a cool-box, switched off electrics, and locked anything valuable away out of sight. Then, with the house shuttered, it was as protected as we could make it. After calling Helen, giving her our sailing details, we walked over with a bottle to visit Bertrand and family. While having a farewell drink together, we handed over keys and a list of   instructions. Then giving handshakes and hugs, it was time to visit Henri and Annette.

Returning home later, we mulled over our year. Weathering a series of financial setbacks we'd ploughed on, and finding jobs, we'd matched the locals at their work. Unfortunately, despited the house being virtually finished, winter rentals without central heating were impossible. And with our website promising a pool for the next season, we really needed to crack on and install one. Though we'd missed out on this year's bookings, we'd done all we could within our budget. Now the farm was in lock-down until next spring.

Stepping out onto the terrace we took in the setting sun while pondering the future. We'd run out of options. We were off to the UK for the winter. And if *that* didn't work out, maybe we'd just have to admit defeat and sell up.

Hah, like that was going to happen! Suppose we had to work seven days a week and save every penny we could, we'd be back to start all over again next year. Bank on it!

Part Two

Back in the good old UK

Chapter 35

Staying with family

We left the farm on the 13th of November, booked on the afternoon ferry from Boulogne. Following an uneventful run up the *autoroute*, we queued for an hour before boarding.

Two hours later, we made ready to descend to the car deck as the ferry entered Dover's Eastern dock. Once disembarked traffic had cleared UK customs, we joined the A2 motorway and headed north.

Joining the A1M later, I drove to Grantham; where after an overnight stop-over with Jill and Dale, we set off north for Durham, and our final destination Burnhope. Arriving to a warm welcome from Stewie and Helen, 'Hugo' was unloaded and we settled in.

Our first night was spent unwinding after the journey; and while we handed over duty free's, our hosts passed on local news. We also got to play with Aaron before his bathtime, amazed at how much he'd grown. Then, as Stewie had an early start the next morning, we all made our way upstairs for an early night.We'd unpacked our cases, so it was on with our nightware; and after taking our turn in the bathroom it was lights out.

Overall, we had a good night's sleep, apart from when Aaron woke a couple of times. Rising early, I caught Stewie getting ready for work, and picked up ideas on local job availability.

As he was leaving, Diane materialised, and over a cuppa we explored our options.

By the time Helen appeared carrying Aaron, we had a few ideas to throw at her. She listened, then said if they didn't work out, the local Asda superstore were hiring for the Christmas pressure period. It would mean working their twilight shift, which wasn't perfect, but at least we'd have wages coming in. It would do as a stop-gap; and as we could job hunt on our days off, we both applied for Asda and were accepted for interview. After a team bonding session, our first shift began together on the shop floor.

By then, our faithful Peugeot had clocked up a staggering 250,000 miles; Stewie remarking jokingly, 'It's been to the Moon and back.'

After checking, I found that at the Moon's closest orbit to Earth the Peugeot could have gotten there – but not back again. However Stewie's joking made us think. We were heading into winter, and though 'Hugo' had done us proud, we'd soon need to spend serious money getting him 'ship-shape.' We sat down and ran through the figures. If we ploughed money into the car out of sentimentality, we'd still have a vehicle with a daunting mileage on the clock. Besides, we really needed more of a workhorse for our life in France.

We shelved the problem for then, concentrating on our jobs and helping around the house. That is, until Stewie came in one night saying he'd mentioned 'Hugo' to a lady seeking a cheap, reliable runabout. She was definitely interested, what did we think? Yes was the answer. But what would we use for transport until we found something else? Helen said we could use *her* car for a while as she hardly used it. And Stewie had his car which she could use in an emergency. The deal was done, and we watched our faithful servant drive off to a life of virtual retirement. And already I was feeling seller's remorse.

A few days later, Stewie came home bouncing with enthusiasm, saying, 'Stew, I've just seen the perfect car for you. It's a private sale, and it's parked up a couple of miles away.'

'What is it?' I asked.

'It's a Mitsubishi Shogun four by four. It's a 2.5 litre diesel, and it looks like it could pull a house down.'

I cocked an eyebrow. 'Well, maybe not a house. But think how useful it could be in France.'

I pushed him for more details, but he could only repeat what he'd seen displayed on the windscreen. What concerned me was, it was parked near a group of houses on the roadside, and the 'For Sale' sheet only gave a telephone number. Normally, I wouldn't have entertained it. However it was worth a look. So collecting Diane, the three of us set off to view it.

We pulled up next to one beast of a machine. Parked off the road, it had huge presence and was in great condition. Everything looked spot on. It had a current tax disc and was MOT'd, according to the information given. There was only one thing left. I needed to test drive it.

Ringing the number on the sheet, I spoke to a guy who said he'd meet us at the car. When he turned up, he had a cast on his leg and was on crutches. He'd appeared from a nearby group of houses, but we didn't see which one. He gave us a story about staying with his sister while selling his house. I suppose we should've known better, but he had the log-book, bill of sale for the car, and proof of identity. Everything seemed to be in order – though he hadn't got the HPI print-out with him. Trusting our instincts, we went for a test drive. My God, the throaty roar of the engine, the torque from the four-wheel drive, the bull bars and commanding seat height. I was in love!

Though Diane was also impressed, she was still hesitant. But after an exhaustive test drive where Stewie and I went over the whole car, even she was impressed. It was just what we needed. With the engine note still throbbing in my ears, we returned to do a little haggling, And with a receipt for our deposit, off we went to withdraw the balance.

Returning the next day the deal was done, and we drove off with a bill of sale and a 'tail-light' guarantee.

Over the next few weeks a few problems cropped up with the car, costing us around £300. It was annoying as we felt cheated. However, once they'd been ironed out, the car went on to give great service. It was the perfect workhorse and could do things that the Peugeot couldn't do– or shouldn't have had to do in its past.

Christmas arrived and we were under the cosh at work, taking on extra shifts and overtime. But let's face it, that's what we were there for. Over the holiday period, we saw all our immediate family and friends, visiting Michael, Miranda and the kids on Christmas day.

After the Christmas pressure period I began job hunting, as the hours had reduced at Asda and people were being let go. Even with us both working full time, there wasn't much left to send to our French bank after paying our way.

On one of my regular visits to the job centre, I saw a driving job advertised at Boots the chemist. I applied for it and got it. The hours were nine till five, and entailed collecting prescriptions from doctor's surgeries for processing. Then, while delivering to care homes and private addresses, I collected outdated medications for return and destruction. Another aspect of the job was providing equipment like wheelchairs and oxygen bottles, issued from the healthcentre. I enjoyed the freedom and sense of purpose it gave, plus the hours and pay-rate were better.

We settled well into life at the Prow's; looking after Aaron to give Helen a rest, and doing our bit in the house including decorating; something we both enjoyed. On the whole we got on fine together, despite the odd tensions as might be expected. Overall though, we couldn't have asked for better hosts.

Working conflicting hours meant Diane and I had little time for socialising. But life with the Prow's was never dull, especially Friday nights when Alan and Pauline came around for drinks and card games. Often, Adam would accompany them, plus other family would drop in if passing.

It was after the Christmas festivities, that our computer inbox began receiving holiday booking en quiries. With a pool to locate and install, plus other jobs to tackle, we applied to our UK bank for a small loan. Surprisingly it was denied. When we asked why, we were shocked. It seems while we were living in France, we'd been issued with a County Court judgement. We hadn't received it, and our credit rating had tanked without us knowing.

After we'd left the Northumberland cottage it'd stood empty for some time. And though we'd paid Royal Mail for a change of address, some of our post had been delivered there. Apparently, the next tenants had used Diane's name and details for identity fraud. So Diane had to contact the company that'd been scammed, and prove we'd changed address and were living in France at the time.

Eventually, the matter was resolved, our name cleared, and our credit rating restored. But we never received an apology from anyone, and it left a nasty taste in our mouths.

After the New Years celebrations, the weeks seemed to roll by quickly. We continued working hard and sending money to France, but at the beginning of March, Diane needed carpal tunnel surgery on her hand. Apart from it being painful, it was a blow to our plans as she couldn't work. With her out of action for at least seven weeks, and rental enquiries coming in regularly, we realised we'd have to get back to France pretty damned quickly. There was too much to do and the season was almost upon us.

With our CCJ erased and finance in place, we handed in two weeks notice at work and had the Shogun serviced. We then visited family in the area, plus friends we hadn't seen for some time. We also laid our hands on an ex-contract Sky dish and box. And needing a new TV, we bought one from Asda – using staff discount of course.

Just before we left, I received sad news. My ex father-in-law, who I'd been close to had died of cancer. It shook me badly. I attended the funeral; and as we'd worked for the same company for years, past collegues also attended, making it easier to get through.

With duty done and everything taken care of, Stewie and Helen threw us a going away party, where most of the Prow family came together to say goodbye.

On the morning of the 24th of April, we said farewell and thanks for everything to Stewie and Helen. Then with a cheery wave, we set off on our travels.

Chapter 36

Playing catch-up

Pulling off the busy A1M headed for Grantham, we were looking forward to another overnight stay with Jill and Dale. Keen to crack on, we were up early the next day, breakfasted and on the road again.

After a trouble-free journey, I pulled into Dover's Eastern docks. We boarded around two pm, and disembarked at four fifteen French time refreshed after a smooth crossing. Re-setting our watches, we cleared customs, left the busy dockyard and passed through the *centre ville* headed for the *autoroute*. And that was where we saw an example of why we try to drive carefully.

Through a cloud of swirling black smoke, backed-up traffic inched forward. Working desperately ahead of the traffic, the crew of a *secours de pompiere* tender were trying to douse a burning truck. And as we drove slowly past, a couple of paramedics were loading a shrouded body into an ambulance.

Welcome to France!

We arrived at midnight on the 26th, and opened the house under Hoppie's watchful gaze. Being ravenous and on an adrenalin high, Diane's quickly-made sandwich and a couple of drinks went down a treat. But after unwinding for an hour, we hit the sheets.

Rejuvinated after a few hours sleep, we drove to Le Lude's *Intermarché* for foodstuffs, and its fuel station for diesel. We had very little actual cash on us, and a problem arose when Diane couldn't find her *Credit Agricole* card. I tried mine, but with scratches to its surface, my card wasn't accepted either, so for a nominal fee we used a UK bankcard.

Back at the farmhouse, François spotted us while out with the dogs. He was impressed by the Shogun – as I was by the work that had been done in our absence. He later showed me I-pad footage of them burning huge piles of brush on the snow covered fields. He said, due to the poor weather, the fires had burned for days. They'd also unearthed another load of scrap in another field, cut down some dead trees, and stacked the wood in our shed.

Catching Bertrand as he set off for his afternoon shift, I thanked him for all his work; then needing to visit the *dechetterie* with 'The Hippo,' I made a new number plate for it bearing the Shogun's licence number. With scrap loaded into the trailer, I drove to the facility, where of course the attendant didn't recognise our new vehicle. After explaining my change of car, he remembered us; and after offloading, I was unhitching 'The Hippo' back at the farm when François arrived. He told me Bertrand's friend was bringing his excavator over the next morning, and we were invited over to discuss future plans.

In my absence, Diane had unpacked and was chatting with family online. With a tank of hot water awaiting us later, we anticipated a nice long soak. Followed by our evening meal and a few glasses of wine, it proves getting joy from life needn't be complicated.

Looking out of the kitchen window, I saw Bertrand's friend Davide drive past in his truck, pulling a backhoe excavator strapped to a trailer. After some ditch clearance for Bertrand, they both came over to examine our proposed pool site. Then tracking in on his excavator, he ripped out stunted trees and levelled the area. To gain extra space for a pool and terracing, he filled three large holes with rubble on the edge of the field.

With that stage of the job done, Davide stated we'd need fifteen tonnes of sand for the pool base, saying it would cost twenty seven euros a tonne. But buying in bulk on his account, he'd deliver it, lay it and level it out for 400 euros. He said he'd return in the morning for my answer. As he loaded up his excavator, I rang Rob to check their pool dimensions, then the quarry to check the cost of sand. With things to discuss, Diane cooked our meal while I brought in wood for the fire. Over dinner and wine, we got our ducks in a row, before watching a video then heading off to bed.

I remember that particular Friday well. It was a gorgeous day with the sun streaming into the kitchen. Davide turned up next door to finish ditch clearing; then, as Bertrand was working, Véronique came over with him to help translate.
After agreeing to his price for the job, I explained what we needed and he got underway.

In an efficient manner, he set up a tripod-mounted laser level at one end of the site. Lining it up on a sensor fitted to his excavator boom, he levelled the area. Working non-stop, he pulled out concrete slabs, rebar and a wealth of scrap, all for a measly 65 euros. Saying I'd source my own sand on my quarry account, we shook hands and he left.

As the equipment trundled off down the drive, we left for Noyant market to catch Rob and Elaine. They'd offered to help us erect the pool when we bought one, as friends had helped them build theirs. Mentioning our Sky TV package, he was also keen to check out the setup and our new TV. Then – completely out of left field, he said they were thinking of moving again: this time to set up a small business.

While we were chatting, Phil turned up to check on our plumbing, as the winter had been colder and longer than any in living memory. Assuring him that everything had survived just fine, I left them chatting and we set off home. It was game on. We were hunting down a pool.

Driving to La Flèche's *Leclerc* then on to *Bricomarché,* we searched for an above ground pool. They were far cheaper than having one excavated, and not subject to strict regulations. But even so, the one we decided on was over 1,500 euros to take away – assembly extra. At almost ten metres by five, it was a hefty piece of kit; but having heard of cheaper ones, shopping around seemed wise. However, first things first!

We'd been invited next door later for a catch up visit. We arrived at eight pm bearing gifts, Bertrand's favourite being a tin of Quality Street chocolates. (Yes, others are available!) We only stayed for an hour, as they needed an early night. They'd booked a well deserved weekend break, and their destination was some distance away.

Back at *La Ferronerrie*, I lit the fire, before enjoying a drink and snacks while video watching. But all too soon we were yawning infectiously, so it was off to bed.

Awake bright and early the next morning, I drank a coffee, then headed out to chop wood. As Diane was still sleeping, I raked over the terracing, levelling the hardcore to receive sand. While out there, I nipped over and opened Véronique's polytunnel. I was pruning in the orchard later when I heard activity in the kitchen. Diane had set the washing machine away and was rattling pans. Breakfast!

The next stage of today's plan, was to inflate a soft tyre at *Intermarché's* airline before setting off for Saumur's suburban shopping precinct. After a cursory look around the mall on arrival, we withdrew cash at an ATM before hitting the city shopping area. We hoped that *Bricomarché, Mr Bricolage,* or *Vive la Maison* might provide a selection of pools. Unfortunately there was no luck anywhere – not even when we tried *Leclerc*. Salvaging something from the trip, we did a food shop before heading home again.

In the afternoon, we loaded up 'The Hippo' with rubbish and drove to the *déchetterie*. Leaving the facility, we were sweating and dirty. It'd been a free for all, as most of Le Lude seemed to have chosen today to turn up.

Nevertheless, job done, we crawled back home. With the trailer unhitched, Diane began cooking while I closed up Véronique's polytunnel. A shower was next on our agenda, then a meal and drinks. After all it was Saturday night. It just *had* to mean *something*.

The sun was cracking the rooftiles the next morning, as my late dad used to say. It was Sunday and supposedly a day of rest; but that wasn't possible with today's schedule.

With breakfast finished, I opened Veronique's polytunnel then my tool-shed. I wasn't looking forward to it, but the whole area was crying out for help. The grass needed cutting, and bushes, shrubs and flower beds all required attention. But after a long period laid up in the toolshed, the equipment needed inspecting. Oil and fuel had to be changed, blades and saw teeth checked and sharpened before anything could be used.

After the servicing, I grabbed the chainsaw. Toppled by the excavator, a large tree lay across the pool site. It needed moving before we could level the ground. Firing up the saw, I began cutting. Meanwhile, Diane got the mower started and set off around the lawns and flower beds.

An hour or so later, I was barrowing logs into the woodshed. Then, stashing the saw away, I grabbed the strimmer and began tackling thickets of weeds.

As the morning progressed, the sun rose on its arc, taking the temperature up with it. Feeling de-hydrated, we were forced inside by the overbearing heat. While gulping cold drinks the phone rang. It was Rob. Could he and Elaine pop over after lunch? Only too pleased to down tools right then, I said yes.

They pulled up at two thirty; and after cold drinks were poured, Rob invited us to his upcoming 60th birthday. The talk then shifted to the newly excavated area. Rob said, once we'd bought a pool, they'd be over to help with the installation – it being a four person job.

We enjoyed their visit, but a couple of hours later they had to leave. I suppose we should have cracked on with the garden again, but we'd lost all momentum. Besides, having sunk a few glasses of wine by then, it could be dangerous handling machinery. After putting away the tools, Diane went in to prepare dinner, while I attended to Véronique's polytunnel and watering both of our gardens.

Now – time to relax!

Chapter 37

We reach for 'The Sky'

I woke up feeling cold and alone. Looking for Diane, I found her working on the computer. She'd been on the internet from four am searching for pools. They were all expensive, the cheapest being those from the U.S. But shipping costs negated any savings to be had from them. It being May 1st and a bank holiday, we couldn't drive out and physically look for one, so I suggested she leave it for now.

With Véroniques's polytunnel opened after breakfast, I got busy with the strimmer, while, Diane grabbed secateurs and began pruning the roses. Surveying the monumental amount of work to be tackled, I realised it would be a very long day.

The next morning, though, we set off with a plan. By then, finding a pool was reaching critical mass. Rob had mentioned seeing a *jardinière,* or garden centre near Angers, and despite getting lost leaving town, we eventually tracked it down. Once inside, though, there were no pools to be had.

Driving on, an advertising board led us to a dedicated pool business. But imagine our dismay, when we discovered that finding a pool suiting our requirements would cost more than 7,000 euros. We drove back home dumbstruck, and searching online, Diane found another large supermarket chain who said they had pools in stock. Unfortunately, when we arrived there they were all too small. Disheartened, we drove home for lunch.

Refusing to be beaten, we drove to La Flèche in the afternoon, where *their Brico* still had the pool we'd liked on display. Biting the bullet, we asked to buy one. There was a three week waiting list, the assistant said. Well, could we buy the display model, maybe at a reduced price?

'Non' was the answer.

Backed into a corner by then, we placed our order.

'Pardon Monsieur, but unfortunately there is a problem,' the assistant said. 'The price shown on the display model is last year's price. The new price is 2,120 euros.'

Well what a surprise! But out of options, we paid 20% deposit and left.

Returning from their vacation the next day, Bertrand and Véronique popped over for a chat. While handing us radishes and asparagus from the polytunnel, Bertrand said François would be back in three weeks. There was also news of Maurice. His ex was still causing problems over the kids, but he now had a girlfriend. She was twenty six years old, and being fourteen years her senior, he seemed to be doing very nicely thank you. Apparently, she'd moved in and was helping with expenses. Nice one Maurice!

Otherwise life continued apace, as we threw ourselves into gardening and landscaping. With the temperature often reaching 30 degrees C and no breeze to speak of, extreme humidity was making life difficult. Therefore, until the air cleared – which was usually after a storm, a midday meal was often followed by a nap. We tended to tread carefully at such times, as it was easy to become ratty and irritable.

Whilst collapsed in a stupor on your bed then, you wouldn't want to be woken suddenly by Jorge in his post van. And to make matters worse, you *definitely* wouldn't want to find a *Leclerc* leaflet in your letterbox promising huge reductions on pool prices!

'Damn, look at this,' said Diane. 'If we'd waited till today, we could've saved more than 400 euros.'

The tearing of an envelope was then followed by, 'Oh great, I thought they'd settled this. It's from Expirian. They want me to write to the company who filed the CCJ against me, threatening them with legal action. They then need copies of police reports, and evidence that we were living in France when the fraud happened. And with our credit rating now re-instated, they'll have our name removed from the company's records and keep all the details on file.'

Sleep was impossible after *that*. And while Diane was working on her letter, I studied *Leclerc's* pool advert.

'I wonder if we could cancel the pool order with *Brico*,' I mused. 'We can't afford to wait three weeks, and we definitely don't want to waste 400 euros if we can avoid it.'

Ringing the bank, I asked if it was possible to cancel a cheque. They said, only if I'd lost my cheque book or had it stolen; in which case I must contact them and the police immediately. Forget it! There had to be another way.

While I was considering a plan B, there was a knock on the door. I opened it, and saw a grinning little guy stood in front of a white van. Oh no, not again! I didn't need this.

By the time I'd been shown everything from clothes pegs, through pots, pans and baskets to clothing, I was mentally drained. Managing to get rid of him eventually, we drove off to Le Lude to post Diane's letter.

The sun was a white-hot ball beating down on Noyant's busy market. In the glaring light, gaudy clothing and flashy knock-off's invited the crowds. Jostling for space, we approached Rob and Elaine's stall. As usual, though, despite arriving early they'd been allocated a stall next to the toilets. At least they had a potential flow of customers!

After discussing our pool seeking adventures, they said it was a pity we couldn't have bought theirs. It would have saved a lot of hassle and helped us both. They'd hit a busy

241

spell by then, so we said we'd ring them, and left to look around the market.

On the way home, we formulated a plan. We'd drive straight on to La Flèche and see what could be done at *Brico*. Arriving, I asked to see the manager. Pleading a family emergency in the UK, I asked, could we cancel our order and have our deposit refunded?

'No problem Monsieur,' he said. We left five minutes later feeling elated; then jumped into the car and drove to *Leclerc*.

When we arrived, they said they'd sold three pools that morning, and we were lucky to get the last one for 1,290 euros. Stumping up for it, we arranged to return with our trailer to collect it, before shopping for wine and snacks to celebrate later.

Back at Ferronerie HQ, Diane had just poured a cuppa, when, toot! toot! Henri and Annette pulled up in their Peugeot. It was the first time we'd seen them since our return. It was also the first time *they'd* seen the Shogun.

'*Tous est un capitalist,*' he accused grinning.

They only stayed for fifteen minutes; and after they'd rattled off down the drive, Diane sent off some emails. Chilled out at last, we ate a late meal while watching a video, before Morpheus beckoned.

Rain was sheeting down in torrents the next morning. Not the best conditions for outside working. We could work *inside* of course, but, having arranged to pick up the boxed pool before lunch, it wasn't worth starting anything. We'd decided to set off for La Flèche early to avoid any glitches. But before we drove off, I needed to check out the trailer lights. They'd been acting up again. Sometimes they worked – then again, sometimes they didn't.

As the rain had stopped, I hitched up the trailer. *This* time the left hand indicator wouldn't work, which could prove dangerous. When I jiggled the connecting plug it began working again. *That'll have to do,* I thought, setting off.

Arriving safely at *Leclerc's* customer service desk, we were directed to the collection point. And in one of those, 'I don't believe it,' moments; while he was loading our pool, a forklift truck driver crashed into the trailer lights. The lenses weren't broken, but *none* of the lights would work after that. Loosening the right hand lens, I found the bulb had been knocked out. With it pushed back in, *both* light clusters worked perfectly. Whatever the problem was, it could wait till we got home.

Pulling up the drive, I reversed the trailer into the barn. After un-hitching, I threw a tarpaulin over it and went in for lunch. It was a heavy piece of kit, so it could stay there until we could get help unloading it. Instead, I spent two hours cutting logs, as the grass was too wet to begin strimming.

Overnight rain abated in the early hours. Wide awake at three am, I sipped a mug of hot milk and read until four. After another abortive attempt at sleeping, I gave up. By seven am it'd turned into a dank, misty day, with feeble sunshine trying valiantly to break through. With the sun growing stronger after breakfast, water evaporated from the terrace like steam from a kettle, so leaving Diane to her computer, I got out the strimmer. I'd already heard the whipcrack of Bertrand's heavy duty *coupe bordeur* coming from the top field. He was edging Hoppie's paddock, as once the electric fencing was installed, anything touching the wire could short out the relay. Unfortunately, at that point Mother Nature intervened. I'd just gotten started when the heavens opened again. With strimming on hold once more, I took in wood for later.

The afternoon saw a marked change in the weather; and working in the field below Bertrand, I strimmed the grass covering the *cave* roof. Moving on, he and Véronique began digging post holes; and with my strimming done by then, I

243

gave them a hand. During the process, Bertrand's mum and dad arrived, and downing tools, we all chatted about the field-work to be done.

Diane wasn't keen when I said we'd been invited for aperitifs later. But showered and changed into cool casual wear, we followed the track to Le Lavendu at seven pm. After introducing Diane to his parents, home-made liqueurs and snacks took precedence; and the dogs, while trying to look unconcerned followed every move from plate to mouth.

Hearing rain pebble-dash the windows an hour later, we made our excuses and dashed back home. And engaged in lighting the fire, I heard the phone ring. It was Kay, upset after receiving bad news regarding a friend. She'd sustained a serious fall and was in the ICU. It was a terrible thing to happen to a young mum.

It was Armistice Day; and following overnight rain, the sun peeped out between ominous black clouds. It looked like the weather could swing either way. Around ten am, Bertrand and Véronique showed up to continue working on the fence.Taking my sledgehammer over, I helped knock in posts – breaking off for a two minute's silence at eleven.

It was a treat watching Bertrand use his chainsaw; cutting posts, shaping stake points, making joints etcetera. Nothing seemed beyond his talents; and Veroniqe also impressed as she de-barked wood with an ancient spokeshave. Sadly, rain stopped play again; and with no sign of it relenting this time, everyone dashed inside for lunch.

The rain eventually eased around three; and emerging, I continued cutting fence-posts as afternoon sun dried the land. Hearing my chainsaw's roar, Bertrand and Véronique came out and began splitting horizontals. Finished on her computer, Diane grabbed the strimmer, and we all worked happily together until six thirty. *All this for Hoppie,* I thought. *I just hope* we *don't have to sell up.*

Finished for the day, I put the tools away and went in for a hot soak. Too tired to concentrate on TV, though, we read for a while then had an early night.

During the early hours there was one helluva crash. Thinking, it might be intruders, I grabbed my axe handle and cautiously checked all the rooms, Diane following closely. Reaching the bathroom, we found that Diane's ornamental mirror had fallen off the wall. Shards of glass glittered on the tiled floor. Could it be the work of Poltergeists? No – just Diane's unsuccessful attempt at mirror hanging. Come on girl, do we *really* need seven years bad luck?

I eventually woke at seven am, Diane at nine. After a substantial breakfast, Diane drove to Le Lude for shopping and fuel. Meanwhile, I cleared the area earmarked for the pool. After taking photos of the site, I then sketched an impression of the finished leisure area.

Wheeling out the *brouette* and some tools, I dug up rocks, and barrowed them to the proposed terrace, where I chiselled them into shape. By twelve thirty pm, I'd scooped out a shallow trench around the area and lined it with dressed stones, the foundations for a wall. But that was enough for then. Diane shouted that my meal was ready, so washed and changed, I sat down to eat.

Waking up as stiff as a board after doing too much the previous day, I limbered up and began again. I spent my morning mixing cement and bonding the base stones in place. After a hard morning in the sun, I broke off for lunch.

As Diane had finished working inside, she offered to help after our meal. So we divided up the work; breaking and levelling hardcore before shovelling sand over it. Then while Diane went off to mow the lawns, I began laying paving slabs.

Bertrand and Maurice showed up mid-afternoon towing an antiquated seed-drill, in preparation for sowing maize on his day off. Waving to them, I went in for a drink, where Diane showed me a letter she'd received from her mum. She co-ordinates a family newsletter, and wondered if we might have a little something to contribute. Really? We had enough material to fill the whole issue.

Stored in the *mouton* shed like a guilty pleasure, lay my horde of pure white limestone rocks. I'd been collecting them for ages and had amassed quite a pile. I intended using them as the terrace wall, making a complete contrast to the paving stones. Reflecting the sunlight as they did, they'd look stunning set off with capping stones. However, I couldn't start yet, as a blanket of fog lay across the valley, making it almost impossible to see. But there was something I *could* do, and it would help us financially.

Heading inside, I phoned Boots my previous employer. Asking for the supervisor, I reminded her that I'd been paid thirty six hours short on my last salary; money we'd been waiting for. She apologised, saying she'd corrected the error, and the money would be in our account by the end of the day. On a roll, I sorted out a rebate due from the tax office, while Diane arranged a transfer from the UK to our French bank. Our account should soon look a lot healthier.

Eventually the fog burned off, and in strengthening sunshine, I mixed cement and began building the terrace wall. Meanwhile, working close by, Diane treated the sun-bleached woodwork of the outbuildings and boiler room with anti-termite stain.

Breaking off for lunch, we relaxed inside with the French windows open. The purpose was to let in cool air of course – not the swift that decided to pay us a visit. After it swooped around in a panic and bounced off a few windows, it finally found the one it'd entered by. According to Diane it was bad luck. *She's right*, I thought, surveying the trail of bird crap it left when it finally escaped.

After our meal, Helen messaged that a letter had arrived from Boots. Should she post it on? I said not to bother, just open it and read it out. Apparently, I'd been underpaid more than I thought, and it was being transferred to our account. I couldn't understand it. I kept track of my hours faithfully. But until I heard otherwise it was staying in our bank.

After an 'interesting' day, we popped a cork, watched a video then headed off to bed.

Rising early as usual, we formulated a plan. After breakfast, we visited the bank at Noyant, where an extremely polite young guy deposited a cheque for us, and ordered us a French cheque book. And at Rob's stall in the market, he re-affirmed their visit later to help fit the Sky system, saying they'd applied for a small trader's licence. Keen to retire the video player, we drove off to *Intermarché* to buy goodies for their visit.

When the market closed at noon, Rob and Elaine drove over; and following an alfresco lunch, the tools came out. After measuring and marking, Rob drove the ladies to Le Lude to find cable and clips, while I drilled the wall and fitted mounting brackets. When they returned the dish was fitted; then taking the TV set outside, we lined up the signal.

Once the system was working, Rob and Elaine left. Spooling out the cable, I clipped it along the eaves, through a hole drilled in the door frame and into the lounge. I broke three drills on the granite during the process, but finally it was done. Scrolling through the wealth of English speaking channels at our disposal, we grinned at each other like kids in a sweetshop.

Chapter 38

Splashing the cash

It'd been happening quite often lately. Up at six fifteen am, I stared through the shutters into a blanket of fog. After a bracing cup of coffee while watching Sky news, Diane began making breakfast. It was still a novelty having all those programmes to choose from instead of old videos, but I could see it becoming addictive. So, with the fog clearing by then, we switched the set off, hitched up the small trailer and drove to La Flèche.

Trawling through *Bricomarché*, we bought cushion flooring for both bathrooms at a bargain three euros twenty five a metre. Then going out to the building supplies section, I bought sixty five breeze blocks. Unfortunately everything couldn't be taken on the one trip. Despite the Shogun being the long wheelbase model, the trailer was too small to take the remainder. I'd only planned on picking up the flooring originally, so I'd have to split the load and return for the rest. However, the forklift driver who brought over a pallet of blocks wasn't on the same wavelength as me. Mercifully, a nice old French couple unravelled the *impasse* we'd gotten into, and after translating for me, we were soon loaded. Thanking our Gallic saviours profusely, we returned home.

With a quick snack under my belt, I rang François, asking if he could help unload the boxed pool assembly. Between the three of us, we manhandled (and womanhandled) it onto a pallet. After thanking him, Diane and I headed off to Saumur for the two o'clock free for all at *Emmaus*.

After a pleasant but fruitless visit, we returned to La Ferroneire, hitched up the 'Hippo,' and headed for La Flèche to pick up the remaining breeze blocks and cushion floor.

Pleasantly knackered after unloading and stacking everything, I garaged the trailer then relaxed with a coffee, only to see Bertrand and Véronique starting work on the fence. Feeling ridiculously guilty, we hid out of sight until they finished. Come on, Bertrand, you don't start working at six thirty on a Saturday night! After all the driving and shopping, loading and unloading sixty five breeze-blocks and the cushion flooring, then manhandling both trailers, and unloading the pool, we'd had enough for today thank-you.

However often, I say Sunday is supposedly a day of rest, it wasn't for me. After breakfast, I forced myself out to mix cement. My spirits soared, though, when I saw Bertrand walking up the drive leading Hoppie by the reins. Sat astride her was an *extremely* apprehensive looking François. As Bertrand pulled up near us, François said she'd begun throwing him off again. It was difficult to offer sympathy and commiserate with him – while all I really wanted to do was laugh.

After lunch all three Charpentiers arrived. They'd turned up mob-handed to translate a form from the *Mairie's* office – though, I noticed Bertrand was as usual carrying a bottle! The letter referred to our *fosse septique,* and new regulations which could soon come into force. We'd deal with them when it happens, I said, as Bertrand opened the bottle.

After a brief visit, (where Hoppie wasn't even mentioned) they left, and I continued cementing until six thirty. By then, I'd had enough and went inside. Sitting down to relax, I heard a loud banging. Looking outside, I saw Bertrand and Véronique working on the fence. It was seven o'clock on

Sunday night, Anna was visiting, and François was returning to Bazaz tomorrow. Couldn't they give it a rest for once?

With a clear day the next morning, I was out cementing at six fifteen. Finishing the terrace wall, I moved on to grouting the *cave* facia. After a late breakfast, I hitched up 'The Hippo,' then Diane and I set off for the quarry. It was time to lay the base for the pool, and for that we needed at least two tonnes of sand. Trundling into *Carriere Roumy*, I introduced Diane to the weighbridge attendant before driving down to the weird moonscape of the quarry floor. It had the desired effect. Diane was overawed – especially when the huge excavator roared over. Explaining my requirements to the driver, he tipped the first bucketful into 'The Hippo.' It landed with such a thump, that the trailer almost collapsed with the shock. Another bucketful seemed to be chancing it, so asking for a *demi* bucketful, I drove off-site with the poor 'Hippo' almost on its knees – so to speak.

After checking in at the weigh station, I drove back ever so slowly. Making it past the head of the drive, I reversed up to the levelled area. Bringing over the barrow, we took turns filling and tipping it, forming large mounds on plastic sheeting. And that was only half the job. With the tyre pressures increased using a new foot-pump, we returned to the quarry after lunch.

By the time we'd shovelled out a second full load, we'd had enough. While Diane went in to make coffee, I swept out the trailer and unhitched the unit. By the time we'd done other chores, it was six o'clock and we were finished – in more ways than one. After a shower and a meal, Diane went online, while I sat stupefied in front of the TV. Then yawning mightily, we staggered off to bed.

While dreaming peacefully in the early hours, I was shocked awake by a loud booming in my ear. Good Lord, what was that? Diane had gone to sleep listening to music through her headphones; and turning over, she'd yanked the earbuds out. The MP3 player was damaged irreparably – along with my night's sleep!

Treating Diane to a cuppa in bed later, I said not to rush. With heavy rain predicted, working outside was a non-starter. However, the sun came out – along with Diane, who'd dressed for work. And *that's* when it began to rain. Would you believe it? Still, it gave us the chance to catch up on paperwork, including a booking for the house rental. It wasn't the first, so getting the pool sorted was now critical.

To that end, we drove to Le Lude after breakfast. It was still raining, but our mission was to find a weed suppressant membrane for the pool area. We had literally tonnes of sand, but we needed a weed-proof base to lay it on. At *Brico,* we were shown rubberised lining, a treated felt, and standard tarpaulin. The first two were very expensive – but would the cheaper tarpaulin do the job? After checking out specialist stores, we returned home soaked and confused.

Dried out and fed, I set off for La Flèche, where we tried their *Brico* and *Leclerc* for membrane without success. Though, we bought a terrace parasol, some paint and a towel rail, so it wasn't a total waste of time.

After visiting *Noz* and surrounding shops, we drove back to find the valley had suffered a power-cut. And as the well-pump was electrically operated, we had no water either. Véronique was in the paddock grooming Hoppie when I told her, '*Ces't normale,*' she said, shrugging her shoulders.

With the shopping stowed away – some of it by necessity in the fridge and freezer, our fate rested in the hands of EDF. As twilight fell power was restored; and as I ran a bath, Kay rang. It wasn't a problem. Diane had plenty of time to chat, as the bath took ages to fill. With us both tired after trashing around, we bathed, forced down a meal, then had an early night – without even glancing at the wine rack.

Seduced into a mini lie-in the next morning by lousy weather, I got up to check Sky news over coffee. Then with the sun appearing, I switched off 'the servant of the devil' and went out to mix cement. I was repairing the path outside the *mouton* shed when Diane got up. 'Breakfast's ready,' she said shortly afterwards.

With dishes washed, the quarry was next. We needed lots more sand, both for the pool base and terrace.Pulling another tonne in the groaning 'Hippo,' the Shogun made it look easy as usual, and by twelve thirty we'd shovelled it all out. As it was seriously hot by then, we adjourned for lunch and a *petit-somme*.

Dragging myself off the bed mid-afternoon, I left Diane attending to booking requests and a deposit she'd received, while I went back to the quarry for yet more sand. At first I'd disagreed with Davide on the amount needed, but the pool itself was 42 square metres, so maybe he was right. Anyway, other building projects needed sand, so no problem.

Half an hour later, the Shogun snarled up the drive again; the poor 'Hippo's' springs sagging. It was the final trip for some time – I hoped, and another tonne and a half to be moved. As I climbed out of the car, Diane shouted that Rob was on the phone. He was asking if he could store some of his stock with us for a while. When I said yes, he said they'd be right over. I'd just finished shovelling when they arrived.

'That's right, turn up when all the work's done,' I joked.

They stayed for an hour after unloading lots of boxes; and over a beer, we discussed the pool installation. They said, when they'd bought theirs, they couldn't find anyone willing to build it for them. It was a pig of a job, so they'd help us as it'd taken them and two friends to build theirs. But first we needed the membrane. Rob had settled for the basic tarpaulin. It was by far the cheapest, and they'd had no issues with weeds afterwards. Soon after, with their storage sorted they left.

Chapter 39

Sand, sand and more sand

With the pool-site measured, we shot off and bought the required rolls of tarpaulin; and after cutting the tall perimeter hedge back, we laid them. Finally, it was time for the sand.

Lawrence of Arabia saw less sand than *we* did over the next couple of days. Filling the barrow, wheeling it across the site, tipping it, then raking it out in extreme heat wasn't *my* idea of fun. But it was a vital step in building the pool we'd promised our guests. Our aim was to lay approximately 72 square metres of sand, up to fifteen centimetres deep to accommodate the pool. With that done, we'd make a gravel pathway around the perimeter to allow for access and cleaning. But looking at it, even with the tonnage we'd bought, running out of sand could still be a possibility.

Off we went again to the quarry, returning with what I hoped was our final load. Swinging around the head of the drive, I noticed a van parked outside the switch room. As we pulled up alongside it, Cigogne staggered out to greet us. He was completely off his face! We had to ring Véronique to come over and make sense of what he was saying.

I'd rung his boss earlier, telling him our electrics were acting up again, insisting it'd begun after they'd fitted the new pump. Slurring his words, Cigone said the pump *might* be the problem, but he wasn't sure. (Oh please God don't let him want to climb down the well!) He then said, he'd be billing me for his visit. No way, I said. If it's the pump, it's covered under warranty. Shrugging, he said he'd return on Monday. Then again, it might be Tuesday. He wasn't sure.

After what seemed like a lifetime the sand was down, though I wasn't too happy with the result. Anything that touched it left an imprint, so how would a huge pool filled with water affect it? I rang Rob, who said it would be fine. The pressure of all that water would keep the base level. Not at all convinced, we opened the box; spreading out its contents and checking everything against the list provided.

Needing a large area to work in, we had a huge clear-up before starting. Anything that could damage the pool's fabric was loaded into 'The Hippo,' while rubble was thrown onto the terrace for hardcore. Then with the site cleared, it was safe to lay everything out.

Taking the rubbish to the *déchetterie* first, we drove on to the quarry for yet more sand. This made eight tonnes in total, which was far less than Davide stated, but seemed excessive to me. However, the pool was the selling point on our website so it had to be right.

We began the build on Tuesday the 23rd It was a gorgeous day with no sign of wind or rain – the first for more than a week. With the forecast boding well for the next few days, we were about to begin when a van shot past. It was Cigogne and his mate heading for le Lavendu.

When they returned after checking out the pump, Cigogne said it was fine. The fault must lie with the switch box. He'd shoot off, bring a new one back and try it out. If it fired up the pump, he'd bill me.

Yeah whatever, we had other fish to fry. We needed to mark out the area precisely before placing mounting blocks around the perimeter. Down to Le lude we went, to buy the correct ones from *Brico*. Bringing back the slabs, I set them out as per instruction, using a complicated arrangement involving planks and a spirit level. Then after catching up with other jobs, I loaded some of Rob's stock into the small trailer for Friday's market after a phone call.

As dusk fell, we trudged back in, Diane checked online messages, and we went straight to bed.

We'd laid the mounting slabs, the day was fine, and here we were at six am ready to go. We'd studied the list, checked off everything, including struts, rolls of galvanized panelling, and the amorphous polypropene lining. But maybe we should start a little later? After all, Diane had the grass to cut, while I had the *mouton* hut and other outbuildings to finish painting. Let's face it, we were putting it off. It all seemed too daunting.

With our jobs finished and lunch out of the way, we'd run out of excuses. Back in the barn, we re-assessed the pile of parts. Well, it wasn't going to build itself, so we sorted out all the components and stacked them in order. Following the instructions carefully, we assembled all the triangular bracing struts for the pool. Taking them outside, I drilled holes in the mounting slabs, installed rawlplugs then bolted on the struts. It was hard work, and drilling the slabs burned out two drill-bits. By late afternoon it'd turned blustery and begun raining; and as it got heavier, we stopped for the day.

Unfortunately rain and wind delayed the build again the next day, so the bathroom claimed our attention. The wall linking it to the main building required work. Smoothing it with the orbital sander, I fitted bracing struts then tongue and groove panelling. But after changing the sink and bidet units, the bath wouldn't marry up. Another trip to *Brico*!

Returning with new couplings I met François, who'd returned Hoppie after a ride out. He'd brought his laptop over, so work stopped while he showed us photos of Le Ferronnerie during the winter. After sending them to our computer, he left. I finished the plumbing then painted most of the bathroom, but after that it was time for our meal.

Overnight rain resulted in an uneasy morning; but without wind, it showed promise for later. If so, work could begin on the pool. But first, we composed a piece for the family newsletter, before Diane checked insurance quotes online. Casting around for jobs to do, I applied second coats of paint to the bathroom and *mouton* hut, before prepping the lounge for painting.

At one point, François came over for Hoppie, but she blanked him; refusing to come down the field to him. Then to further annoy him, Lupé found some freshly deposited horse manure to roll around in.

'Oh, he has lain down in horse-shit. He must stay outside,' he said tartly.

When Hoppie finally deigned to saunter down the field, François spent half an hour washing and grooming her. After painstakingly removing ticks, he released her back into the field, where she immediately rolled around in a mud hole. Diane had just returned from La Flèche, and we had a quiet snigger as François walked away shaking his head.

Following an upturn in the weather, work began on building the pool. While Diane assembled some framework in the barn, I began digging out the bankside below the terrace. It needed to be excavated in three places to receive the mounting blocks for side struts. But when we tried fitting those struts there was a problem. Checking the instructions, I re-positioned the mounting blocks before drilling them. It'd been a long hot afternoon; and fuzzy-headed, we thought it was time to call it a day.

The work had been frustrating, with little to show for it. Also, sinking into the sand while we worked left us feeling unhappy with the base. One consolation was, the weather had improved dramatically, so a beautiful sunset stretched into a balmy evening enjoyed by us on the terrace.

We slept badly that night, both of us worried about the pool. And it didn't help our mood when we woke up to rain.

Mid-morning, François turned up. He'd promised to pop over sooner, but he apologised, saying he'd had an accident in his car; though, nothing serious thankfully. When he asked how the pool was coming along, I said we weren't happy with the level of the plot. It seemed to be sloping. Nipping over to Le Lavendu, he returned with Bertrand, carrying a home-made tool he used when landscaping. After some tutting and shaking of his head, he agreed to get Davide back to re-grade it. Utterly dismayed, I realised this meant starting over again, and moving eight tonnes of sand and the *tapis de sol* to get to the earth below. What a waste of time! Nevertheless it had to be done. The pool must be perfectly level, or the volume of water could be unequal on both sides. Standing on a *tapis de sol* or groundsheet, the pool could shift during use, causing the framework to twist.

We worked half-heartedly on other jobs for the remainder of the day, then, after a bath and our meal, we watched a programme called, 'No going back,' showing people like ourselves who'd opted to live abroad; some of them having lots more problems than us. It did nothing to help our mood, though, so we opted for an early night.

Worrying about mounting delays, I couldn't sleep. And it didn't help, when gunshots, from what I took to be hunters continued late into the night. When I mentioned it to François later, he said, 'It is not hunters. It is something to surprise the birds.'

Ah – a bird-scarer. So what were they targeting, owls?

Chapter 40

A foundation course

It was the beginning of May, and with rainclouds gathering overhead pushed by a westerly wind, we were better off working inside. I began in the bathroom while Diane fielded booking enquiries online. Mid-morning it brightened considerably, so, wheeling out the barrow, I shifted fifty six breeze blocks to the terrace site. Then with a batch of cement mixed, I began laying them.

As the day improved, cobalt blue skies peeped through lingering cloud. And as I worked methodically, Bertrand appeared, telling me that Davide would call by later to inspect the site. If he agreed with our findings, he'd turn up in the morning to correct the problem. He went on to say, even though François was a named driver on his car insurance policy, he was having problems getting his claim settled. Furthermore, he wasn't allowed a courtesy car. Well what a surprise! However, Véronique had saved the day; loaning him *her* car – while she used her bike.

Oh, wait till I tell Diane!

As Bertrand left, I continued cementing, finishing my third barrow-load as dusk settled. I was cleaning up when Bertrand and Davide appeared. Inspecting the site, Davide scratched his head and agreed that it didn't look level. But they insisted the site didn't need to be dug up again, suggesting, I lay concrete under the strut mounts to compensate, and construct a retaining wall along the lower edge to prevent slippage. I agreed it might work, but mentioned the manufacturer's warranty stipulations and our concerns as to client's safety. Reluctantly, he agreed to return and fix it for free. However, he was booked solid for the next couple of days. Damn!

Fuelled up on toast and coffee by six-thirty am, I opened the shutters to another glorious day. Tee-shirt off and sunscreen on, I began work on the terrace, which was coming along nicely. And with cement mixed, I was soon engrossed in the job. However, sunny or not, Diane stayed inside painting.

I continued until the cement ran out; driving to *La Poste* after lunch with Diane's insurance paperwork. With the diesel rumbling throatily, I proceeded to *Intermarché*'s garage to inflate a tyre. It had a slow leak which I'd meant to get fixed at *Robles Pneu*. But with no other reason to visit La Fléche, I'd been topping it up with my footpump. Sadly, that had now broken. An unfortunate coincidence, as, arriving at *Intermarché,* I found *their* pump had *also* given up the ghost. Sighing inwardly, I called into Gilles' garage to have it checked. (Yes I know, I know.) And of course, Alberte found a puncture. But not a *normal* puncture. Oh no! This one would be extremely difficult to fix due to the huge tyres.

Of course it would!

Long story short, I was ripped off again. In England, I could have had a remould fitted for less. But, I didn't dream it would be so expensive when I let him go ahead. Why do I never learn?

Diane hadn't been feeling well all morning, but when I got back and told her the story, she felt worse. I couldn't blame her. That garage would be the death of us.

Despite feeling rough, she'd begun laying cushion floor in the bathroom. Bought in a *Brico* sale, the weathered driftwood pattern looked realistic, plus it was warmer underfoot. We finished it together, then after re-hanging the door, we packed in.

Besides not feeling well, Diane had another reason to leave the bathroom in a hurry. When she was laying the cushion floor earlier, she'd heard footsteps in the hallway. She called out to me but got no answer. Well she wouldn't, would she? I was in Le Lude – and she was alone in the empty house!!

I rang Chris later, after trying unsuccessfully to text him throughout the day. Using his mother's house phone, he said he'd lost his mobile, and dealing with all the hassle that it caused had cheesed him off. It hadn't been the best of days for any of us, so after dinner, we balked at watching TV, and had an early night instead.

It was the end of May, and with time marching on, Diane checked the weather forecast. Sunny all day, with a light breeze and zero chance of rain, it couldn't be better. Kitted up for a sand moving marathon, we set off to barrow the eight tonnes from the pool site. Davide was due the next day, and though *he* should have done it, and the excavator would have made short work of it; we decided the risk of damaging the membrane was too great. No good crying over spilt milk. We just got on with it.

Though the skies clouded over at one point, it was still humid. Taking turns shovelling and barrowing left us with with three huge piles of sand. Rolling the membrane up in sections, we then tidied up the site. It was six fifteen by then, so I prescribed a hot bath, a meal, and a bottle of plonk while watching TV. Being dog-tired though, the TV and wine were put on hold in favour of another early night.

Our first guests were arriving in less than five weeks, and here we were, waiting for our newly laid pool base to be dug back up.

Davide arrived at eight fifteen; and after a brief discussion, he produced aerosol paint cans and marked the boundaries; then with a laser-level clipped to his excavator boom, he lined up on a tripod- mounted sensor and began.

It was like watching a master sculptor at work, as his machine skimmed earth from the surface, swivelled around on its turntable, and like a human arm, laid it exactly where it was needed. When an area was levelled to his satisfaction, it was tamped down firmly. Sometimes only a wafer thin scraping was required, but at other times a bucketful was distributed to widen the boundary.

With the site levelled to perfection, the membrane was laid back down. Then Davide took about ten minutes to reinstate the eight tonnes of sand – a job which would have taken us hours to do. Working in from the boundaries, he deposited bucketfuls of sand; avoiding the membrane by using the extended dipper arm. With the sand laid, he drove off site, leaving Diane and I to finish levelling it. We then laid out paving slabs, post supports, and finally base rails. By six thirty, we'd done all we could and went inside.

The nightmare continued the next day, as we began assembling the pool in earnest. After a couple of hours, we broke off to seek *tapi de sol,* used to protect the pool's base from the abrasive effects of the sand. We should've had it ready, but we'd been unable to find any before now. This time, after no success in Le Lude, we thought we'd try Saumur with its plethora of shops.

We set off after lunch, and with it being Saturday, we nipped into *Emmaus* for a quick visit first. We eventually found some *Tapis* at *Brico*; and after a quick scoot around *Gifi*, I drove home. With everything at hand for the pool build by then, we planned an early start in the morning.

Bright-eyed and bushy-tailed after breakfast, we began assembly. Following the instructions, we fitted the upright posts, attached the bottom rails around the perimeter then laid the *tapis*. And with the first of the two wall sections waiting nearby, the top rails were attached. Next, we attempted to feed the rolled wall section into the slotted bottom rails, but found that the gap between the top and bottom rails was insufficient.

Getting inside out of the sun, we checked the plans. Our conclusion was, the mounting blocks were set too high. Feeling quite sick by then, we had to dismantle it all and dig out the blocks. After re-setting them a centimetre deeper, it was all to do again.

We laboured on through the afternoon, hot, sweaty and cursing; our day ending at seven thirty when we went in absolutely knackered to eat. After a hot soak, it was another early night, dreading what we'd wake up to.

More problems surfaced the next morning, as we tried feeding the first roll of galvanized panelling along the track. However careful we were, sand kept falling into the track causing the panels to jam. Most of the problems occurred simply because we were short-handed. After saying it was a four person job and knowing we were on with it, Rob and Elaine had gone off to an event in the UK, and no-one knew when they'd return.

Heaving and straining, we'd unrolled the ten metre panelling along the tracking. It was within a metre of the end post. But that was it. It just wouldn't budge any more. Completely dispirited and barely speaking to each other by then, we secured what we'd managed to achieve with ropes then abandoned it.

I rang Rob later and they'd just gotten back. He promised they'd be over in the morning, saying, between the four of us we'd have it finished in no time. He said he'd show us where we'd gone wrong. I couldn't give a toss about that. I just wanted the damned thing finished!

Chapter 41

A pool with a view

It was a hot blustery morning. I just hoped the wind would drop before Rob and Elaine arrived. We breakfasted, did jobs around the house, and made sure that everything was ready for the build ... then we waited. They eventually arrived around one pm; and out at the site, they decided it would be easier to begin the side panel assembly again. With four people to keep control of the panelling it would unroll easier. So out it all came again, the measurements were re-checked, a couple of the blocks were adjusted and the rails re-fitted. Then we were shown the easy way to do the job.
They'd apparently followed a French manual and an instructional video when building *their* pool. This showed both rolls of panelling linked to each other; one person pulling, two keeping the panelling in the tracking, and the fourth unrolling it. Now why couldn't they say they had an instruction manual and video before we began? More to the point, why wasn't one provided with our kit?

From then on everything went smoothly – that is, until a freak gust of wind blew the panelling over and wrenched out the track. That was it, they said, they were leaving. They had somewhere else to be. And by the way, could I get them some of their stock from our shed.

Promising they'd return on Sunday, they left. But that meant another four days lost. Totally frustrated by then, we rolled up the panelling, stacked everything else in the barn, and switched to the terrace project.

We packed in at seven pm and sat down to our meal. After rounding off the meal with home-made strawberry ice cream for the comfort factor, we tried to relax watching TV, but the pool issue dwarfed everything. We really needed to get it finished – urgently.

Other outstanding jobs took up the next few days, as we did everything possible to spruce up the house and gardens ready for visitors.

With Friday's temperature still showing 30 degrees C at six pm, we'd put in a long shift working on the the terrace. Calling around on his way to deliver hay to the pony club, Bertrand seemed puzzled that the pool he'd seen half-erected a couple of days ago was now dismantled.

We had a big push on Saturday, finishing the downstairs bathroom and upstairs bedroom. Then, while Diane graded the angled bankside, I drove to the quarry for *genti,* or gravel to spread on the terrace. Being overloaded as usual when I returned, I became bogged down while reversing nearer to the terrace. Preoccupied with manoevering, I failed to notice pool struts that Diane had neatly lain out on the grass. The air was blue when Diane realised I'd driven over them, and after that, we were best kept apart.

It took hours of work trying to straighten them out properly, but worse was yet to come. An email arrived, saying Rob and Elaine wouldn't be coming in the morning as promised. They were visiting friends.

With both of us fuming after that, I shovelled out the gravel and unhitched 'Hippo.' Not trusting ourselves to speak to each other, Diane drove off to do some shopping, While, I finished the wall and laid the gravel.

After we unloaded the car on her return, we were hot, tired, and dispirited. But above all else, we were mad at Rob and Elaine. They'd promised to help us, then let us down repeatedly; this time at the eleventh hour to visit *'friends.'* What did that make *us* then? I'm afraid an injection of alcohol seemed obligatory after the email; and the evening spiralled into a bacchanalian music fest that ended in the wee small hours.

Not *too* early the next morning, we walked out to the terrace with our coffee to hold a council of war. We decided it was no good relying on anyone but ourselves. And with our stress levels off the chart, a special effort should be made to keep our tempers in check. Using our new found knowledge, we'd work our way through it somehow; we always did.

The day was sunny and calm; and despite some hair-raising moments involving chairs, ropes, and pegs to hold everything together, we did it. As we finally bolted the two ends together, the large ovoid shape was complete.

As the sun reached its zenith, the reflected heat rose to the high 40's. Climbing out of the structure dizzy with dehydration, we removed the ladder before going inside for drinks and a rest. After raking the base later with the sun setting behind us, everything was ready for fitting the pool liner in the morning.

We intended celebrating our achievement; but showered and fed, we just couldn't be bothered. Besides, Diane was suffering from a touch of sunstroke. Trying to be sensible for a change, we went to bed. What a day though!

It was another extremely hot day, the temperature soaring quickly to thirty five degrees C. With the ladder in place early, we climbed into the pool, laid the liner, and secured it to the walls. Then using the angle grinder, I cut out openings for the skimmer and pump. As I was taping the cut edges Véronique appeared, followed by Bertrand nursing a hangover after his parent's golden wedding celebrations yesterday.

Not so welcome later were Rob and Elaine, who arrived to check on progress. Maybe it was a guilt trip, but after giving us some advice they left us to get on with it. However, Rob did caution against tying the liner to the pool-rim in extreme heat, as the material may have expanded. When cool, it could contract and cause damage.

Frustratingly, it still wasn't cool enough by nine pm, so we packed in, had lots of ice cold juice, a snack and a cool shower before bed beckoned.

Thankfully, it was cooler and overcast the next morning; allowing us to climb into the pool, tie the liner, smooth out the wrinkles and run in enough water to cover the base. Diane then took on the onerous task, of crawling around on hands and knees for ages, smoothing out the creased surface.

Meanwhile, after mixing cement, I worked my way around the outside, filling in gaps in stone-work and checking that the tracking hadn't shifted. I then did a quick trailer run to the quarry for more *genti*. Barrowing it to the terrace, I met Diane climbing out of the pool totally dehydrated, her knees badly blistered from the hot rubber base. It would be stupid attempting more until the temperature dropped. So, hooking the hose over the pool rim and turning it on, we sat in the kitchen taking in fluids and chilling out.

Knowing it would take days to fill the pool, we turned off the supply after a couple of hours, during which we watched England play Trinidad in a World Cup match. Beers stood chilling in the fridge, but needing to be on my A game in the morning, they stayed there.

During the night, I was woken by a loud knocking noise *in the room*. Sat up fully alert, I then heard another double knock! Climbing carefully out of bed, I grabbed a torch and my 'cosh,' then had a good look around.

There was nothing to be seen!

It was extremely hot when we visited the pool after breakfast. Dividing our labour, Diane continued in the pool while I laid *genti* on the terrace. Needing lots more, I drove to the quarry for another load. By then it was 38 degrees C, and after shovelling it out and barrowing it to the terrace, I was ready for a long cool drink in the kitchen. Burnt to a frazzle, Diane climbed out of the pool and joined me inside.

Levelling the terrace after lunch, we grabbed pots of *crepi* and painted the surrounding walls. By mid-afternoon, Diane was suffering from sunstroke and covered in insect bites, so I suggested she go in, have a shower and a lie-down. After clearing up, I too had a cooling shower. The temperature eventually dropped a little, but it was still in the high twenties when we settled down to sleep.

The following morning, we were working in a heatwave trying to fill the pool from the well. Limiting the drain on our joint water source, we used the hose three times a day for short periods only. We felt guilty, as Bertrand also needed water for his animals and birds, and we both needed it for our gardens. But what else could we do? If we switched over to *eau- de-ville* the water was metered, and with that huge pool to fill, it would be prohibitively expensive. .

After switching on the pump, I went off to another hard day in the garden. Unfortunately, after hoeing between our burgeoning veggie crops, I forgot to turn off the water after the last fill and went off to bed. Visiting the bathroom at two-thirty am, Diane found that the system was dry. Nipping out quickly, I turned off the pump, allowing the level to build up again. By the time we got up for the day, things were back to normal.

At the end of the week the pool was half full. And it only needed apertures for the skimmer and water-pump, which we cut while standing in waist deep water. The rest was mainly cosmetic; laying paving stones for the ladder to stand on, and pea-gravel between the panelling and the lawn. Standing back, we smiled at each other. At last we had our pool!

Chapter 42

A brush with celebrity

Sat deep in thought at the top of the pool ladder, I stared down through the shimmering water. Reflecting the blue liner and azure sky, it looked deep and inviting. My reverie didn't last for long though, as I was interrupted by François, home from college. Ostensibly he'd popped over to 'inspect' the pool, but he had an ulterior motive. He needed our help for his upcoming English exam. After giving the pool his blessing, he made a bee-line for the terrace wall. Eyeing it up, he shook his head and said, 'It is not straight.'

'Oh,' I said. 'Which part?'

'All of it,' he said bluntly.

I tried explaining that I'd gone for an English dry-wall look, but he didn't seem impressed. With my workmanship trashed, he then asked what I intended doing with the scrap in the top field. I said I'd gather it up and trailer it to the *dechetterie,* but it would have to wait. After discussing his syllabus, he headed off home as I continued working.

Hearing an engine soon after, I looked up and spotted a familiar car on the bottom road. Ah – Rob and Elaine. Parked up, they made their way over to check out the pool. I said, due to all the hassle we had doubts regarding its construction. However, Rob said they'd felt the same way after finishing theirs.

'Nothing's perfect,' he said. 'But you've saved a big bill for professional help. Anyway, we're here to invite you for lunch on Sunday.'

Declining graciously, I said, with our first guests due soon, we couldn't spare the time. Replying waspishly, Elaine stated that she'd bought a load of food especially.

Too bad, you shouldn't take us for granted, I thought. *And where were you last week when you promised to help us?*

They hung around for a while, but the atmosphere was a little strained. After their departure, I headed out to the barn … and found a load of scrap. It was all neatly stacked and I know François meant well, but I didn't *want* it in there.

With the pool now established, fencing and posts awaited collection at *Brico*. But as it was Saturday, a trip to Saumur was on the cards first. After lunch, we scoured *Emmaus* for a bathroom cabinet; but unsuccessful, I bought Diane a birthday gift at *Intermarché*. Equally important, we found a pool skimmer and net when swinging by *Brico* to collect the fencing and posts.

Back home in the late afternoon, we checked our materials laid out in the barn. We also had fencing and posts, wood for a job in the en-suite, and tarpaulin for the terrace bankside. So no excuses then, it was time to crack on. Unfortunately, rushing to complete the jobs, the hose we'd left running into the pool was forgotten. Once again the well was sucked dry, and this time I had to apologise to Bertrand.

Another Father's Day; and after laughing at my cards over breakfast, I began working. With no time to delay, I started stone-painting the terrace breeze-blocks. While raking the pool embankment, Diane spotted Bertrand heading our way. He'd called over, to discuss how to best use the well. After checking on Hoppie, he returned as we set the tap running. However, half an hour later the flow stopped. Luckily, Bertrand was working in his garden, so shouting him over, he checked our water tank and found it empty. Knowing that *his* water pressure was okay as he'd just used it, he thought our pump must be at fault. What, again?

Oh great! No water for drinks, showers or the toilet. He suggested I fill our twenty five litre container from his standpipe while he rang the plumber. As it was threatening rain by then, I filled it and followed Diane inside.

Chris rang later; and enjoying a laugh with him, I forgot our problems for a while. But with the humidity rising, it came as no surprise when a squall rolled through the valley. With the doors and windows thrown open, cooling breezes circulated throughout the house. Refreshing though it was, the curtain of rain that followed robbed us of our Sky signal. With a feeling of *déjà vu,* we watched Billy Connolly on video while sharing a bottle of *rosé.*

Diane's birthday didn't get off to a brilliant start, as we were still without water. After popping over to check on the situation, Bertrand returned home to phone Mr B, reminding him of our plight. With Diane's celebrations on hold, we waited for Cigogne and his crew to arrive.

In the meantime, François turned up with his new lurcher puppy, a gangly, excitable replacement for the recently deceased Hermé. While offering his help if needed, he also wanted to discuss his school projects.

Shortly after breakfast, a brace of vans rattled past us containing 'the team.' After examining the pump down the well, Cigogne returned with François to give us his evaluation. It seems the pump was running okay – but not pumping water. Well since it was under warranty, what were they going to do about it? I asked. As usual, the answer was a non-commital shrug. Nevertheless, he went back, removed it, and took it to Angers for inspection, assuring me he'd return to fix the problem in the morning. Meanwhile, he'd connect us up to the *eau de ville* to tide us over. With the high cost of metered village water however, pool filling was put on hold, while I began erecting the fencing I'd bought.

To top off a memorable birthday, Diane pulled a muscle in her back and had to lie down. However, she rallied later when the Charpentiers arrived to wish her 'Appy Birsday.'

Feeling much better when the painkillers kicked in, she took a call from Chris wishing her Happy Birthday. After a hot soak in a herbal bath, the Sky signal had returned, so she relaxed watching TV.

The pool stood half full, and there was no news regarding the pump. With the clock winding down rapidly until our first guests arrived, desperation was setting in. As Diane still had back pain she took on lighter jobs – like chasing a client who'd paid his deposit, but not yet the outstanding balance. Meanwhile, I loaded the trailer with yet more rubbish, and took it to the *dechetterie.*

My final job was cleaning out a blocked drain, before settling down to watch England play Sweden in the World Cup qualifiers. At a vital point in the game the phone rang. It was a booking enquiry from someone wanting five star accomodation, plus a list of extras thrown in for free. *This is our new life,* I thought. *We'd better get used to it.*

As the pump was still a no-show in the morning, it was one hell of a shock when the water clouded over. With Algae forming on the liner, the previously clear water now resembled pea soup. Borrowing Bertrand's large hose and adaptor, I reluctantly switched over to *eau de ville;* my mind imagining euros gushing into the pool. Unfortunately, we had no choice.

While I tended to the pool, scrubbing the liner as it filled, Diane nipped off to *Bricomarché* to buy chemical additives and a P.H level indicator. Thankfully, with the filtration unit fitted and chlorine added, the water began to clear.

The next morning, Cignone returned with the pump. It was okay, he said. The problem was, it was set higher up the well than Bertrand's, so, as the level dropped, ours ran dry, while his continued running. With it coupled up and us reconnected to the well, we were back in action.

The water colour changed often over the next week, requiring the P.H levels to be monitored carefully. It was a worrying time, as on one occasion the water turned almost black. Oh, it was great fun, wading up to my waist in gunge, cleaning the slime off the liner base with a brush. Thankfully, it was pumped out through the filter, and it felt wonderful afterwards when I went for a shower.

With a week until our guests arrived, I began decorating the en-suite bathroom; finishing by staining the beams and knocking together a z-framed door. By then Diane had gone through the house like a whirlwind, but there was still so much to do.

I woke feeling sluggish after a windy night. Six days to go, and I couldn't sleep properly for worrying about outstanding work. How would we get it done in time? Thankfully, Nadine had offered to fly over to help us, and we were picking her up at Tours off the noon flight.

We began working at seven o'clock, breaking off for breakfast at ten. A quick drive to Tours saw us pulling into the car park as the plane was landing. Parked up, we rushed into the passenger lounge and waited near the arrivals terminal. Glancing around at the clock, I did a double-take. Waiting to enter the departure lounge was the celebrity chef Hugh Fearnley-Whittingstall, with his son Oscar. Aware how I value *my* privacy, but being a fan of his, I sidled over, quietly introduced myself, and said how much Diane and I enjoyed his TV shows. He replied, 'Thanks a lot, cheers.' Wishing him good luck, I casually moved away. I doubt anyone else even heard me.

As Hugh and Oscar vanished into the departure lounge the arrivals doors burst open, and there stood Nadine struggling with her luggage. Hefting it into the car boot, we headed home.

Chapter 43

We have paying guests

After a welcoming lunch on the sun-dappled terrace, I loaded up 'The Hippo' for the *dechetterie*. Leaving me to it, Diane showed Nadine the pool and our improvements, plus a list of outstanding work to be done. But before any of us did *anything*, Nadine was desperate to have a dip in the pool.

After unloading at the *dechetterie* later, I drove over to the quarry for more sand. Yes more! However, on the way back Sod's Law kicked in yet again. Passing the mushroom *cave,* I was held up in a traffic jam. A live power line had come down across the road, torn from an insulator during last night's storm. After waiting for some time an EDF van pulled up, and before long traffic began moving. Arriving home, though, I found the whole area was now without power.

With the sand unloaded, we did what we could without electricity. The service was finally restored at eight thirty pm, allowing us to save the contents of both the fridge and freezer. After an 'interesting' day, the evening turned into a wine-fuelled music singalong; which ended late for Diane and Nadine, who'd stayed up to watch the awesome might of an electrical storm.

On the Friday, I was woken early by a loud bang. It turned out to be Bertrand shooting a pine marten, which in addition to stealing eggs had attacked six of his new ducklings.

These, and twenty pullets, they were his fattening stock for Christmas.

Being wide awake afterwards, we ate a hearty breakfast before Diane and Nadine cracked on with inside jobs. Meanwhile, I had a list of ten to tackle outside, including the last section of fencing, so it was all hands to the pumps. We hadn't Nadine's help for long, as she was headed home on Monday's flight. So like Diane, she was working flat out.

Mid-afternoon it began raining; and after rushing to get in the washing, it hung festooned around the room drying. When dry it was ironed, as we worked on into the evening. After a late finish then a shower, a bottle was opened to celebrate a job well done.

Up with the larks on Monday, I did some strimming while Nadine adjusted to flying home. Following last minute packing and a filling breakfast, it was a rush to the airport.

With its usual efficiency, the Ryanair flight arrived bang on time, and after a group hug and special thanks, Nadine strode off into the departure lounge. After watching her plane take off, we headed for Le Lude to do food shopping.

We'd been experiencing starting problems with the Shogun lately, so when we left *Intermarché,* it came as no surprise when I found the battery was flat. Dumping everything into the car, I phoned Gilles' garage. Alberte the mechanic arrived in a van and jump-started 'The Shoggie,' but suggested we return to the garage to test the battery. As we drove in, Bertrand, who was working on his vintage car, strolled over to check out our problem. After testing, Alberte declared the battery had two dead cells, which encouraged Gilles to begin pricing batteries. Peering over his glasses, he said a heavy duty battery, plus the call-out and inspection charge would cost me 100 euros.

While a battery was being sourced, Bertrand, with his head under the bonnet noticed the alternator belt was loose; something which had escaped Alberte's notice. When I pointed this out, our subdued mechanic tightened it. Once fired up, the battery held its charge; but insisting I leave the car on test overnight, Gilles lent me a car to get us home.

Saturday morning, and with lots still to do before our guests arrived, we had a major problem. As the clients had booked the whole house, we'd arranged to rent Phil's caravan for *our* accomodation. However, he'd rung last night, saying he'd suddenly decided to use it while following the Tour de France. Aaaah! We were out on a limb.

We were at Gilles' garage when it opened. After holding charge overnight the battery was fine, so paying 48 euros for the call-out and extras, (no dead cells then?) I handed him back his old Citroën and drove off. Right, let's get back and sort this out. People were renting our house for a week, and we had nowhere to stay.

Ringing around locally, there was no accomodation to be had; so with the clock ticking, we booked a pitch on Le Lude's *Aire de le Loisire* campsite. Then, driving to *Brico,* we bought among other things, a two person tent. Charging back to the farm, we began tackling our list of jobs. The largest was cleaning out the pool, followed by rigging up a gazebo. Other small, but essential jobs then followed, swallowing up our time. And after storing stuff in the granary and the *cave*, I then found, I had both hornet's and ant's nests to contend with. But finally everything was done.

After a shower then a bathroom tidy, we sat completely drained waiting for our guests. When there was still no sign of them by seven pm, a worried Diane rang them on her mobile. They were surprised to hear from her. Believing they'd booked to arrive the next day, they were staying overnight in a hotel in Paris. It was pointless playing the blame game; that's life. Well ours anyway.

Waking at nine am after a lie-in, we drove to *Brico* to buy more camping gear: chairs, a gas cooker and a lamp, plus anything else we could think of for a week under canvas. Leaving the store, our attention was grabbed by four English guys, driving an Austin Healey, an E type Jag, and two MG's. They were heading south after visiting Le Mans. We chatted for a while but the clock was ticking. With our accommodation waiting, it was back home to eat then pack for the campsite.

Mid-afternoon, François rode by on Hoppi, saying he'd cut the top triangle of our field to prevent *challon,* or thistles from spreading. But as this fenced off section belonged to the late Monsieur Ami, he'd left it where it lay as it didn't belong to either of us.

We gathered all our equipment as he rode off, and fifteen minutes later, we were laying it out on our pitch. After trying for some time to set it up – and making a dog's breakfast of it, an old French guy and his granddaughter offered to help. Being pressed for time, the young girl said they'd finish it for us while we went back to receive our guests. During the conversation, Diane's phone began buzzing. It was a message from the guests. They'd arrived at the farm and were waiting for us. Aaahh!

Tearing up the drive, we found the family waiting. Apologising for the delay, we gave them a quick tour explaining everything, while giving special reference to the pool. Diane showed them the welcome pack in the fridge, a list of directions to shops and other info, and they were happy. Then leaving them to it, we shot off back to the campsite, promising to return in the morning.

Back at our pitch, our tent had been set up perfectly and everything was ship-shape. Thanking the old man, I handed him a bottle of wine as a thank-you, before sorting our equipment. *Finally we could relax,* I thought. However, as I sat down my chair collapsed! Then later, while watching the World Cup final at the site clubhouse, I broke *another* chair. I was beginning to think we were cursed. To help lift my spirits, though, France threw the game away after Zinadin Zidane was sent off for a foul. Aw, what a shame!

After a surprisingly comfortable night's sleep, the shower block's amenities claimed our attention. Then it was breakfast for two! During the tidying up there was a call from our guests. The grille wasn't working. Not a problem, Diane assured the group leader, it's French, therefore it's different. We drove over and found everyone enjoying themselves, either sunbathing or splashing about in the pool. Another girl was doing exercises on the lawn in a temperature of thirty degrees C. Hey, if that's what floats your boat! After Diane demonstrated the cooker, the mother invited us to have a drink and chat with them on the terrace.

Driving into town afterwards, we browsed around the shops before heading back to the site, where we read and relaxed. After a day spent finding ways to fill in time when we felt we should be working, Diane served up a meal and a couple of drinks. Then it was off to our airbeds, feeling tired, but strangely content.

Chapter 44

Living the dream

Our second night's sleep in the tent wasn't as blissful as the first. We woke up as stiff as boards after tossing and turning all night. But following a trip to the shower-block then a hearty breakfast, we took a stroll around the site as it stirred into life. Our morning was then spent reading, before an urge to get off site sent us walking into town in the afternoon.

Feeling hot and uncomfortable when we returned at six thirty, the site pool looked inviting, but we were directed back to the office for tickets. Paying for entry, I asked if shorts were okay for swimming, and was assured they were. In the changing rooms, though, it was a different story, as the attendant insisted I borrow speedos from the office. Yuk!

Nevertheless, the swim was sublime, the pool cool and refreshing, though, the facilities were overated in their advertising. Annoyingly, I ended up with sunburn, and spent a painful night dozing upright in the car.

Over the next couple of days, we became enmeshed in campsite life. But after a shower and breakfast that first morning, checking on our house-guests became our priority. They were doing fine and enjoying the solitude, so returning to the campsite the pool was hard to ignore.

The afternoon saw us invited to an evening shindig at one of the caravans, as the owners were headed home the next morning. Arriving after dinner, we met lots of people, drank our fair share of wine, and had a few laughs, before wandering off at eleven thirty as the party ended.

Up early the next morning, I made coffee, but Diane didn't appear as usual to claim her cup. *Strange,* I thought, looking into the tent. Oh boy! She was a mess. She'd tripped over a guy rope while going to the toilet block during the night. Her hands, knees and face were scraped, so I went over to deliver apologies for her absence, while wishing the caravanners goodbye. Diane waved them off from a distance, and after treating her wounds, we visited *Intermarché* to buy meat for a cookout later. It was no surprise to me that she wasn't feeling up to the *moule et frites* festival in town, or the firework display afterwards.

Going for a morning stroll at seven am, I came across a pegged out section on the riverbank hosting a fishing competition. After watching the enthusiastic participants for a while, I returned to the tent. On the next pitch along, a French family had arrived, and were trying to erect a caravan awning – much to the amusement of everyone nearby. Soon, another family joined them, and before long, the corner site was taken up with caravans, awnings and tents. Setting up a giant air fan and a huge fridge, the group began partying, so using our get out of jail free card, we walked into town to check out an upcoming jazz festival.

Returning onsite, we found a chaotic crowd embroiled in a rescue mission. They were trying to help a guy who'd collapsed in a toilet block. People were panicking, some were screaming, saying he was a diabetic, and asking when the paramedics were going to arrive. *Step back and give the poor bloke some air for God's sake,* I thought.

Oh you certainly see life on a campsite!

The travelling pastry van pulled up tooting its horn. And as Diane went for our breakfast snack, I continued packing. It was Saturday and our guests were leaving, so driving to the farm for ten am, we found the family had cleaned up, dishes were washed, and bed-sheets were whizzing away in the washing machine. After a quick inspection, Diane returned their damage-waiver cheque. And after writing a nice comment in the visitor's book, they drove off. Thankfully, the only problem they'd had was with the boiler. But they were impressed when a new plumber we'd found arrived quickly to fix it. It was a different story when we had a good look around, though. We found some minor damage, and a thorough clean was required. It wasn't bad, though, and was a valuable lesson for the future.

After a comprehensive clean and pool check, things were almost back to normal. We timed ourselves; aiming to finish no later than three thirty pm. On a change-over weekend, new arrivals could check in at four pm.

Our next visitors were a family booked for a fortnight, beginning on the Saturday. But this group might prove awkward. The husband had asked if his brother and wife could stay over for a few days, plus, could another brother park his caravette onsite for a while. Apart from expecting this for free, there were by-laws to consider, as well as the effect on our neighbours. A regretful no was our answer; accompanied by directions to the local campsite.

We thought it could also present a problem when they left. What state might the house be in? But that was next week. There was a lot to do before then.

Sipping coffee while stood at the kitchen window, I watched Madame Renard's friend tear past in his Lada Niva heading up to the woods. Some said he made *eau-de-vie* in a still up there, whereas François swore he put out food to attract deer for hunters. How would I know? He never stopped, or even acknowledged my existence.

With the house tidy and jobs done, we decided to kill two birds with one stone. Setting off with our sketch pads to

Luché Pringé, we'd check out its campsite. Then driving to Mansigné, we'd also check theirs, before heading to the man-made beach. As it was the sketch pads weren't even opened, but we had a great afternoon on the beach.

Arriving back, I cleaned out the pool, checked the P.H and chlorine levels, then as it was 39 degrees C at four pm, I went in for a swim. Absolutely gorgeous!

Visiting garden centres took precedence over the next week, searching out plants and equipment. We got back at two pm one day with the temperature at 44 degrees C, and found Bertrand tearing around the field on his old combine harvester cutting the rape-seed crop. Wearing vintage motorcycle goggles, a bandanna, shorts, tee shirt and flip-flops, he was a sight to behold. Unfortunately, the cutting caused dust, chaff, and insects to settle on the pool. While skimming the surface with the net, we scrambled to get the cover on.

The weather broke after the heatwave, with a predicted storm lashing the area. As thunder and lightning swept across the valley, we lost the Sky signal, the computer crashed, and the pool cover was swamped. But looking on the bright side, it was cooler and made sleeping easier.

We'd managed to ring Michael before everything went pear shaped; then Nadine rang, asking if we were okay. We assured her we were. It was just another day at the office.

Back online after the storm abated, Diane checked out the car tax, as we hadn't received a reminder. While she checked her e/mails, I took some photos for her updated advert. Unfortunately the USB cable for transferring them to the computer was missing. After scouring the house, Diane contacted Nadine to ask if she'd seen it whilst visiting. She rang back saying she'd found it in her hand-luggage!

Shelving that plan until we found a replacement, we addressed storm damage in the garden. Finished at seven forty five, we bathed, then relaxed with a couple of beers on the terrace.

Waking to a sunny Friday, we ate breakfast then began fitting solar lighting on the pool bankside. Then with the garden watered, Diane drove into La Flèche for the USB cable and last minute shopping. Grabbing a broom, I began at the head of the drive, clearing clippings left by the *commune's* hedge-cutting tractor. With our guests due the following afternoon, first impressions were important.

Returning with the cable, Diane transferred the photos to our website. Though frustrated by the snail-like dial-up, she was grateful for Nadine's help connecting it to the French system during her visit. Luckily, she'd just closed the computer down; as a 'BOOM,' signified more thunder and lightning. After one particularly close strike, we lost the computer signal, TV and lights. We tried reading by candlelight; and though it was fun, we decided it was easier to turn in for the night.

The storm raged on until the next morning, when we awoke to carnage. With our visitors due around four pm, I strode out, to be confronted by a smashed table and parasol on the terrace. Leaving Diane to sort out other damage, I uncovered the pool, cleaned the outer panelling and terrace furniture then drove to *Brico* for a replacement table. I found the only ones available were coloured green, but due to time constraints, I had to take one. I'd use it elsewhere later.

After setting up the table, we shared the remaining jobs. Then just before four the phone rang. The family were in Le Lude and heading our way.

When they arrived, they were a nice couple with a grown daughter and three grandchildren – two girls and a disabled boy. They loved the house and pool; and living in London, they appreciated the wide-open landscape and covered car parking in the barn. The brother with the caravette had gone to the campsite, while the other, a soldier on leave from Afghanistan mightn't make it, they said. As a patriotic supporter of our troops, I felt guilty then. But if they'd had their way, there'd have been at least ten using our home.

After giving the family the grand tour, we left them to it and drove to the shops. Heading back to the campsite past the farm, I was concerned to see smoke gushing from the chimney. The temperature was over 30 degrees; so worried that there was a problem, I drove up and knocked at the door. Were they cold, I asked? Did they need extra blankets? Getting a blank response, I mentioned the smoke. 'Oh no,' said the Dad. 'Everything's fine.'

He'd decided to burn my decorative varnished logs to see what the fire looked like when it was lit!

Chapter 45

The Amsterdam connection

Back on the campsite we'd secured a better pitch. And being experts by then, we soon had the tent erected and everything squared away. We felt smug – until we realised we'd left our stove at the farm. Dammit!

We woke early the next morning, famished and covered in insect bites. Our evening bar-snack was a distant memory, and due to the missing stove, breakfast *de jour* was a cobbled together cold snack and a bottle of lukewarm water.

Mmm. Delicious!

With breakfast plates washed, a stroll into Le Lude to check out its *vide greniere* seemed like a good idea. The skies had cleared by then, and walking around, we met Jean from the *cave* and the guy who ran the *dechetterie*. We only made one purchase – a stove. The stall-holder wanted five euros when I asked the price, and before I could speak, Diane jumped in with, 'Three euros, okay Monsieur?'

Returning to our tent after a long walk around, we lay reading inside until the sun sank behind some trees. We could have used a swim; but settled for a shower, a meal, and a few drinks instead. However, still wide awake at two thirty am, I dressed quietly and went for a walk around the site. It was deserted as I'd expected; and with the moon covered by cloud, I felt like a vampire as I strode past sleeping campers.

Calling over to the house after breakfast, we found it deserted, so we emptied bins, checked the pool, watered the garden and picked up our mail. It seemed the families had congregated for a party at some time. We took away three empty champagne bottles, two one litre wine bottles, and a dozen varied beer containers.

Returning to the campsite for our sketch-pads, we drove through picturesque countryside seeking inspiration. Parked by the river in La Flèche drinking coffee from our flask, we were unable to drum up any enthusiasm for drawing. It was as if we were living in a vacuum. Our schedule had become a routine of calling around to the farm to check on the family, tending to the pool and gardens and disposing of rubbish. We did some work when we could, but only when the family weren't there. They'd paid for privacy – though, we were invited for drinks and a chat occasionally.

Apart from looking after the gardens and servicing the pool, we attended to business, like visiting *Hotel Impot*, Anger's tax office. But frustrated at being unable to do much else, we decided visiting some of the area's attractions seemed a good idea, not having had the time before. We drove to many chateaux in the area, enjoying d'Ussy, Brezac, Chambord – which was special, and Villandry with its wonderful gardens and fish pools.

One of the most enjoyable to us though was our own Chateau Le Lude; where on one open day, a stall selling mole deterrents took our eye. Being troubled by molehills on our lawns, I asked the stallholder's advice. He sold plants which repelled moles, he told me, but they had to be laid out in regimented lines, exactly five centimetres deep and fifteen centimetres apart, and laid at a forty five degree angle. What happens if doing all that doesn't work? I asked. Sucking in his breath, he suggested we poison them, shoot them with a shotgun, or put explosives in their tunnels. Then what about the lawn? I asked. A wry shrug was his answer.

Besides these excursions, we booked a canoeing trip on the Loire, and relaxed watching local *boules* competitions. But the campsite itself was a rich source of entertainment, with its karaoke bar, grand BBQ night, and the interaction between the diverse mix of holidaymakers.

On the Thursday, Diane decided to walk into Le Lude alone, while I drove to the quarry to pay our monthly bill. We met up afterwards at *Intermarché*, where we chatted to an ex-pat English couple in the car park who went on to become good friends. While loading their French-plated car, they'd noticed our GB sticker. Apparently, they'd lived half a mile away from us for two years and we'd never met them. They were a font of knowledge and had a circle of ex-pat friends. After an initial chat in the car-park, they invited us to visit them at their home on the Monday.

Racing a threatening storm, we made it back to the tent safely, despite mini-whirlwinds gusting across the site. Sat outside drinking and chatting by lamplight later, the air had cleared so we hoped sleeping would be easier.

We'd booked to go canoeing the next day, but at first it didn't look promising. Though, with the weather being overcast and cold, at least flies weren't a problem.

Arriving at reception at two pm, we met an instructor. After basic instruction, like a swan with two cygnets, he shepherded us upriver in his kayak. Once he deemed us safe to navigate unaided, he left us to it. We set off on the placid river, the sun strengthening by then and dragonflies skimming the water ahead of us. With our paddles cleaving the mirror-like water, we glided past the château gardens, headed for 'The Barricade,' a huge log jam upriver.

When we arrived children were diving and swimming. After watching their antics, we explored the backwater, paddling beneath overhanging willow trees. At peace with the world, two and a half hours just slipped by.

Our usual Saturday excursion to Saumur was preceded by a visit to the house.When we arrived to check the pool, a guy introduced himself as our guest's soldier brother. He and his wife were sat alone at the terrace table. Remembering my thoughts on his service, we left them in peace and drove to Montreux Bellay.

After strolling by the river then climbing the long staircase into town, we found a quaint old restaurant for an early lunch. Then with the bill settled, I drove off to Saumur, where we bought a few items at *Emmaus,* before buying food and drink at *Leclerc.* It seems hypocritical saying this, but we felt overwhelmed by crowds of tourists, mostly English. I understood then how the French must feel.

To crown my day, I was forced to *buy* a pair of speedos before I was allowed to swim in the damned campsite pool.

As we ended the first week of our fortnight's stay on the site, Marika the Dutch receptionist came over to say we'd have to move pitches. A couple had pre-booked our site weeks before, and were due the next day. It was raining at the time, but as soon as the sun had dried the site, we lifted the tent bodily and carried it to another pitch two spaces away. Job done!

We'd begun prepping our meal when a Seat hatchback drew up nearby. With the boot emptied, a young couple began setting up a huge khaki-coloured polytunnel tent. Their toddler son ran around playing until it was finished, then they all disappeared inside.

It's a bit cramped brewing up in a car – but necessary when your tent is completely drenched after an overnight storm. I'm sorry if it sounds like it was always raining. That *definitely* wasn't the case. But when a rainstorm hits in France, it's usually dramatic and worthy of a mention.

After a shower and breakfast, Diane charged up her phone, using the pitch socket and our extension cable. I'd been trying to contact Michael for two weeks, on his house phone, his mobile, and by texts – all without luck. We'd try again later, but after posting off birthday cards to Dylan and Ben, we were meeting up with our two new friends Ron and Joan. Taking the road out of Le Lude, I passed the old château gate-house, and found their place a little way along. It was a small but pretty house, with well tended gardens, a barn and guest cottage. When we pulled up they were entertaining family visitors, but made us welcome. One of the young girls had been stung by a wasp; the second time in a matter of days, she said, and the discussion on how to tackle the critters helped break the ice.

After an entertaining inaugural visit, we returned home to check on the pool. It was as well we did, as the increased temperature had turned the water dark green. Luckily, the family were out for the day, so we gave the pool a shock treatment which began working almost immediately. Some partying had obviously taken place, as all the garden chairs were drawn up around the co-joined terrace tables which were draped with solar powered lights. Another clue was the pile of *sixty five* empty bottles we took to a bottle bank – emptied since our last visit *two days* before.

Back at the campsite, I was sat outside reading when the tall young guy from the polytunnel tent passed on his way from the toilet block. Stopping, he said, 'I find it strange that you have a large car and a small tent, whereas, I have a small car and a large tent.'

And that was my introduction to my new friend Johannes, a soldier from Amsterdam. That meeting was followed by an invitation to pop over for drinks later, where we met his wife Guda and their son Jappe.

After yet more overnight rain, Johannes came over with a fly sheet and ropes, which not only made the tent more waterproof but extended our living space considerably. Following another pleasant evening, where Johannes and I drove one helluva distance for Indian takeaway, we were invited to their tent again the next evening. However, there was a stipulation. I must dress in dark clothes.

Turning up mistified, I discovered I was accompanying Johannes on a metal detecting expedition. Apparently, he planned to investigate the perimeter of a local archeological site – without permission and with me as his lookout! To trot out a well used phrase, what could possibly go wrong?

Driving slowly along a woodland track without lights, we arrived at the site perimeter. Johannes was soon out, kitted in camouflage and sweeping the area with his metal detector.

Then all hell broke loose, as barking dogs and shouts from close by told us we weren't alone. Ducking low and racing across the site, we saw lights come on across a nearby road. Some guys then climbed into a van, which started up and headed our way. Skirting the edge of the site, we shook off our pursuers and made it to the car.

'I'll just make one or two quick passes,' Johannes whispered, and 'beep beep,' he had a signal. Under a centimetre of gravel in the car park, he found a Roman cistercese coin.

'This makes it all worthwhile,' he said.

Really?

Anyway, we made it back safely, and the ladies seemed impressed by our commando mission. After a few beers everything took on a rosier glow; and after cleaning the coin, Johannes said it was the best example of its type in his collection.

It was the end of the week, and our Dutch friends were leaving. Handing back their flysheet, we waved them off. Then, dismantling *our* tent, we headed back to the farm.

We arrived to find our outgoing family had made an attempt at cleaning up, but bearing in mind their disabled son's needs, Diane just handed them back their damage waiver cheque and wished them a safe journey.

Following a thorough clean up, the house was ready for our next visitors. But *this* time when we moved out, it was into Ron and Joan's cottage at Le Lude. After hearing of our camping experience, they made the offer unconditionally. And for the remaining bookings until the end of the season, it became our home away from home.

At the season's end, the house was locked down; and after a long tiring drive, we boarded the ferry back to the UK.

Chapter 46

Could this be the end?

We arrived at Stewie and Helen's on the seventh of November. Our mission, once we'd settled in was to find work again – quickly. As before, Diane signed up for Asda, while based on my previous experience with Boots, I filled a similar vacancy at their Newcastle branch. These jobs would sustain us until our second letting season in France.

Not wishing to bore the reader too much, I've condensed the next section.

After another eventful winter with the Prows, running the farm as a business became our main focus. And with a successful letting season supplemented by e/bay marketing behind us, we headed off once again for Stewie and Helen's in October, where Diane threw herself once again into the eager arms of Asda. As a departure for me though, I found a short term job as quality controller at a supplier to Nissan North-East. Then, moving on when the contract ended, I valeted and delivered vehicles for a van hire company.

At the end of a profitable 2007 season in France, October found us headed back to the UK yet again. This time we were staying with Nadine in Coxhoe near Durham.

By then, Diane was a regular seasonal worker with Asda, whereas, at first I was jobless. Registered with various agencies, I also chased other jobs, including a few weeks working at a recycling centre renovating garden machinery.

Then, during an agency interview, where I was offered a totally unsuitable job, a placement officer stepped in after reading my CV, saying she had a better job to offer. She arranged an interview at Durham Castle for a job as concierge and night security officer.

That position turned into one of the most satisfying I'd ever undertaken, working in magnificent surroundings alongside students and masters alike. The hours were eight pm until eight am four days a week. After checking students and staff out in the evenings and collecting their keys, I locked the halls of residence, Tudor-like kitchens, the grand banqueting room and student bars among many others. Following the lockdown, I did regular security patrols throughout the night.

On my first shift, the atmospheric chapel with its ornate carvings gave me thought for reflection. And, climbing up spiral stairs to the minstrel's gallery, I imagined medieval players seated at their instruments. In the master's lounges, the odours emanating from weathered old leather furniture, cigars and brandy, lent an air of opulence which was both timeless and re-assuring.

Three occurences stand out in my time there. On one occasion, I was called out to confront intruders on the castle battlements. Not knowing how many there were, or what I was walking into, I pretended to radio imaginary security guards for help, shouting out loud that police were on the way. At that, three teenage boys leapt out of nearby bushes. I collared one, while the other two jumped the low stone wall and ran away. Escorting my trespasser off the premises, I sent him home with a caution.

The second was when a fire alarm went off in student accommodation. I had a limited time to assess the location, before the fire service turned out automatically. After doing relevant checks, I found it was in outsourced premises in Durham city, and I had to run down to meet the responders.

Luckily it was a minor incident involving overloaded circuits; but I arrived to find dozens of students and a fire crew waiting for me, as I held master keys for the building.

And last – but very *definitely* not least; I was securing the grand hall one night. It was the end of term, the students had left for Christmas holidays; and, though their rooms were available for rental, none were occupied at the time. Knowing that I was alone in the building, I locked the huge oak door behind me, switched off the lights, and set off by torchlight along the room. Weaving between rows of refectory tables and bench seats, I was acutely aware of stern looking figures staring down from old oil-paintings. And through stained glass windows, moonlight cast a kaleidescope of colour around the room. While, high above me in the Minstrel's Gallery, suits of armour appeared to be moving. Heading for the door at the end of the room, the only sound was my echoing footsteps – until suddenly the silence was broken – by a loud *cough* behind me.

Now, I've had the hairs stand up on the back of my neck before, but never like *this*. Striving to stay calm, I forced myself to walk slowly to the door, insert the key, then with the door opened, I spun around. There was nothing there.

Apart from those occasions, the job was mostly routine, but rewarding on so many levels.

Unfortunately, while minding the boys for Nadine one day, I fell while chasing after Ben, who'd run off in the park towards the main road. The accident left me with torn rotator cup and shoulder strap ligaments which impeded my mobility in my job. And as I never seemed able to find time for reconstructive surgery, the injury still affects me today.

In 2008 Britain was hit by a financial meltdown, as the pound plummeted against the euro. Bookings were down as foreign travel for Brits became prohibitively expensive, and my pension and other sterling transactions were devalued substantially.

On the farm we'd been living in a caravan we'd towed from the UK, while visitors enjoyed our home. This year it was imperative that we find work to tide us over the winter.

But first, our final visitors arrived from England.

Following some sketchy planning, Chris drove down with two friends, Mark, and Paul – A.K.A Vasey. As unattached guys they had a great time, sampling the food, wine and beers of the area. We didn't even have to ask for help, they piled in enthusiastically. And when they weren't working, they visited areas of interest to them, including Le Mans, and an adventure park with a go-kart track. Most nights were spent partying together, and the quiet farm was often enlivened by loud music, as using brooms, mops or whatever came to hand, we sang along to pop groups. They only stayed for a week – but what a week!

It was soon after they left that we began winding things down. Locking up the house and caravan, we left once again for the ferryport. Due to a change of circumstances this time, our destination was Hull, where we were staying with Kay in her small rented flat as a stop-gap. Once we'd found work, we'd seek alternative accommodation. Unfortunately, just as Diane joined Asda, and I registered with agencies, someone shopped Kay to the council regarding over occupancy. We were forced to find a B+B immediately.

However, in the rush to move out, we rented a bed-sit by phone, in what later seemed to be a halfway house. We'd spotted a single woman and a male/female couple on our initial visit, but once moved in, apart from female staff, Diane found herself as the only woman in a building housing seventeen men. As it was, they were all polite and friendly, so we decided to tough it out while looking for somewhere more suitable. The facilities could have proved a problem, but with juditious planning, we managed to nab a bathroom after cleaners had been in, and were first in for meals. Also, with a garden to relax in, Kay within walking distance, and Hull to explore, things could have been worse.

Once settled in, we established a routine. Diane was working the night shift at Asda, while I worked at Hull General Hospital in the catering department on dayshift. Until something better turned up, it would have to do.

It seems hard to believe looking back, but due to the financial slump in both France and the UK, we spent the winter of 2008, and the whole of 2009 in Hull.

As Diane continued to work at Asda, the agency found me various jobs, both in hospitals and social care. The contracts, mostly short term were not what I'd have chosen. But they were all that was available at the time.

Having befriended a young lady at the jobcentre who realised I was keen to work (unlike many she dealt with,) I was offered jobs. One was as carer for a quadraplegic guy. I often drove him out in his mobility vehicle, helping him to vicariously enjoy his passion for flying radio controlled model airplanes. And working at both of Hull's main hospitals in various roles, I serviced I.C.U units and oncology wards; regularly coming into contact with suffering and death.

Thankfully it also had its lighter side, as on another contract, I had many a laugh working as part of a deep cleaning team dressed like C.S.I in haz-mat suits.

Spending 2009 in the UK enabled us to build up our French bank account for our return in April 2010. By then we'd traded in the thirsty Shogun for a Renault Laguna, as not only was it uneconomical on fuel, it was developing problems.

As previously mentioned, the men in our lodgings were invariably polite, and left us to our own devices – except for one particular day. After her night shift, Diane was trying to sleep, while I in turn tried to keep quiet – a difficult task in a bed-sit. Suddenly, loud heavy metal music boomed out along the landing. It was impossible to ignore, and almost blasted Diane out of bed. Nipping quickly along the landing, I knocked on the door of the music fan. It was opened by a tall thirty something guy, and I explained that Diane had worked a night shift and was trying to sleep. Asking politely if he could turn down the volume, he replied, 'Sure, no problem mate,' and the noise subsided.

I'd just gotten back when the volume was ramped back up even louder. Before I could return to remonstrate with the guy, the manager shouted at him to turn the noise down. All went quiet for a few minutes, then 'BANG,' our door shuddered violently, and a voice shouted, 'Get out here you old bastard.'

Half asleep, Diane jumped, and said, 'What's happening?'

'God only knows, but I'm going to find out.'

'Be careful,' she said.

'BANG,' again. This time, I opened the door and saw the raging young guy. 'What's your problem?' I shouted. And at that, he shouted,'You're my effing problem.' And running forward, he slammed me back against the door. Bouncing back, I leapt at him, grabbed him in a neck hold and forced him down. As I squeezed harder, he shouted, 'Gerroff you're gonna break my glasses.'

Furious by then, I shouted, 'I'll break your bloody neck if you don't get back into your room.'

Too late, the manager shouted up the stairs, 'Come on lads, let's stop the brawling eh?'

To which I replied, 'This is your job. Get him into his room and keep the noise down.' Then throwing the idiot to one side, I went back into our room.

That wasn't the end of it, though. Later there was a polite, but firm knock on the door. I'd already heard the manager talking to someone with an authoritive sounding voice, so replying like a worried old man, I asked, 'Yes, who is it?

'It's the police,'a voice stated.

'Can you prove that,' I replied. 'Some maniac along the landing just attacked me. It could be you for all I know.'

He held his warrant card up to the spy-hole in the door. I took my time reading it then opened up. There stood a police sergeant, with a WPC behind him. After asking both Diane and myself what'd happened, the sergeant despatched the WPC to take a statement from my assailant while he took ours. A few moments later, crashing and yelling preceded my aggressor being marched along on his tip-toes, hands cuffed behind him.

'What's happened here then?' the sergeant asked.

'Oh, not much sarge. He just told me in graphic sexual detail what he'd like to do to me,' she said calmly.

'Right sir, I don't think we need bother *you* any more,' said the sergeant, and the trio departed.

The next morning at breakfast, the weirdo was back after spending a night in the cells. The trouble had arisen because he thought I'd complained to the manager about the noise. I warned the so called manager to keep him away from Diane and myself, or I wouldn't be responsible for my reaction. After he had a quiet word with him over a beer on the doorstep, the guy left.

Soon after that the fire alarm began clanging, and the building was cleared. The lunatic had stuffed tea-towels in the microwave, switched it on and walked out.

It was soon afterwards that we left for France.

Chapter 47

A tragic end

Our intention when we returned to France was to contact *Immobiliere's,* with a view to selling the house. We had no bookings, but we'd built up funds to carry us through. We'd tried our best to keep our dream alive, but we'd had enough of living like nomads. The dream was turning into a nightmare. We still had a small mortgage to pay, but rejected ideas of borrowing, either from family or financial institutions. We hadn't lived in la Ferronerie for almost eighteen months; and though we'd always paid our way, squatting in other people's homes had lost its appeal. And that last experience in Hull had been the final straw. There was no sign of an economic revival anytime soon, and forced with an unknown period of living like this, we called time.

Contacting Jane's agency and others, we put the farm on the market. Then meeting up with our neighbours who were pleased to see us back, I had to shoot down their plans, saying they were unviable. Once again, I gave Bertrand the opportunity to buy most of the land, saying if he wasn't interested, we'd be forced to sell up and move. Once again, he declined. After that meeting, our relationship with our neighbours soured. They became distant, avoiding us whenever possible. However, they agreed reluctantly that there was nothing else to be done. So that was it then, our friendship had died.

We could understand how they felt, up to a point. Their help had been invaluable over the years. But on the other hand, Bertrand had often treated our farm as his own; especially when we were away in the UK for long periods. Though realising he kept it viable while we were away, we'd heard rumours that he was claiming E.U farming subsidies, and that under French law, a farmer working a neighbour's land for seven years can claim it as his own. As crazy as it sounds, and in the absence of any proof, we'd experienced enough chicanery to give it some credence.

The first viewing we had was from a medically retired policeman, who loved the property and agreed to the asking price immediately. He was even prepared to buy most of the furniture. After signing the *compromise de vente,* all went well for a while. We then told Ron and Joan that we were leaving. Though they were sorry, they understood why, and agreed to take some of our things when offered them.

Then came the body blow! With the sale underway and half of our furniture shipped to the UK, the buyer backed out. Apparently, he was a Walter Mitty character, who believed he was due a large pay-out for injuries sustained on duty. When the bank checked out his story, they refused to lend him the money.

We were then told that his girlfriend had raised the deposit independently. Yet again the deal fell through, when *her* bank refused the funding. Technically, under French law, we could have been entitled to two payments of 10% of our property's value as compensation – certainly one. However, with the *notaire* acting for both buyer *and* seller (a common practice to share costs,) all we received after the debacle was a cheque for about 3,000 euros paid into our account. When asked why it was so little, the Notaire said the bank had refused the loans, so technically the fault wasn't the buyer's, though he'd mis-represented his prospects. And the amount could vary greatly depending on the ability of the buyer to

299

pay. It was frustrating, as the correct compensation payment could have enabled us to stay in France. Unfortunately, hiring lawyers to pursue it would have dragged us through the French courts; and if we lost, could have incurred untold costs. So, not prepared to take the gamble, we sucked it up and moved on.

We spent most of April through to July trying to sell the house, before putting the sale into the hands of another *Immobiliere* and returning to the UK for Nadine's wedding. It took place near Darlington on 10th July; and staying with Jill and Dale, we travelled up together for the event.

Returning to Grantham after the nuptials, Dale asked us where we'd like to live when we returned. He loved the Scottish Borders, and with nothing to lose, we drove to Scotland to check out properties. After arranging to take over the tenancy of an unfurnished cottage near Melrose from September 1st we returned to France.

At the end of August we received shocking news. Diane's dad had sustained a massive heart attack while on holiday in Canada, and after resuscitation, he was in intensive care in Vancouver. Unable to do anything from France, our search continued for a house buyer, while keeping in touch with family in the UK.

Then, with everything on hold, we left the house sale in the hands of our *Immobiliere,* and drove back to take up the tenancy of our cottage almost a fortnight late.

Before we left the farm, Ron and Joan took charge of a feral kitten we'd been nurturing. Our first encounter with the tiny mite was when we heard a mewing noise, and Diane spotted it hanging onto an end beam on the barn. We'd spied a pregnant cat recently at the back of the granary, and this was obviously her kitten. Putting on a heavy glove, I climbed the ladder, rescued the struggling and spitting infant, and placed it back in the granary. After another incident later, it seemed the mother had abandoned it. So, leaving food and milk in the barn regularly, it began a long journey towards trusting us. Since then we'd taken responsibility for it; and now, Ron and Joan had taken on the role until we returned.

Settled back in the UK, we learned that Dale had been saved by Joanne's partner Blair using CPR, and after a spell in hospital, he was medi-vacced back to the UK. As he was then transferred to a specialist heart unit, we visited Jill and stayed over. When he could receive visitors, the family took turns attending the hospital. Released later into home care, he declined the offered wheelchair and walked out of the hospital with dignity, to be greeted by delighted family.

Meanwhile, our French agents kept in touch with us. They said to keep quiet about written agreements with Bertrand regarding our land; then mentioned threats from him when prospective buyers were shown around. He'd even rung one prospective buyer, saying the well water was poisoned, which was crazy as he also used it.

We had little time for all of that, though, as Dale's health hung in the balance. Eventually, the agents found a buyer for our house, though, at a reduced price; saying if we agreed, they'd fly over to Edinburgh with paperwork to get things moving. Meanwhile, we were living in an unfurnished cottage, with half of our furniture in storage near St Albans after the aborted first sale. The remainder was still in the farmhouse in France. All we had were two canvas chairs, and a second-hand TV bought from a charity shop. As for sleeping, I'd constructed a bed/settee from boxes of books, topped off with an airbed. It would have to do for now.

Come December, we did a Christmas run, visiting family and dropping off presents. Stopping over at Grantham, it was good to see Dale back home and looking much better.

As January arrived, the house sale was still unsettled, and our furniture remained trapped in storage. Our discomfort while waiting for our furniture to arrive meant nothing though; as on January the 13th Diane received a dreadful phone call. Her dad, who'd been in hospital awaiting heart surgery, had died overnight hours before the scheduled operation. Even more poignant, it was the day after Jill's birthday. Of course Diane was devastated and wanted to be with her mum. However, other family were much nearer than we were, so we had to trust their judgement.

We later travelled back to France to collect some of our belongings, which Ron and Joan had kindly stored in their barn for us. Our accommodation was 'Rosie's Cottage' named after Joan's mum, and it provided us with a much needed break. They said they'd been looking after the kitten, and even thought of trying to catch it and adopt it when we'd gone, as the often gruff Ron had grown fond of it. Sadly, one day when they arrived to feed it, it never showed up. They hadn't seen it since, despite visiting the farm daily with food. We were forced to accept the unthinkable. Bertrand, a stated cat hater could have killed it, and possibly its mother too.

As the house was virtually sold, we told Ron and Joan to take anything in the garden, barn or toolshed – things which weren't part of the agreement and no use to us in the UK. After a farewell drink together the previous evening, the removal began. All of our carefully packed belongings were loaded into two vans and we waved them goodbye.

With the house locked up and all services switched off, we drove away soon after them. In the rear-view mirror, I could see the pool cover flapping in the breeze, but there was no sign of our neighbours. After dropping off the keys at the agency, we headed for the ferry. The dream was finally over.

The End

Epilogue

After returning to the UK in 2010, Stewart and Diane settled in the Scottish Borders. Restless, Diane found a seasonal job working at nearby Floors castle in their gift shop. The following season, Stewart became a visitor guide at the castle. In 2015 they married, and in 2021, Diane retired. However, Stewart is still working; enjoying the stimulus of meeting visitors from both home and abroad in a setting of living history.

Family members written about in both books are now married with children; Nadine has three, Helen three, Kay four, Michael four, and Chris one. In total, Stewart and Diane are the proud grandparents of fifteen grandchildren – for now anyway.

The French dream is remembered fondly by all who lived it, though it was often hard, and sometimes dangerous. But the enterprise eventually proved profitable, and taking all things into consideration, no-one involved would have missed the experience.

Printed in Great Britain
by Amazon

84081797R00173